URBAN TRANSPORTATION PLANNING

URBAN TRANSPORTATION PLANNING

BY ROGER L. CREIGHTON

UNIVERSITY OF ILLINOIS PRESS

Urbana · *Chicago* · *London*

Third printing, 1972

To J. Douglas Carroll, Jr.

who pioneered in this work

CONTENTS

FIGURES

TABLES

INTRODUCTION

DURING the past two decades—at first somewhat slowly, and now more swiftly—there have been assembled a body of data and a set of procedures by which teams of persons with different skills have been able to prepare long-range plans for coordinated transportation systems to serve metropolitan areas. These plans have not been simply designs based on intuition and judgment, but are based on rigorous processes, including computer tests, which demonstrate that the recommended plan maximizes performance in relation to an accepted goal.

Unfortunately, the factual bases for this planning, and the planning processes themselves, are understood by relatively few people. This has occurred despite extensive publication of the components of this work in technical journals, and even despite good reporting of the entire processes in the final reports of several metropolitan transportation studies. A substantial gap exists between the thinking of those with experience in this field and those who *should* know: political leaders, executives in the fields of transportation construction and management, leaders in the fields of metropolitan and regional planning, and those whose professional work lies with urban problems.

This knowledge gap is hurtful in the confusion which constantly surrounds debate on what to do about "the transportation problem." Proposals are made and contested; charges and counter-charges are hurled; simplistic solutions are proposed with sublime assurance, as if one new mechanism, or the construction of some type of transportation used in another city, would suddenly solve all problems. And these large matters are discussed without any organized framework, without any attempt to establish the proper scale of investment, without any consideration of goals, mostly without any data, and with no understanding of the nature of travel and the characteristics of transportation facilities. It is almost as if people delight in having an area in which anybody can speculate because nobody knows anything about the subject.

Free speculation and uninformed debate would be an interesting pastime if it were not that the problems of urban transportation are so serious. The toll of accidents is appalling; 53,000 lives lost on highways in the United States in 1966[1] is the equivalent of wiping out entirely more than three divisions of troops, and the loss of such manpower—even in the scale of a World War II—would have shaken an entire government. The economic losses from congestion, both in the movement of people and of goods, are very difficult to measure, yet they exist and damage our national productivity. There is the frustration which comes through possessing, on the one hand, the most modern of technologies, and, on the other hand, having such slow, costly, dangerous, and unpleasant travel within our cities. The building and rebuilding of our cities—the environment in which more and more of the world's population is living—is wrapped around the mesh of transportation systems; yet how to weave these systems together, and how to keep them in equilibrium with the demands for travel, is not understood.

The main purpose of this book, then, is to try to convey ideas on travel and transportation planning to as broad a segment of the public as possible, and most particularly to the people who make decisions in this area: political leaders, engineers and urban planners, government executives, and businessmen and civic leaders. To be specific:

1. We need to communicate the presence of a large and increasingly systematic knowledge about travel, land use, and transportation networks.

2. We need to have a better understanding of the capabilities of existing comprehensive transportation planning processes as a means of determining optimum transportation plans.

---

[1] National Safety Council, *Accident Facts, 1967 Edition* (Chicago).

3. We need to be aware of the limitations of our habitual thought processes when dealing with complex subjects such as transportation and cities.

4. We need to examine the implications of the data and of transportation planning processes on the theory and practice of metropolitan and regional planning.

The focus of the book is upon ideas rather than facts and upon the framework of planning methods rather than upon detailed techniques. Data are presented mainly to convey ideas about general magnitudes and about the workings of urban phenomena which are critical to transportation planning, not as facts per se. "The facts" have an uncomfortable quality of changing slightly over time and from city to city. Likewise techniques of planning vary from study to study, and detailed information on these techniques is best found in manuals or in the technical journals such as those cited throughout this text. This book attempts to fill the need which exists for a general work which surveys the urban transportation planning process and illustrates how it has been used to develop transportation plans.

Content

We may start with the idea that a city or metropolitan area (the terms are used interchangeably throughout this text) is a continuously self-modifying system:

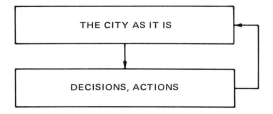

Prior to the coming of the major metropolitan transportation studies, decisions to modify the transportation facilities of the city tended to be localized, scattered, and short-range. The major transportation studies may be said to have created a new situation:

The new situation is different only in degree from the earlier situation. Transportation planning such as is described in this book is a venture—one might almost say an adventure—to be more far-seeing, more comprehending, and better able to deal with complex problems. Decisions and actions are still reactions to events, but the planning process has extended our ability to see into the future, and to anticipate both the good and the bad effects of alternative programs.

We may add further detail to the preceding diagram and show the major elements of the transportation planning process in the context of the real world, and of human actions to modify that world.

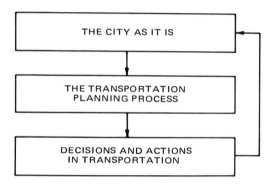

The five elements of the transportation planning process are described briefly below.

1. *Data.* Planning must start with data which symbolically represent the concrete things being planned. These data may already be possessed in the form of human memory or they may have to be gathered at considerable expense, as in the transportation planning process.

2. *Simulation models.* The data are used to develop models which simulate (a) selected activities of the present world and (b) the way certain of these activities change over time. This element of the planning process incorporates both the forecasting stage and the testing stage as will be described in Chapters VIII and XI.

3. *Goals.* A planner must have a set of goals, either his own or

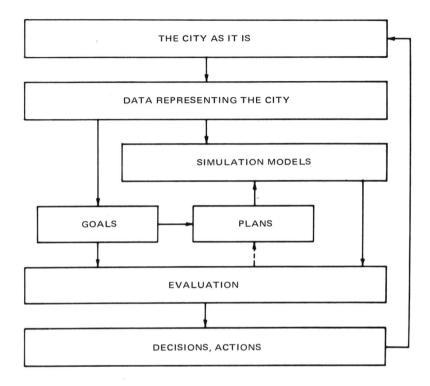

preferably those he employs on behalf of others. It is important that these goals not be those whose use preordains a conclusion of some kind. Goals suggest planned changes, and are used in the evaluation element.

4. *Planned changes.* Plans are proposed changes which may modify events or activities. These proposed changes can be represented within the simulation model, producing a different result than would have been the case had they not been instituted.

5. *Evaluation.* Once the results of the simulations are known, they must be evaluated against the goals which have been pre-established. If the evaluation results are not satisfactory, new changes must be planned.

6. *Decision and implementation.* At the conclusion of the planning process, some decision and implementation must be made.

This connects planning to the sphere of action; without this connection, planning would be meaningless.

The product of this process is a strategic plan for the construction of metropolitan transportation systems, that is, networks which are designed to work as complete entities. The strategic plan defines the general locations of new facilities and the sequence of their construction. The strategy determines the investments which the public should make in new or reconstructed facilities, both road and mass transportation facilities. We are not concerned here with such things as roadway geometrics or the mechanical features of mass transportation vehicles in and of themselves, but only as these bear upon the large-scale actions which governments are going to have to take consistently over many years in order to achieve the goals of their communities.

Without strategic plans, actions taken in the transportation field are more likely to have the failures of any piecemeal approach. That is, there is apt to be a greater incidence of poorly coordinated facilities, and especially of facilities which do not give the public an adequate return on investment.

Strategic plans are chosen through an examination of alternative strategies, and this process of examination discloses the probable effects of each alternative. At the end of the process the representatives of a community may not choose the most economical solution; what is essential, however, is that these representatives make their decisions in full view of the probable consequences of alternative strategies.

The Coordination Dilemma

Transportation planning does not exist in isolation, but is related to other planning and decision-making of great importance to society, as illustrated in the following diagram.

There can be no debate about the need for single-function agencies, such as transportation agencies, to prepare long-range plans for their own construction programs. If they did not, they

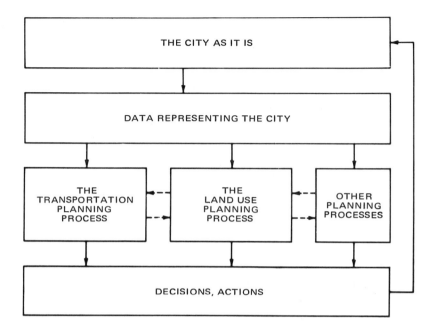

would be acting shortsightedly. It is essential that single-function agencies have the skills and know the principles and methods for planning their own work.

However, there is also a need for coordination of different planning programs. One might even go further and say that, in theory, all such planning ought to be done together. This is based on the premise that any action in one part of an urban area or in one functional activity will have an effect upon all other parts and all other functional areas. Therefore, it is reasoned, all these actions ought to be planned together for the good of society. In particular, there needs to be close coordination between the two fields of transportation planning and land use planning.

However, before multi-function planning coordination can become a meaningful reality, three conditions have to be met. Effective coordination depends upon (a) being able to assess the impact of an action in one field upon another field, (b) having control over the two or more programs being coordinated, and (c) knowing the goal or goals toward which the coordinative action is being taken and being able to assess its worth, since it will inevitably cost something to achieve.

Unfortunately, these three conditions are not met in the current state of the art of urban studies. While research has been going forward recently on the relationship between transportation and land use,[2] current understanding of this relationship is not well quantified. We can observe that transportation affects land use and vice versa, but methods for estimating the extent of the impact are still being developed.

Second, while there is control over the location of new transportation facilities within a metropolitan area, there is, *at the level of the metropolis,* no control over whether people will build, or when, or where. This fact will be demonstrated more fully later in this book. Governments are too fragmented, and, being democratic governments, they bend to the popular will over time. Without such control, coordination between land use and transportation planning can only be a partial activity.

Finally, there is as yet no consensus on the goals of metropolitan areas and even less understanding of how alternative land development forms will work to improve performance toward these goals. Thus, even if transportation and land use could be coordinated at metropolitan levels, there is no assurance that the resulting action would produce a substantial benefit for the residents of an urban area.

The foregoing does not suggest that coordination is undesirable or permanently unworkable—quite the contrary. It does suggest that we have to be realistic. If coordination of multiple programs is going to be attained, and particularly if land use planning is to be coordinated with transportation planning, there must exist the ability to measure the important relationships (and they are not all important) between different functional activities, an agreed set of goals, and the ability to evaluate objectively the impact of alternative arrangements of human activities upon the quality of human life. Out of this there can come a sound national and regional land

---

[2] *Urban Development Models,* Highway Research Board Special Report 97, Washington, D.C., 1968.

development policy and this can then be meaningfully served and supported by planned transportation systems.

Antipathy toward Expressways

Currently there is a widespread antipathy towards any form of transportation planning which deals with expressways. This antipathy is caused by a number of factors. The automobile and the truck, in increasing numbers, have created congestion, killed and maimed people, increased air pollution, and changed the appearance of cities, too often for the worse. Expressways have created, or threatened the creation of, relocation problems. Expressways have taken park lands and destroyed historic buildings. The central cities through which new expressways are planned are reeling from the continued pressures of poverty, racial strife, and municipal insolvency. The threat of further losses of tax base—no matter how small—and of further objections from citizens is enough to cause even the strongest mayor to block any further action in transportation except that which may conveniently be tucked away underground.

Under such circumstances it may be wondered why anyone should be concerned with methods of planning urban expressway systems. Is it not all a futile exercise? The answer to this must be strongly negative.

We have to take a long-range view. Cities are currently passing through extremely difficult times. Urban rebuilding has been stalled by lack of adequate resources, by a pattern of atomized ownership, and by a failure to industrialize the construction industry. But these difficulties will in time be overcome; eventually urban areas, and particularly central cities, will be made more malleable, and they will be redeveloped. When this situation comes about, there will be a need to have plans for transportation systems whose capacities are in equilibrium with the demand for service. And those are the kinds of plans this book is about.

Approach

The nature of transportation systems and of the urban areas they serve is such that a kind of thinking different from the conventional has to be used when preparing plans for them. An urban area is a unity, a whole. But it contains thousands or millions of people, spread over hundreds of square miles of land, making twice as many person trips per day as there are residents, and these trips flow over thousands of segments of a transportation system. All of these things are linked with one another in varying degree.

Conventional thinking and conventional planning tend to approach the city as if all Gaul were still divided in three parts. Conventional thinking is dominated by categories and classifications. Inevitably it deals in contrasts, as in expressways *versus* transit. With conventional thinking we try to break the world down into components so that we can deal with the parts more easily. We then reason, "If this (category) occurs, then that (category) is bound to happen." The failure of the conventional thinking is partly in the crudeness of the categories and partly in other errors, such as in assuming that trends always behave linearly.

However, when we measure cities and urban travel, we see (if our measures are fine enough) that this world does not work in categories but in continua. Each individual trip, each parcel of land use, even each street segment, when seen at the metropolitan scale, becomes an extremely small particle. When these particles are arrayed in any one of a number of orders, they form continuously varying patterns. The measures presented in this book show, for example, that from a land use and transportation viewpoint there is no such thing as "central city" and "suburb." Legally these are entities, but from the functional viewpoint of transportation the names are gross classifications which hide the fact that the two are merely segments of a quite smooth gradient of population density which decreases as one moves outward from the center. Even the term "city" becomes a false classification. What "city" stands for is a variable concentration of population at higher density than that of the lower density "rural areas" which surround it, but which has, in modern times, no sharp line of demarcation separating it from the country.

What is needed, then, is a method of reasoning about metropolitan transportation which can deal with continua—a kind of integral calculus, if you will, instead of the geometry of the conventional thinking. As will be seen, the methods described in this book deal with continua by simulating the behavior of the extremely small particles comprising travel within the metropolitan transportation system, and then observing and evaluating the results.

The direct implication of dealing with a continuously varying subject is that there can be no simple answers or categorical solutions to transportation planning problems, and the reader will find none in this text. However, the reader can know what is involved: what travel is like, how it is distributed in space, what needs exist, and what criteria should be considered in establishing policies for the allocation of limited public resources. With this knowledge, he will have an increased ability to make better and more realistic judgments.

Limitations

As previously indicated, the main purpose of this book has been to communicate ideas on travel and transportation planning in order to increase understanding and to improve the quality of decision-making in the transportation field. To succeed in this purpose, we have to deal with an unusually large span of material, ranging from measurements of cities to the basic methods of transportation planning, and from computer methods to the subjective area of human values. The breadth of this subject matter necessarily limits the depth to which any given aspect can be taken. It has been necessary, therefore, to select those things which are important to the purpose of the book and to go into them only in that detail required to make the more important quantities and technical processes understandable. In making these selections, I have tried to make the relationships between data and theory clear, as well as the relationships between the planning process and the view which is taken of the city. Footnotes will lead the technically minded reader to the publications describing detailed methodology.

Most of the material for this book was drawn from the author's work experience as assistant director of the Chicago Area Transportation Study and as director, from 1961 to 1966, of the long-range planning program mounted by the New York State Department of Transportation for the six upstate metropolitan areas.

While the material used in this book is drawn from two case examples—the Chicago and Niagara Frontier studies—this does not impose a narrow view. The Chicago study in the years 1955–61 was the leader in developing new planning and testing methods. Its work strongly influenced the course of transportation planning throughout the United States and elsewhere during and since that time. The Niagara Frontier study followed the general methods used in Chicago, adding improvements from time to time. While the detailed techniques used by other transportation studies throughout the country may vary from those described here (for example, the gravity model may be employed instead of the opportunity model in travel forecasting), the basic planning processes used are all very much alike.

The processes which are described here are ones which will be improved and extended; areas where improvement is needed have been suggested in Chapter XVI. Nevertheless, the process which is described here remains as a kind of core or basic process which needs to be used to develop initial plans, and for continuing planning, as a rigorous method for designing the major networks of expressways and rapid transit systems in urban areas.

Acknowledgments

An enormous amount of credit is due to others. First, the greatest credit should go to J. Douglas Carroll, Jr., under whose leadership the transportation studies gained their greatest forward movement. Second, I want to thank Messrs. J. Burch McMorran, E. Burton Hughes, and William A. Sharkey of the New York State Department of Transportation, and the Rockefeller Administration of New York State, for their unfailing support of transportation planning and research. During more than five years of work in New York we were never once criticized for any position we took on a professional basis, and this is the kind of support which professionals really appreciate.

Last, but not least, I want to thank those who worked on the staffs of the Chicago and Niagara Frontier studies. The names of the principal staff members are given in the appendix, but space unfortunately does not permit the listing of all those who contributed in so many ways to the success of those studies.

The Ford Foundation, working through Rensselaer Polytechnic Institute, made possible my taking the time to put down these ideas on paper, and I am greatly indebted to them, and particularly to Paul N. Ylvisaker, Louis Winnick, and Dean Arthur A. Burr, for their support.

The text has been read, in its various stages of development, by Professor George C. Hemmens, Professor John T. Howard, Professor William I. Goodman, J. Douglas Carroll, Jr., John R. Hamburg, and Professor Britton Harris. The reviewers' comments have been very helpful, but they are not responsible for any of the faults of the book. I wish to express my appreciation to them for their assistance, and also to John Patton, who assisted with library research, and to Ann Patterson, who typed the manuscript.

The following figures are reproduced, by permission, from the three volumes of the *Final Report* of the Chicago Area Transportation Study: Figure 1, 2, 4, 9, 10, 11, 12, 13, 14, 15, 16, 17, 18, 20, 22, 23, 26, 27, 29, 30, 31, 35, 54, 55, 56, 57, 58, 59, 60, 73.

The following figures were redrafted or prepared from figures or data contained in the *Final Report* of the Chicago Area Transportation Study: Figure 7, 8, 19, 32, 38, 39.

The following figures are reproduced, by permission, from the two volumes of the *Final Report* of the Niagara Frontier Transportation Study: Figure 21, 40, 41, 42, 49, 50, 51, 52, 53, 74, 75.

The following figures were redrafted or prepared from figures or data contained in various published and unpublished reports of the Niagara Frontier Transportation Study: Figure 3, 5, 6, 25, 28, 61, 62, 63, 64, 65, 66, 67, 68, 69, 70, 71, 72, 76, 77, 78, 79, 80, 81.

Figures 45, 46, and 47 were redrafted from an article by Roger L. Creighton *et al.* in Highway Research Board Bulletin 253.

Figure 24 was redrafted from Figure 30 in Volume I, *Final Report*, Pittsburgh Area Transportation Study.

The photograph of the model of Wichita's commercial land use pattern was taken by James A. Veon, Administrative Assistant, Wichita-Sedgwick County Metropolitan Area Planning Department.

Special thanks are due to those who approved the use of the foregoing materials and who assisted the author in collecting them. Among these are E. Wilson Campbell, John J. Howe, and Frederick Petrick of the Chicago Area Transportation Study; John K. Mladinov and Mildred Black of the New York State Department of Transportation; and Robert Kochanowski of the Southwestern Pennsylvania Regional Planning Commission.

PART ONE

THREE VIEWS OF THE CITY

Successful attempts to develop long-range transportation plans for metropolitan areas require an understanding of travel, of transportation facilities, and of the structure and growth of cities. These are the materials with which the transportation planner must work.

The surveys which have been made as parts of urban transportation studies portray the city with a much finer level of detail than has heretofore been possible. As a result, we can view certain urban phenomena in a new way, as continua made up of many small particles. This conception suggests that planning methods need to be adopted which are different from those based either on emotional statements or on conventional reasoning.

Chapter I looks at basic problems and policy issues of transportation; Chapters II–V examine travel, land use, and transportation facilities. Data are drawn from the Chicago and Niagara Frontier studies; data from other cities could have been used equally well and would lead to similar conclusions about cities and urban travel.

I

PROBLEMS AND POLICY ISSUES

PRIOR to the industrial revolution—and this applies in those parts of the world where that revolution is still going on—the prime difficulties faced by men in transporting themselves and their goods over the surface of the earth were physical ones. These were how to overcome the frictions of land travel and how to overcome the shifting winds and dangers of the seas. These frictions may not today appear real to most people, but many who have traveled in eastern countries no more than twenty years ago can remember seeing carts being dragged through rutted roads with both men and horses in the traces: a harsh reminder of the difficulty of movement.

Mechanical progress, however, provided engines for propulsion, better materials for vehicles and ships, and better surfaces (both rail and road) for vehicles to use in traveling on land. The investments in smoother, all-weather road surfaces and in rails actually reduced the physical frictions of travel, and at the same time mechanical power was applied to the vehicles. Thus, the physical difficulties of travel were abated.

But then population increased and crowded into cities. The difficulty of transportation became no longer how to overcome distance but how to thread through masses of people and vehicles. In the relative scale of difficulties facing men, the physical problem was greatly diminished and—partly as a result of this success—the more serious transportation difficulties became the conflicts between and among people.[1]

[1] Toynbee calls this a change from an "external" to an "internal" challenge; see Arnold J. Toynbee, *A Study of History* (Somervell abridgment, Oxford University Press, New York, 1946), p. 205.

These conflicts between people take a variety of forms. There is, of course, the problem of direct conflict within the traveled way—the dreadful accident problem which killed 53,000 persons in the United States in 1966 and injured 1,900,000.[2] There is the problem of mutual delay: increasing densities of people and vehicles over-crowding transportation facilities, delaying each other by their own numbers. There is the problem of conflict between people in motion and people in their site-based activities: people at one time needing linear spaces for speed, at other times the broader areas of land for their activities—accessible, but without the noises and disturbances of travel. There is the problem of making difficult decisions in the allocation of human and material resources between types of trans-portation, and between transportation and education, housing, and recreation.

There is no doubt that these conflicts are going to become more intense as time goes on. Population will continue to increase. The land surface of the earth will remain constant, and hence regional densities must rise. Requirements for speed will go up. There will be more traveling as the resources which people can devote to trans-portation rise. (With higher income, the proportion of disposable income available for transportation rises.) All these things will pack people more closely together—both in motion and at rest—and hence will increase potential conflict.

When we turn from the difficulties themselves to techniques for reducing difficulties, the contrast between the old and the new is quite sharp. Once transportation difficulties could be reduced mark-edly by mechanical improvements. A new engine, a new railroad track from Boston to Worcester, a new road, a steamboat, an air-plane: these meant the overcoming of the physical obstacles of distances and ground friction. Routes for these vehicles could be planned and built one at a time, and each new route meant a marked reduction of some particular friction.

In the tighter urban world of today, however, these mechanical techniques are no longer assured of their earlier high rate of profit-ability. Transportation facilities are already everywhere; land is in-

[2] Disabling injuries. National Safety Council, *Accident Facts, 1967 Edition* (Chicago).

creasingly scarce; people are living (in regional terms) at higher densities; people are traveling more; and the standards of what people want in the way of living conditions are going up as fast as modern communications can convey the idea of what the rich are doing.

The technical task of the present, then, is how to organize things so as to reduce the present and future conflicts between people. It is also to make sure that the resources which are being allocated for transportation capital improvements will earn a high profit for society. This is, of course, not exclusively a problem in social relations any more than it is exclusively a problem in engineering. Rather, as will be shown later, it is an enormously complicated assignment stretching across many skill groups, including engineering, city planning, social science, economics, the design professions, and politics. From the transportation viewpoint, the technical task must eventually be expressed in terms of plans for entire networks (as opposed to single facilities) of all types of transportation facilities, for entire urban areas or regions. In this sense, the result is a physical design. From a larger viewpoint, however, transportation planning, if it is to make its greatest contribution, must eventually be combined with planning for other things in an urban area or region (particularly land use) which will help to diminish conflicts between people.

This book is about planning for transportation systems in urban areas. There is, however, no point in proceeding into this subject without examining the importance of transportation planning and how it relates to the larger goals of the individual and society. For this examination we must look at the magnitude and nature of the conflicts of transportation today.

Magnitude and Nature of Conflicts

We hear and read a great deal about "the transportation problem" and about attempts to find "solutions" to this problem. Some of the confusion which surrounds this subject is because of the dual meaning of the word "problem." Some people use the word "problem" to mean a mathematical problem, and this implies that a solution is possible—at least, in terms of the mathematics which most people have studied. But "problem" also means a vexing or perplexing question, like the problem of crime—a problem which is apparently beyond our powers to eliminate completely, and hence which has no solution.

It is only in this latter sense that the transportation problem exists: as a vexing difficulty, or as a troublesome matter. This is because transportation problems are defined by the things which we don't like as individuals or which society as a whole doesn't like. What we don't like, or view as a potential danger or irritant, is a problem. What we do like is a good thing and becomes a goal which we strive to achieve. "Problems" and "goals" are obverse sides of the same coin, being defined by us in relationship to ourselves as individuals or as a society.

Because the transportation problem is relative to us, it is likely to be changing as our views change. Many of our views are constant (since we remain human animals with certain physical needs), but others are modified as time and technology change, as we live in different places, as our productivity increases, and as all the various parts of our environment shift and change in time.

At any given time, then, we can fairly define "the transportation problem" as the *summation of the things which people don't like about transportation*. Certainly such a definition will include all kinds of minute, peculiar dislikes, ranging from the old lady who doesn't like curved streets because they confuse her to the man who dislikes the lack of interurban trolley service because he enjoyed a hot summer ride on one as a boy fifty years ago. But out of the mass of dislikes, we can classify some which are commonly held, and regarded seriously, by very large numbers of people, and which thereby represent what society considers the transportation problem.

1. *Accidents.* Accidents are, on the whole, the most dramatic and terrifying of transportation problems. In 1966, approximately 55,000 persons were killed in transportation accidents in the United States, 96 percent of them in motor vehicle accidents.[3] We are so

---

[3] National Safety Council, *Accident Facts, 1967 Edition* (Chicago).

used to this attrition—the two or three persons killed in our home cities and counties each week—that we forget how rapidly the gruesome score is added up against us.

Accidents can never be completely eliminated; they are bound to occur when large numbers of individuals, each inevitably making a certain (albeit very small) proportion of wrong judgments, travel in vehicles which may be faulty, on a variety of ways with varying degrees of built-in safety, and under a variety of weather conditions. Moreover, accidents are more likely to occur when drivers are less well disciplined and as long as society tolerates the drinking driver. (Two studies reported by the National Safety Council in *Accident Facts, 1967 Edition*, found that over half of fatally injured drivers had been drinking.)

Table 1. *Motor Vehicle Deaths per 100,000,000 Vehicle Miles of Travel for Selected States, 1966*

Rhode Island	2.7
Connecticut	2.9
Maryland	4.6
New York	4.8
Oklahoma	5.2
North Dakota	5.6
Missouri	5.8
Texas	6.2
Alabama	6.7
New Mexico	7.0
Tennessee	7.4
Puerto Rico	10.1

Source: National Safety Council, *Accident Facts, 1967 Edition* (Chicago).

Even if accidents cannot be eliminated, they can be reduced drastically. As Table 1 shows, there is a great disparity between accident rates per one hundred million vehicle miles of travel. Connecticut is three times as safe a place to drive in as Puerto Rico. Reductions in accident rates come as a result of actions on many fronts, including more effective disciplining of the driver, elimination of the drinking driver, safer vehicles, and safer roads. What we are concerned with in this book is what can be done from the viewpoint of transportation and land use planning.

To show how costly accidents are and to emphasize the seriousness of the need for all accident reduction programs, we can make a simple comparison. The estimated cost of motor vehicle accidents in the United States is $10,000,000,000 per year.[4] By comparison, the capital funds invested each year to build new and safer roads is $8,645,000,000 per year.[5] Less money is being spent on improvements than is being paid for accidents.

2. *Congestion.* People actively dislike congestion, presumably because congestion represents two significant wastes. These are excessive operating costs and wasted time.

Excessive operating costs can be measured with a fair degree of precision. An automobile being driven at an average speed of five miles per hour because congestion forces it to make many stops and starts, costs about 5.0 cents per mile to operate. In contrast, the same vehicle moving at an average speed of thirty miles per hour, costs about 2.5 cents per mile to operate.[6] Thus, congestion can increase vehicle operating costs as much as 2.5 cents per mile.

Similarly, congestion drives up the costs of providing bus service, contributing to the financial difficulties of mass transportation and to the need for higher fares. Forgetting for the moment the greater tire wear and fuel costs inherent in congested driving and assuming that a driver is paid $4.00 per hour in direct wages and fringe benefits, it costs the bus company 80 cents per mile to run the bus at five miles per hour and only 20 cents per mile at twenty miles per hour. This is simply because the bus goes farther in an hour at

[4] National Safety Council, *Accident Facts, 1967 Edition* (Chicago).

[5] U.S. Statistical Abstract, 1967, Table 587.

[6] Rochester Metropolitan Transportation Study, "Basic Corridor Plan for Expressways," New York State Department of Public Works, Albany, January, 1967, Table 23. The lowest operating cost for a vehicle is at an average speed of thirty-five to forty miles per hour. The Rochester costs were based on an earlier study by George Haikalis and Hyman Joseph, "Economic Evaluation of Traffic Networks," presented at the 1961 Annual Meeting of the Highway Research Board in Washington, D.C. See also Paul J. Claffey, "Running Costs of Motor Vehicles as Affected by Highway Design," National Cooperative Highway Research Program Report 13, Washington, D.C., 1965.

high speeds. If the same bus were driven on a freeway at seventy miles per hour, the labor cost of moving the bus one mile would drop down to less than 6 cents.

The waste of time inherent in congestion is universally condemned, but measuring its cost to society is a difficult assignment. The cost of the truck driver's time and the cost of renting his vehicle can, of course, be computed readily. The Chicago study in 1962 used a figure of $4.00 per hour as an average for all trucks.[7]

Estimating the value of a person's time is much more difficult. There is clear evidence, however, that given a choice, people will pay for higher speed, and hence time. Studies of the choices people make between free and toll facilities permit the value of time to be deduced; values of $1.14[8] and $1.42[9] per automobile hour were calculated in this fashion. A more recent study based on data from a sample of workers using free and toll roads to travel to five industrial plants allowed calculations to be made giving a value of $2.82 per person hour for commuter trips of over five miles.[10] Any average numeric figure such as the $1.50 per vehicle hour or the $0.85 per person hour used in the Chicago study merely gives a scale to the point: time has value and people dislike to waste it in congestion and slow travel.

3. *Inefficient Investment.* A third thing which people don't like about transportation is paying for it, particularly in taxes. Yet this is a surface reaction, because closer examination will generally reveal the grudging response that taxes are necessary to produce the transportation services people require. Certainly the test of years of voting in a representative democracy would indicate that people will pay for transportation improvements.

[7] Chicago Area Transportation Study, *Final Report*, III, 10.

[8] G. P. St. Clair and Nathan Liederer, "Evaluation of Unit Cost of Time and Strain-and-Discomfort Cost of Non-Uniform Driving," Highway Research Board Special Report 56, Washington, D.C., 1960.

[9] Paul J. Claffey, "Characteristics of Passenger Car Travel on Toll Roads and Comparable Free Roads for Highway User Benefit Studies," Highway Research Board, Washington, D.C., January, 1961.

[10] Thomas C. Thomas, "The Value of Time for Commuting Motorists," Highway Research Board Record 245, Washington, D.C., 1968.

What is universally condemned, however, is waste in the use of public funds. This deeply felt emotion stems from the fact that anything given over to inefficiency through taxes has no mitigating benefit whatsoever to us and to the things we want. Wasted or inefficient investment is thus a deep-rooted part of the transportation problem.

The visible part of waste or inefficiency is quite rare. This is the group of cases where something is built which is obviously never going to be used, or where public funds are stolen or misappropriated. These are the things which make the headlines when they do happen, but by and large this is not very often.

The more subtle but infinitely larger and more important kind of inefficiency has to do with low productivity of investment in transportation facilities. This may be the case either with facilities which have just been built or with facilities which have been in place for a long time. A few simple examples may be given. If a short section of four-lane expressway, capable of carrying well over 50,000 vehicles per day, is built in an area which will produce only 5,000 vehicles per day, then that is an inefficient investment. If a street is widened at a cost of $1,000,000 per mile, but its capacity is only increased from 1,500 to 2,000 vehicles per hour, there is a probable case of inefficient investment; too much is being spent for too small a gain in capacity. If a transit line is extended at a cost of $10,000,-000 per mile, and only a few hundred additional passengers are served, that would be an inefficient investment.

These are the kinds of inefficiencies which most people never think about. Most people are not accustomed to thinking of public roads or transit lines as investments which should produce a high rate of return. Yet the amount of money spent for new, fixed transportation facilities such as roads and rail transit lines (excluding rolling stock) is enormous—about nine billion dollars[11] per year in the United States. It is impossible to estimate the magnitude of inefficiencies, either in what is being newly installed or in that which has been long in place. All that can be said is that if, through careful planning and design, the productivity of new investment could be

---

[11] Estimated from U.S. Statistical Abstract, 1967, Table 587.

increased by only 2 or 3 percent, there would be extremely large gains for society in terms of faster, safer, and less congested travel.

4. *Inaccessibility.* Good access is a kind of freedom, and inaccessibility is a loss of freedom; this is why inaccessibility is one of the problems of transportation. Without access, land cannot be developed, people cannot move to jobs or to hospitals, schools, or recreational, cultural, or educational opportunities. Lack of access was held by the McCone Commission to be one of the causes of the 1966 riots in Watts,[12] although one must be careful here because it may not have been so much the lack of transportation as the lack of social access bred by racial prejudice which was at the root of the disturbance.

As in other difficulties of transportation, inaccessibility is quite relative. In the premechanical era, access meant any means of getting oneself or one's products physically to a particular site. Now it is not a question of getting there, but of the speed, cost, and pleasantness of getting there. Our demands as a society call for much closer proximity to one another in time, at least, if not in cost or space. It is only with this proximity that people can specialize and obtain the high productivity which we have. More and more, then, the pockets of relatively low accessibility must be reduced, whether within urban areas or in regions like Appalachia.

5. *Ugliness.* Like inaccessibility, ugliness is a relative matter. What could be tolerated in the nineteenth century, when the nation's attention was focused on expansion, cannot be tolerated in the twentieth century. Now we have to look at a very long stay with more people in a limited land area. And as time goes on these people will have more education, wealth, and perhaps leisure to give them the opportunity to be critical about appearance.

In the transportation field, the ugliness which people dislike lies both in the transportation facilities themselves and in the urban or rural backgrounds against which the transportation facilities are seen. The beauty of a road, or of any other transportation facility,

[12] *Violence in the City—An End or a Beginning?* Report of the Governor's Commission on The Los Angeles Riots, Los Angeles, 1965.

is inseparable from its background. Rural or mountainous backgrounds are admirable foils for the sweep of the ribbon of a road—for drama and surprise, or for serenity.

But in most cities, these conditions do not prevail. The prevailing background of buildings is small in scale and mostly unattractive. Transportation structures have to be larger to carry many people, and they are seen close-to. Further, they are often extremely common and unimaginative, if not brutal, in their own right. They tend to dominate their neighbors, the houses and small stores. Only rarely, as when the Eisenhower Expressway enters the Chicago Loop *through* the Post Office Building, or in the river drives of Manhattan, are buildings able to dominate the transportation structures.

So, ugliness of the urban environment does not help transportation ugliness; the net result is that the rider of transit or the driver in his car has ugliness as his constant partner. This is a real problem.

6. *Strain and Discomfort; Noise and Nuisance.* Travelers of all kinds have strain and discomfort to contend with in their journeys. The passenger on mass transportation must wait for his vehicle or his transfer, sometimes in bad weather, sometimes in unattractive surroundings. The airlines passenger has to wait and tolerate delays in schedules. The automobile or truck driver is under constant strain in tight driving conditions, and at least one study has measured the physiological stresses he and his passengers endure.[13] Probably the same could be done for the Manhattan subway passenger. People don't like these strains and it is one of the tasks of those concerned with transportation to reduce them as much as possible.

From the viewpoint of the person on the ground, transportation facilities always have some degree of noise or nuisance which is objectionable. This may be the howl of a jet, the dust from a road, or the rumbling noise of a transit or rail line. Mostly these problems are not serious and can be tolerated, but there are places and times where the nuisances created by transportation facilities are substan-

---

[13] Jaime F. Torres, "Development of Criteria for Evaluating Traffic Operations," vols. I and II, National Cooperative Highway Research Program Project 3–1 (Cornell Aeronautical Laboratory, Inc., Buffalo, N.Y., 1966).

tial. This is simply another manifestation of the increasingly social nature of transportation problems.

7. *Air Pollution.* Air pollution is an increasingly serious consequence of the expanding use of motor vehicles in urban areas. Gasoline engines are never completely efficient in their combustion of fuels. They produce, along with harmless emissions like carbon dioxide and water vapor, a considerable number of harmful emissions. These include carbon monoxide, aldehydes (which are irritants), nitrogen oxides, and at least nine carcinogens. Some of these exhaust materials react in sunlight under certain conditions to produce ozone, one of the components of smog.[14]

As population increases and with vehicle ownership rising faster than population, the total amount of pollutants going into the atmosphere is bound to increase. Some of these pollutants can be reduced by new devices installed on automobiles, trucks, and buses. And, of course, not all air pollution is produced by motor vehicles operating over the roads; airplanes, factories, power plants, trash burning, and domestic furnaces contribute to the problem. Nevertheless, vehicle-caused air pollution is a serious problem, especially in the denser parts of metropolitan areas, and this is something which must be considered in the development of transportation policy and of regional settlement policies as well.

These, then, are seven components of "the transportation problem." These are not the only components; more will be brought forward later in this text. But these are enough to indicate the dimensions of our needs. And these difficulties, by their nature, demonstrate that there can be no instant solutions. As long as there is cost, time, or energy required, or danger, inconvenience, ugliness, or discomfort in moving from place to place, there will continue to be a transportation problem. As long as people are discommoded or even threatened by the construction of any transportation facility (rail, road, or airport), or by the noise, fumes, vibration, or dust

[14] Howard R. Lewis, *With Every Breath You Take* (Crown Publishers, New York, 1965), pp. 91ff.

coming from a traveled way, there is a transportation problem. As long as people have to pay taxes for transportation facilities or services, there is a transportation problem.

The Issues

The problems which have just been listed are descriptive of conditions which exist and which people do not like; the issues, however, are what to do about these problems. There is generally little debate about the nature of the problems; instead, debate centers on the best methods of lessening the impact of these problems. Methods of solution are the real issues.

There are two broad classes of means for reducing the impact of transportation problems. One of these classes contains the means of management, administration, regulation, and education. Accidents, for example, could be reduced drastically in number if penalties for driving under the influence of alcohol were made so severe that people simply would not drive when drinking. More driver training and more rigid enforcement of traffic and speed regulations would also reduce accidents. Air pollution, in another example, could be reduced by regulations controlling engine exhaust emissions.

The second class of problem-reducing actions consists of making capital investments in new transportation facilities or in funding the operation of certain transportation services such as mass transportation facilities. Here problems are reduced by providing new channels for movement—channels which will reduce congestion and provide transportation which is safer, more pleasant, and more efficient.

In this book we are concerned only with this latter class of means for reducing transportation problems. And within this class, our focus is primarily upon making improved provision for the movement of people by the planning of physical facilities such as roads and rail rapid transit lines and the provision of services for moving people such as by bus. Goods movement is dealt with only as roadways allow for truck transportation of freight.

Capital improvements to reduce transportation problems are especially important when urban areas are expanding, because building new transportation facilities in patterns which are based upon sound planning principles can prevent the creation of transportation problems in new areas as well as alleviate problems in built-up areas.

The capital investment issues can be listed as follows:

1. How much capital investment should be made for new or reconstructed transportation facilities within a given time period?

2. How much of this capital investment should be placed in road systems and how much in mass transportation systems?

3. Within the road systems, what types of roads should be built or reconstructed? Where in the urban area should new roads be built? What pattern of roadways, by type, should be formed?

4. Within the mass transportation system, what types should be built and operated? Where should they go? What kind of a system should be formed?

The foregoing are the fundamental questions that have to be faced when considering capital investment as the means of making reductions in urban transportation problems. Not included within the above list are such issues as the substitutability of communications for transportation or the use of new inventions to move large numbers of people and goods in ways which are fundamentally different from individual transportation of people in vehicles over roads or group transportation in public conveyances. It is important in planning to keep close to possible new developments like these, but in the past two decades there has been no evidence that either substitutability or novel means of transportation will have any substantial effect upon transportation within urban areas.

The main thrust of this book, then, is about planning which recommends directions to take when faced with questions of the amount, type, location, and pattern of capital improvements. Inevitably, this revolves around physical planning, although it is physical planning at the largest, strategic scale.

We must, however, expand consideration of problems and issues beyond those of the transportation world alone. Transportation is intimately related with population, with economic productivity, and with the distribution of population and production facilities in space. Thus transportation problems are related to the other problems of urban areas, although the nature and closeness of the relationships are not always well known.

A list of the major categories of urban problems would include at least the following seven items:

1. The transportation problem.
2. The pollution problem: air, water, land.
3. The housing problem or, more broadly, the inability of urban areas to adjust to change.
4. The social problems, such as (a) overpopulation, (b) class segregation, (c) loss of freedom and individuality in the larger cities, (d) crime.
5. Health problems.
6. Education problems.
7. Economic problems: low productivity and maldistribution of economic opportunity.

Again, the problems are descriptive of undesirable conditions; the issues are to what extent and how these problems are going to be reduced in their impact upon urban dwellers.

Once more there are two groups of methods for making reductions in these problems. There are administrative, social, economic, and governmental actions which can be taken. These are probably the most important kinds of actions which can be taken because they are related most directly to the social, economic, and governmental nature of the problems.

But since we are concerned with transportation, our interest lies in the physical changes which are proposed. It is mainly the physical arrangements of people, buildings, and activities which must be served by transportation.

The physical issues can be enumerated as follows:

1. How large should urban areas be?
2. What patterns should they take (i.e., compact, linear, star-shaped, or clustered)?
3. At what densities should they be built and what should their density gradients be?
4. What should the internal arrangements of their land uses be?

These are easy questions to ask, although they cloak an almost infinite number of urban settlement patterns which can be conceived as combinations of size, shape, density patterns, and internal land use patterns.

But there is a more fundamental issue, one which is rarely raised in the United States. Can urban development be controlled? If urban development cannot be controlled, then it cannot be planned, and all the foregoing questions are merely rhetorical.

At this point, the distinction of scale must be raised. Urban planning must deal with a variety of scales. At one extreme is the scale of the small housing development, the shopping center, and the residential neighborhood. At the other extreme is the scale of the entire metropolitan area and even the region which surrounds it. There is no doubt that it is possible to control and to plan the developments at the lower end of the scale. It is even possible to make plans for certain functional activities at the metropolitan scale. Transportation, as will be shown, is a case in point. But the reason planning is possible for these metropolitan functional activities is that control exists which makes planning meaningful.

However, at the metropolitan scale, there is a very serious question as to whether it is possible, in the United States, to draw meaningful physical plans. The reason is that the growth of the metropolitan area, and of regions, is the result of hundreds of actions by individuals who have the right to build on their small parcels whenever they want, and where governmental controls pertain only to the micro-scale of development and even then are often modified to suit the developer's needs. In Europe, which has a different tradition of land ownership and a tradition of strong governmental controls, the possibility of realistic metropolitan planning exists. But the evidence which is brought forward later in this book suggests strongly that metropolitan planning in the United States under our current economic and governmental procedures is impossible.

This leaves transportation planners in a serious dilemma. On the one hand, in the transportation field there exists the potential for developing and implementing metropolitan transportation plans. On the other hand, there are a perceived set of major urban problems which planners would like to help reduce in magnitude. But there are very few controls, and governmental acts of construction are small in scale compared with the size of the problems. Further, the effectiveness of transportation actions in reducing these other urban problems is not known.

Under these circumstances, the best that can be done is to prepare transportation plans to the best of one's ability, trusting that in time greater understanding of urban development and firmer controls will allow a more productive coordination to take place.

II

TRAVEL: CHARACTERISTICS AND LOCATION

BASIC to any planning is an understanding of materials. Materials are viewed here in a broad sense. The engineer, for example, must understand not only the strengths of the materials used in a bridge but also the loads that will be imposed on that bridge. The materials of the transportation planner include not only the physical ways and vehicles within which people and goods move about but also travel itself, and the activities which generate travel. In this chapter, attention is focused upon urban travel.

Travel is the movement of people and of goods between activities which are separated in space. It is a necessary concomitant of the activities of individuals and of the groupings of people (such as businesses, governments, and private institutions) within society. Without travel, people could not specialize their activities and maintain or increase their over-all productivity.

The planner has to deal with travel in measured terms, not subjectively or intuitively. The subject is too large and the daily movements of people and vehicles are too diverse to permit any other kind of examination. Therefore, we have to start with fact. For transportation planning, the principal data on travel have been generally gathered by massive origin-destination surveys, including home interviews, roadside interviews, and interviews of the drivers of commercial vehicles. The interviewing processes are described more fully in Chapter VII.

The data which are presented in this book are drawn mainly from the work of the Chicago Area Transportation Study[1] and from

[1] Chicago Area Transportation Study, *Final Report*: vol. I (Survey Findings),

the Niagara Frontier Transportation Study.[2] Other sources could have been used equally well, and would have provided similar sets of information.[3] The Chicago data, however, have the advantage of having been portrayed by use of the Cartographatron, and these displays are still the most exciting graphics of travel ever made.

It is convenient to divide presentation of travel data into two parts: that part which describes the general characteristics of travel (such as time, purpose, mode, and length) and that part which describes the geographic distribution of travel. These are now taken up in order.

The Characteristics of Travel

A limited number of sets of data is reported here for the purpose of giving the dimensions of urban travel. Having some of these dimensions at his fingertips is absolutely necessary for either the transportation planner or the civic leader, because this helps him to see things in their proper proportions as well as to understand how the phenomenon "travel" works.

It is not just numbers and sizes, however, which the data show, but a very high degree of regularity and sense in the ways in which people move about the metropolitan area. This contrasts strongly with the prevailing conventional wisdom about travel—a "wisdom" which suggests that people are individually either stupid or capricious in traveling at all, in their choice of mode, in their appraisal of costs, or in their choice of routes of travel. The numbers and characteristics of travel, as they gradually become visible, demonstrate time after time that regularity, economy, and sense exist.

1959; vol. II (Data Projections), 1960; vol. III (Transportation Plan), 1962. Often cited as CATS.

[2] Niagara Frontier Transportation Study, *Final Report*: vol. I (The Basis of Travel), 1964; vol. II (Travel), 1966. Often cited as NFTS.

[3] For example, see *Report on the Detroit Metropolitan Area Traffic Study*, Parts I and II, 1955 and 1956; Pittsburgh Area Transportation Study, *Final Report*, vols. I and II, 1961 and 1963; Penn Jersey Transportation Study, *Reports*, vols. I and II; *Measure of a Region* (Tri-State Transportation Commission, New York, May, 1967).

1. *Trips and Travel in Relation to Population.* In large cities, where trips made by nonresidents are a small percentage of the total, trip-making is directly a function of population size. The trip production rate of the population in the Chicago study area in 1956, for example, was 2.0 person trips per day. (A person trip is defined basically as a one-way journey of a person five years of age or older in an automobile or a transit vehicle to a destination outside the block of trip origin.) By contrast, the Niagara Frontier in 1962 had a weekday trip production rate of 2.3 person trips per person. Smaller cities with lower densities and higher car ownership rates tend to have higher trip production rates than larger cities.

With a population of 5,170,000 persons, the Chicago area's total trip production was 10,212,000 person trips daily in 1956. These were trips made in vehicles, as indicated by the preceding definition. An additional 3,921,000 walking trips were also made each day; this was estimated on the basis of a sub-sample taken of walking trips during the latter part of the home interview survey.[4] Walking trips were defined as one-way journeys of persons five years of age and older outside the lot of trip origin, except that social-recreation trips by persons under sixteen years of age inside the block of trip origin were not included. All of the preceding figures are for weekdays and do not include data for Saturdays, Sundays, or holidays.

Turning to vehicle trips, which include truck trips as well as automobile trips, there were 1.2 vehicle trips made per person per weekday in Chicago. The total number of weekday vehicle trips having destinations in the study area was 5,944,000, not including 16,000 vehicle trips that passed completely through the study area. More than 86 percent of these vehicle trips were by automobiles; the remainder were trucks. Average car loading was 1.5 persons per car.

The unit used to measure journeys is the trip, but the unit used to measure amount of travel is the person mile or the vehicle mile. Person and vehicle miles of travel, because they account for trip length, provide a better measure of impact upon street and transit systems than the trip unit does.

[4] Roger L. Creighton, "Report on the Walking Trip Survey," Chicago Area Transportation Study, Chicago, 1961.

In the Chicago area, 8.0 air-line person miles of travel—about ten miles over-the-road—was generated for each resident each weekday, as recorded by the home interview survey. This included trips by bus, subway, elevated train, and surburban railroad as well as by automobile.

The average vehicle garaged within the area traveled 21.0 miles each day over the road. The total (unweighted) vehicle miles of travel within the study area was 36,200,000 each weekday. Of this, 33,700,000 were driven by vehicles garaged in the study area.

2. *The Uses of Vehicles.* Eighty-six percent of all vehicle trips in the Chicago area of 1956 were made to move people, and 14 percent were made to move freight. However, the average truck has a greater impact upon the road system than the average passenger car because of its greater length and weight and slower acceleration rate. More than one-fifth of all weighted vehicle miles driven on roads in the Chicago area were driven by trucks in 1956.[5]

The vehicle miles of travel produced by trucks is distributed throughout the city fairly evenly in relation to passenger car travel, although there is a tendency to greater proportions of trucks in commercial and industrial areas. In time, truck travel is more evenly distributed across the working day than is automobile travel. As shown in Figure 1, truck travel peaks at 10:00 A.M. and 2:00 P.M., which is off-peak as far as automobile travel is concerned.

3. *The Regular Cycles of Travel in Time.* People have very definite rhythms about their urban trip-making. Over the year (as the Chicago study's long-term traffic counting program showed) there is a very slow cycle of changing trip-making, with winter being generally about 12 percent below the annual average and summer about 12 percent above the annual average. During the five weekdays, travel varies about 5 percent about the mean—low on Mondays and Tuesdays and high on Fridays. Each of the two weekend days—within most of the urban area—is generally below the

---

[5] In the weighting process, a tractor-trailer was considered as equal to three automobiles; a medium truck, two; and a panel or pick-up as one.

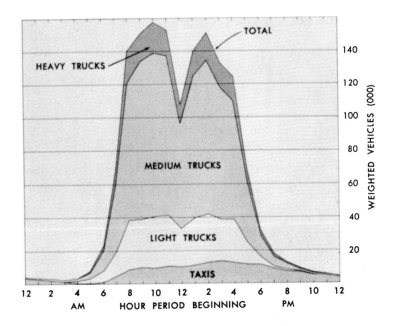

Figure 1.
Hourly distribution of truck and taxi trips, Chicago area, 1956.

average weekday in trip-making. (Weekend peaks occur mainly
on outlying roads connecting urban areas with vacation or resort
regions.)

Within the average weekday, however, there are tremendous
peaks and valleys in travel. Figure 2 shows the pattern of hourly
travel for the Chicago area in 1956. For comparison, Figure 3 shows
the pattern of hourly travel for the Niagara Frontier in 1962. In
each case the peak travel period is in the afternoon hour beginning
at 5:00 P.M. and the second peak is in the morning hour beginning
at 8:00 A.M. The least travel occurs between 3:00 A.M. and 4:00
A.M. This peaking is clearly the result of the day-night cycle in which
people go out from their resting places in the morning and return
in the evening. The greater ease of travel in the lower density Niagara Frontier may account for the third, evening peak of travel which
shows up in that survey.

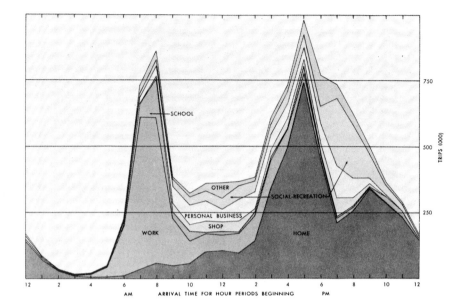

Figure 2.
Hourly distribution of internal person trips, by trip purpose,
Chicago area, 1956.

4. *The Activity Linkages of Travel.* Home is the base from
and to which most person trips are made. Over 86 percent of all
trips made by people in the Chicago area had either their origins or
their destinations at home.

When trips are examined as to land use at origin and destination, the same things shows up: 92.8 percent of all person trips have
origins and/or destinations on residential land. Thus, as in the day-
night time cycle, most travel orbits out and back from the home.
Only 7.2 percent of person trips are made with both origin and destination at nonresidential land uses.

Truck and taxi travel, however, has a substantially different
pattern. Sixty-one percent of such vehicles make their trips from one
nonresidential activity to another, and 82.0 percent of truck and
taxi trips have a nonresidential land use at either origin or destina-

tion or both. This demonstrates how commercial vehicle trips are extensions of nonresidential (chiefly commercial and industrial) activities.

5. *The Purpose of Person Trips; Land Use.* Table 2 shows the purposes for which person trips in the Chicago area were made in

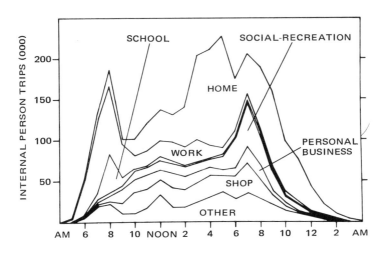

Figure 3.
Hourly distribution of trips, by trip purpose, Niagara Frontier, 1962.

1956. These are "destination" purposes. A table showing "origin" purposes, that is, the kind of personal activity which a person is leaving in order to make his next trip, would be almost identical. Thus a person going to home has his next trip coming from home. The only differences that can occur between "origin" and "destination" purposes are the result of situations such as a person's driving to shop, then walking to a restaurant to eat a meal, and then proceeding by car to his next destination. Since walking does not count as a trip, the purpose at destination and the purpose at origin are different. Such differences are, however, very small in proportion to the great mass of trips.

"Home" is the largest single trip purpose, as might be expected. It is the base from and to which trips cycle during the day. After "home," "work" is the largest purpose, followed by social-recreation and personal business.

Just as "home" is the largest single trip purpose, residential land as a whole generates the most person trips (see Table 3). Commercial land is the second largest generator of trips, and since its area is quite small—only about 3 to 5 percent of developed land within the typical American city—it generates trips at very high rates per acre.

Table 2. *Purpose of Person Trips Made in the Chicago Area, 1956*

Purpose at Destination	Percentage of All Person Trips
Home	43.5
Work	20.6
Shop	5.5
School	1.9
Social-Recreation	12.8
Eat Meal	2.1
Personal Business	10.2
Serve Passenger	2.4
Ride	1.0
Total	100.0

Source: CATS, *Final Report*, vol. I, Table 38.

Table 3. *Land Use at Destination of Person Trips in the Chicago Area, 1956*

Land Use at Destination	Percentage of All Person Trips
Residential	54.9
Manufacturing	7.6
Transportation, Communications, and Public Utilities	2.7
Commercial	24.0
Public Buildings	7.7
Public Open Space	3.1
Total	100.0

Source: CATS, *Final Report*, vol. I, Table 38.

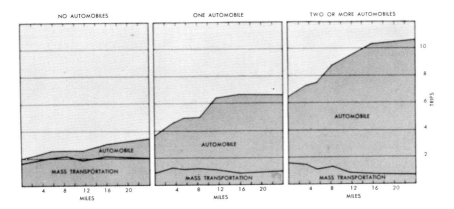

Figure 4.
Trip production per family, by mode, for families with zero,
one, and two or more automobiles, by distance from the Loop,
Chicago area, 1956.

6. *Trip-making of Families Related to Location of Residence and Car Ownership.* One of the more complicated—and more interesting—regularities of urban travel has to do with the production of trips by families and their choice of mode of travel as related to car ownership and distance of residence from the center of the city. Figure 4 shows, in its first section, how families that do not own cars use transit for most of their trips, whatever their distance of residence from the central business district. (Even families without automobiles make some trips in automobiles—as passengers in a car pool, for example.) Families without cars make more trips when they live farther away from the core, but their proportional use of transit still remains very high.

The second and third sections of Figure 4 show how ownership of either one or two cars cuts drastically into transit riding. Those who own cars, whatever their place of residence, make two and three times as many trips as those who do not own vehicles, and they make most of their trips by car.

7. *Trip-making and Age.* Who makes all these trips? An age cross-section taken from data of the Niagara Frontier Transporta-

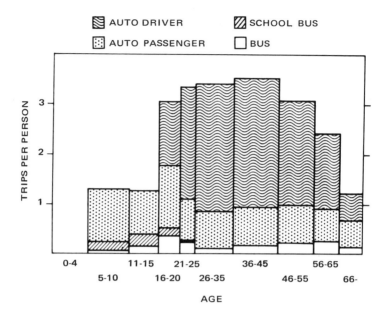

Figure 5.
Daily trips per person, by age and mode of travel,
Niagara Frontier, 1962.

tion Study (see Figure 5) shows that persons between 16 and 55 are
well above average in trip-making, and that the group making the
most trips consists of those persons between 36 and 45 years of age.
From the age of 45, trip-making steadily declines, and those over 66,
like those under 16, are well below average in generating trips. Age
also affects choice of mode. Under 16, of course, all persons must be
passengers since they cannot drive. Transit use is heaviest, proportionately, for those under 20 and over 56.

8. *The Time-Use of Automobiles.* From time to time statistics
are shown which "prove" that if one more automobile is produced,
all the highways of a country will simply be filled up, and the whole
transportation system will jell. What these statistics ignore is that
automobiles spend most of their time parked, and in the highest

single six-minute period, only 24 percent of all vehicles are likely to be in motion.[6]

One of the first graphs of the time usage of automobiles was produced by the Niagara Frontier Transportation Study in 1965, and this diagram is reproduced as Figure 6. Part of the reason for the lateness of the appearance of this graph is that it was not until computers became sufficiently fast and big and until more important problems had been solved that time could be set aside for the production of such curiosities as this.

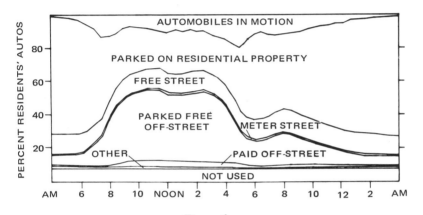

Figure 6.
Automobiles in motion and at rest, by time of day,
Niagara Frontier, 1962.

It is most interesting to see how, in an urban area of over a million people, most cars are parked so much of the time, and how most of them are parked without charge to the driver, not only at residential places but at industrial and commercial establishments. Only a very small minority of cars pay for parking.

9. *Trip Length.* Of all the data presented in this book, data on the distribution of trips by their lengths are probably most impor-

[6] Niagara Frontier Transportation Study, *Final Report*, vol. II. Figure 6 shows 20 percent, but this is for the peak 15-minute period.

tant. These data are the basis for the important theoretical developments of the 1950's, and it is essential to carry this knowledge into planning for the road and mass transportation systems of cities and for the placement of their land uses.

Most trips are short, and there is a steady and very regular decline in trip frequency as trip length increases. Generally, in the larger urban areas 20 to 25 percent of all person trips, by all modes of travel, are under one mile in length; another 20 percent are between one and two miles in length; another 12 to 15 percent are between two and three miles in length. Thus, *half of all trips are under three miles in length*. As length increases, fewer and fewer trips are made. Each interval of a mile between ten and twenty miles contains generally fewer than 1 percent of trips. All trips over twenty miles in length total up to less than 5 percent (see Figure 7).

Of course, the shorter trips, despite their greater frequency, produce less of an impact on the street system. Medium and longer trips, because of their length, exert a greater degree of traffic wear and tear. It is by siphoning these trips off onto specialized facilities that some of the most important improvements in transportation can be made.

The amount of wear and tear imposed on the street system by trips of different lengths can be calculated readily. The number of trips in each trip length interval (usually one mile) is multiplied by the average length of that interval; the sum of these products is the total (air-line) vehicle miles of travel driven on the streets of the area. The percentage contribution of each trip length group to the total can then be found. The results of such a calculation are shown in Figure 8 for the Chicago area as it was in 1956.

Figure 8 shows that 50 percent of all vehicle miles of travel are made by that 17 percent of all trips which are seven miles in length or greater. By contrast, the 66 percent of all trips under four miles in length only produce 27 percent of the vehicle miles of travel.

The Geographic Distribution of Travel

One of the prime difficulties which plagued transportation planners until 1956 was the difficulty of making geographical pre-

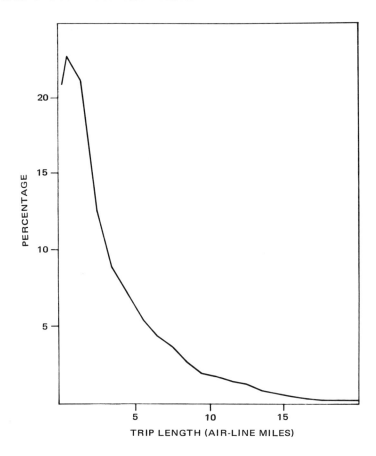

Figure 7.
Trip length frequency distribution of automobile trips,
Chicago area, 1956.

sentations of origin and destination data in a way which would be meaningful, either to the planner or to the layman. This revolved around two problems: the problem of aggregation and the problem of the mechanics of visual display. It is necessary to digress into these problems in order better to understand the geographical displays of the Chicago data which are presented later in this chapter.

Consider first the problem of aggregation. Take a metropolitan

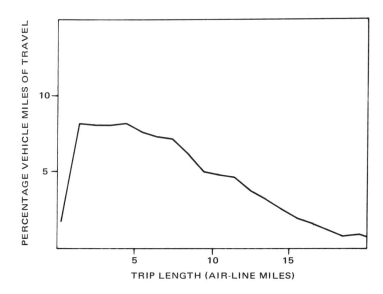

Figure 8.
Frequency distribution of automobile vehicle miles of travel,
by trip length, Chicago area, 1956.

area and say that its population is 5,000,000 persons. That is all that
is known: the metropolitan area has a population of 5,000,000.
However, if we divide the metropolitan area into two parts, for
example, central city and suburb, then we can make comparisons;
we know twice as much and can speculate on relationships. If we
divide it into four pieces, we know at least four times as much—
actually much more, because between four pieces of an area there
are six relationships. The more we subdivide the area, the more we
know about it; that is, the smaller the units we use to summarize
data by, the more we know about the whole.[7]

However, the problem of presenting travel data by smaller and
smaller units gets progressively more difficult. Anyone who has ever
used statistics knows that a table with more than ten rows and ten

[7] And, by contrast, the less we know about each individual piece. The errors
of samples creep in when the data are more finely presented. Thus there is a bal-
ancing of the extent to which detail can be dealt with.

columns is almost incomprehensible; actually, the limit should be much smaller, perhaps five by five. But data on origins and destinations, to be useful in estimating what volumes will use a new road, must be presented by many small units—often as many as three to five hundred zones within an urban area. A table with a few hundred rows and columns, such as is sometimes seen in the reports of the older transportation studies, is practically meaningless except as evidence of work done.

To make such data meaningful, the desire line map was invented. In the desire line map, a straight line is drawn from the center of an origin zone to the center of a destination zone—theoretically, one line for each trip. Where multiple trips go between zones, the bundles of trips are represented by bands, the width of each band being proportional to the number of trips.

Upon completion of such a map, one had a fairly good picture of where people wanted to go. And one had a nice bill for drafting, since a city with a mere 100 zones in it would have 5,000 lines to be drawn by hand. To cut down on this expense, the numbers of zones had to be reduced to a few: 20 zones would require only 200 sets of lines to be drawn. But this meant that the data were once again aggregated by such large units that meaningful conclusions could not readily be drawn. Impasse.

In California in 1947–48, to get around the problem of hand-drawing of desire lines (and other problems as well), it was decided to create very small zones using a grid scheme, each zone one-tenth mile on a side.[8] These grids, having an x-y or Cartesian system of identification, could be handled readily within even the simple card computers available at that time. Furthermore, the computer could calculate, knowing the x-y position of both origin and destination, what the other zones would be through which that trip would have to pass, assuming that its desire was to travel in a straight line. In this fashion, the desire line miles of travel could be summed up for each zone and a map colored to show the intensity of travel desire lines through each square mile zone.

The Detroit Metropolitan Area Traffic Study (1953–55) im-

[8] "Traffic Survey of the Sacramento Area," State of California, Department of Public Works, Division of Highways, Sacramento, 1947–48.

proved on this method. By an ingenious system, data cards produced by the computer were sorted in inverse Y sequence and were then fed into a tabulating machine which was wired to print the values of the intensity of desire lines directly in their proper position on a map.

The study area in Chicago was twice as big as Detroit's. The trip data were coded directly to the block of origin and destination and these could be summarized either into 4,800 quarter square miles or into 500 zones. It was the quarter square miles which we hoped to use for trip desire line density calculations. But with the card calculator and printer speeds of those days, this job was impossible to do within any reasonable time.

This problem was posed by the Chicago Area Transportation Study to the Armour Research Foundation. They studied the matter and then proposed to build a machine which would actually draw each individual trip as a straight line on the face of a precision cathode ray tube, there to be summed up on a photographic plate. A contract was thereupon let and within a year the machine was operational.[9]

The following paragraphs are taken from the first volume of the final report of the Chicago Area Transportation Study. They describe the essential features of the Cartographatron and the way in which it was used.

In the simplest of terms, the Cartographatron is a combination of an electronic computer, a television picture tube, and a camera.

Before the Cartographatron could be operated, travel data had to be prepared for its use. The travel data were transferred from punched cards to magnetic tape and in the process of making this conversion, the desire line length and direction of each trip were computed. The completed magnetic tape contained information on the origin, directon, and characteristics of each trip. This magnetic tape could then be read by the Cartographatron.

The panel of this machine contains selectors which permit an op-

[9] One has to express a word of appreciation here for the support exhibited by the Policy Committee of the Chicago Area Transportation Study in this and other instances of innovation.

erator to select for display only those trips having desired characteristics. Thus trips can be selected, according to their length, purpose, time of arrival, land use, zone of origin, direction, mode of travel or any other of a total of twenty-two trip characteristics.

For any trips so selected, the Cartographatron converts the numerical data on the tape into voltages which then generate a blip of light on the face of a cathode ray tube, moving it precisely at the correct angle from the trip's origin to its destination. The speed at which this blip of light moves is a function of the trip's factor—that is, the number used to expand that sampled trip to its correct proportion of the total universe of travel. The slower the speed, the greater would be the amount of light generated on the face of the tube and hence the greater number of trips represented.

In the Study Area, all of the trips are traced between quarter square mile grids. Trips with origins and/or destinations outside the cordon line are traced either from the centers of the political unit to which they are coded or, in the case of trips starting outside ring "8," the trace starts at the sector point of entry.

At all times during the running of a tape, a camera with its lens open is focused on the face of the cathode ray tube. Each blip of light is recorded on a photographic plate, the weight of each line being directly related to the speed of the moving blip. The photographic plate accumulates the records of thousands of trips, with varying *densities* of desire lines as more of these lines accumulate in some places than in others.

The Cartographatron, in processing data as described above, completes a single trip desire line in one ten thousandth of a second, or 20,000 trips in seven minutes. By other methods, this would have required many hours of machine processing and additional hours of cartographic work. Further, the Cartographatron permits the selection of trips to be mapped. All of the characteristics of a trip (mode, purpose, time, etc.) are recorded on the same tape. By use of the selection panel on the Cartographatron, it is possible to select only those trips of immediate interest, and to map them.

To place the Cartographatron operation in its proper perspective, the size of the travel inventory must be considered. Trip records from all surveys combined require more than 378,000 punched cards. In terms of magnetic tape, this equals nineteen reels. This is the travel inventory file which, when expanded, accounts for each of the

10,500,000 daily trips. Allowing time for the changing of reels, it takes about 7 minutes to run one reel. A map of the entire file can be prepared in approximately four hours.[10]

The purpose of the Cartographatron as originally conceived was twofold: first to display the density of trip desire lines in each square mile of the study area, and second, to gain knowledge by displaying the patterns of different kinds of trips. The first purpose failed: measuring the density of desire lines, even with the most precise optical instruments, was an inaccurate and clumsy business. The Detroit procedure, with its slow digital calculations, was superior. However, our great need to measure density evaporated because better planning tools were created, and so this failure was cancelled by other successes.

But in providing knowledge, the Cartographatron was a brilliant success. A new microscope had been built, and we could peer into it and see the little bursts of light which represented the trips of a household, spraying out to their several destinations and then shooting back home again. This was actually possible to see on the monitor tube on the face of the machine.

Once these patterns were accumulated on photographic plates by a camera focused on the large, precision cathode ray tube, we had as fine-grained a picture of metropolitan travel as anyone could desire. And with this accurate mental picture we could see better how a system should be designed.

No longer were we slaves to the notion that all travel goes to the central business district or that we should build roads "to serve people who go from here to there." Travel turned out to be much more evenly spread, more scattered in direction. Different types of trips, different modes of travel, different land uses all generated their own unique patterns. The complexity was enormous; our ignorance had been very great.

In the following pages, illustrations and text describe the patterns of trips made by people and vehicles across the Chicago study area.

[10] Chicago Area Transportation Study, *Final Report*, I, 97–99.

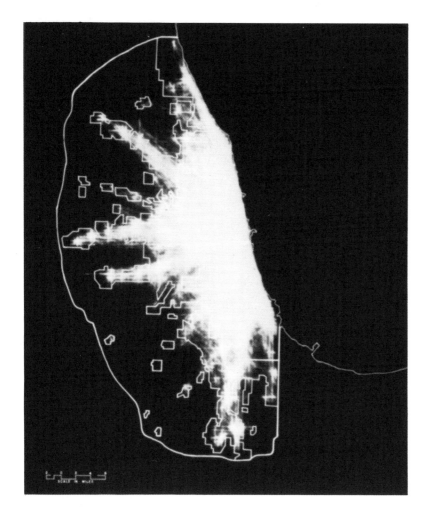

Figure 9.
Desire lines of internal automobile driver trips.

1. *Automobile Trips.* The geographic distribution of the automobile trips recorded in the 1956 home interview survey in the Chicago area is shown in Figure 9. More than 4,811,000 automobile driver trips are represented on this display.

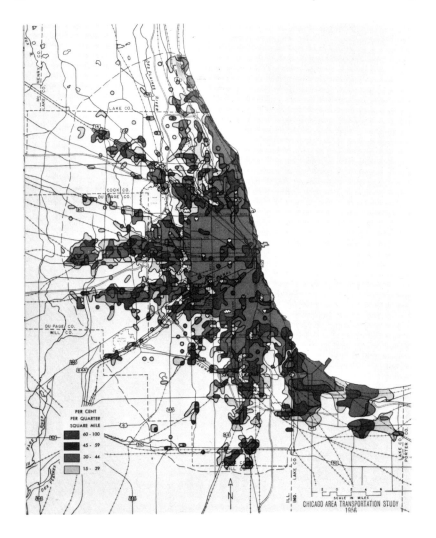

Figure 10.
Developed land, Chicago area, 1956.

A first observation is that the presence of automobile travel
made by residents[11] coexists with the extent of urban development,

[11] And their guests, and residents of temporary quarters such as hotels and
motels.

and the correspondence is quite exact. (See Figure 10 showing urban development in the Chicago area.) The intensity of this automobile travel increases where the density of urban development is greater, although the correspondence is not linear, since transit starts to carry increasing proportions of travelers in denser parts of the urban area.

It is worth noting that the pattern of travel is not in any single predominant direction, but is omni-directional. As will be shown later, there is more radial travel than circumferential travel, but in

Figure 11.
Model of automobile trip destinations, Chicago area, 1956.

Figure 9 this fact cannot be discerned readily. The conclusion which must be drawn from the fact of omni-directional travel is that transportation facilities have to serve people so that they can move in all directions with nearly equal ease.

Since the Cartographatron displays do not show differences in density very well (especially when printed on paper instead of being recorded on a photographic positive), another kind of display must be shown to portray density. This is achieved in a block model such as is illustrated in Figure 11. This latter figure shows automobile driver trip destinations in each quarter square mile of the Chicago area. The blocks record density quite accurately.

Figure 11 again demonstrates that trip-making is a function of land use. The over-all pattern is like the pattern of land development. What is surprising about this display is that the density of automobile driver trip destinations is so flat. It appears to be only twice as high in the city of Chicago as in the suburban areas, while population densities in the city are nearly four times as high.

This figure should be compared with Figure 12, which shows

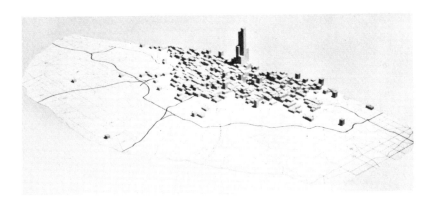

Figure 12.
Total floor area model.

the density of floor area in the Chicago area (suburban areas excluded because their floor area was not measured). The high peak of floor area in the Loop and the central area surrounding the Loop is not matched by an equivalent peak of automobile driver destinations. The reason is that mass transportation carries the heavy volumes of people that go to this concentrated area.

2. *Truck Trips.* Truck trips are shown in Figure 13. The pattern is similar to that of automobile driver trips, but is slightly more concentrated toward the core. The core area is where there is a greater concentration of the commercial, wholesaling, and manufacturing activities which are served by trucks. Suggestions are often advanced to build special truck roads or truck expressways, but an inspection of Figure 13 shows how uniformly truck trips are distrib-

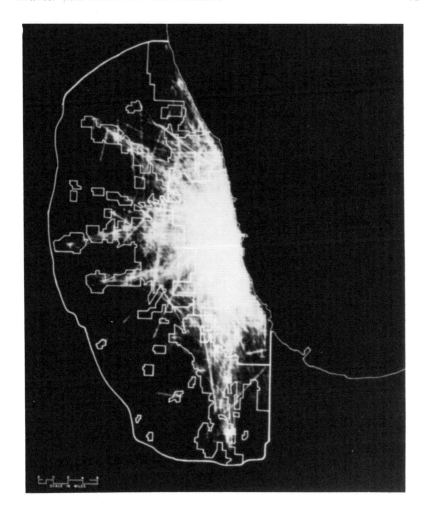

Figure 13.
Desire lines of internal truck trips, Chicago area, 1956.

uted, and hence how unwise it would be to create a separate network
to serve them.

3. *External Trips.* Many persons conceive of travel which
enters an urban area from the outside as consisting only of two kinds

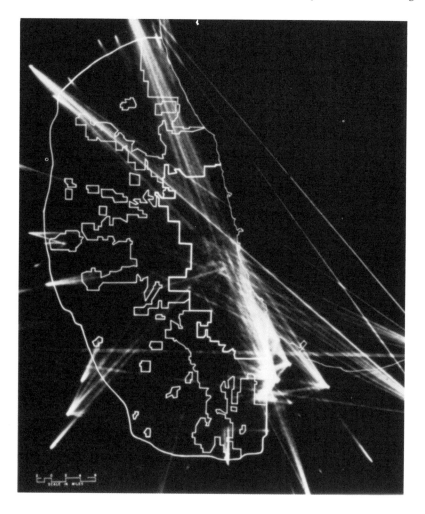

Figure 14.
Desire lines of all external vehicle trips, Chicago area, 1956.

of trips: those made by persons who want to go completely through
the urban area, and those made by persons who want to go to the
central business district.

   This impression is a false one, as shown in Figure 14. External trips spray out from their sector "entry points" to destinations throughout the entire urban area. The central business district attracts only its fair share. Those trips which go all the way through the urban area are exaggerated in their importance by the fact that the Cartographatron is given exact points between which these trips must run, and the light beam of the tube superimposes these trips on top of each other, whereas the single trips to more scattered destinations tend to get lost in the reproduction process.

4. *Bus Trips and Rapid Transit Trips.* The traces of bus trips and rapid transit trips are shown respectively in Figures 15 and 16. Seeing these at identical exposure and weighting as automobile driver trips, one gains an indelible impression of the extent and nature of transit travel as compared with that of the automobile.

Bus trips take place within a much more restricted area than that of automobile travel—an area which is coincidental with the areas of high-density settlement of population. Where population density exceeds 17,000 persons per square mile of land in urban use, as it does in most of the city of Chicago and in large parts of the nearby communities of Evanston, Oak Park, and Cicero, then bus service can be provided on a fairly economical basis. Where densities fall below that level, the provision of bus service becomes marginal or unprofitable: service levels are lowered, and most people select and use automobiles for their trips.

Rapid transit travel, on the other hand, is seen as a specialized means of moving people for long distances to the central business district (CBD) of a metropolitan area. More than 80 percent of rail rapid transit trips in Chicago were to the central area, which is a 13.6–square mile area centered on the Loop. This area had, in 1956, more than 1,164,000 person trip destinations to it, of which 26.5 percent were by rail rapid transit. Where the CBD is sufficiently large in terms of employment, the movement of people to the CBD over existing rail lines can be done economically. The principle of using existing facilities to the utmost is a sound one here, especially when the alternative would mean extremely heavy costs for the construction of new pavements or new systems for the movement of these same people over identical distances.

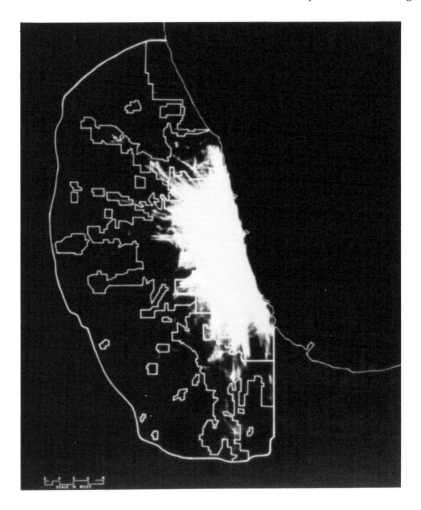

Figure 15.
Desire lines of internal person trips using buses,
Chicago area, 1956.

5. *Short Trips and Long Trips.* One of the things we wanted
to ascertain later in the course of our work in Chicago was whether
the patterns of trips of different kinds indicated the existence of
distinct and identifiable communities. The term "community," like

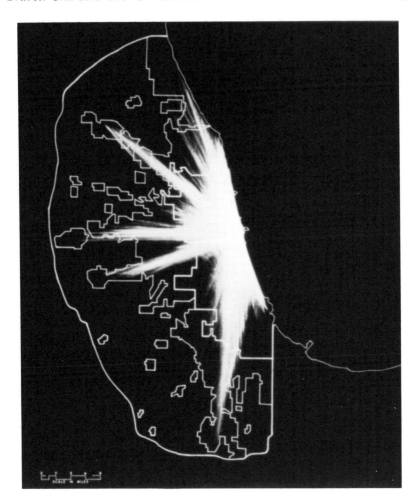

Figure 16.
Desire lines of internal person trips using rapid transit,
Chicago area, 1956.

the term "neighborhood," had been developed by city planners to
have a special meaning: a part of a city occupying an identifiable
area of land, whose population of twenty or forty thousand persons
had fairly strong place-ties and might be served by common facilities

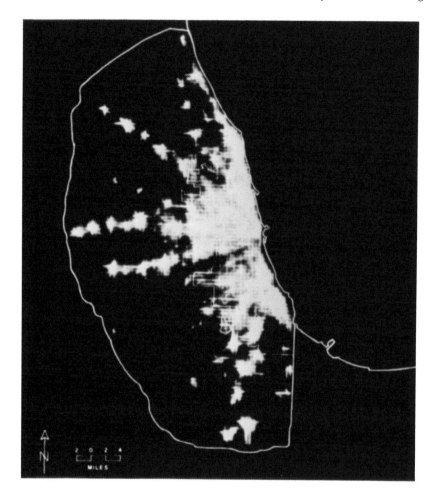

Figure 17.
Automobile trips less than three miles long.

such as a major shopping center, a junior or senior high school, and other public and private facilities.

To test out this idea, a Cartographatron display was made in which trips of only one- and two-mile lengths were shown. It was reasoned that if there were communities in existence, these short trips would identify their areas, since there would be more trips made within the community than between the community and adjacent communities.

The resulting display is shown here as Figure 17. The existence of communities could not be proved by this device. In the suburban areas, where the small suburbs were grouped around railroad stations and were in turn surrounded by farmland, a distinct "community" pattern was shown. However, this seemed to be more a case of absence of other places for people to go on their short trips than anything else. Within the mass of completely urbanized area (the city of Chicago and the near-in suburbs) the short trips blurred together. Only the voids created by river barriers, forest preserves, and industrial strips seemed to prevent all the short trips from covering the entire area.

The idea of communities forming themselves naturally while cities grow in their present fashion thus does not seem to hold up.[12] This is not to say that the idea of community is undesirable, or that if a whole city were to be planned from scratch they could not be created. What it does say is that when cities grow as they do now, their patterns of travel suggest that people move in one direction for shopping, in another for schooling, and in other directions for their other purposes. As a result, the service areas of the different activities (schooling, local government, shopping, fire protection, social, religious, and so on) are quite independent and do not coincide in the way in which planners, using conventional reasoning, would like.

By contrast with the short trips, Figure 18 shows the pattern of trips of ten or more miles in length in the Chicago area. Here is seen how a metropolitan area is knit together. There is a clearly evident radial direction to travel—not surprising with the greater concentration of work opportunities in the core area (not just in the central business district itself but in the much larger warehousing and industrial areas around the center). Even with this radial travel in evidence, there is a very large amount of travel in other directions. If the central area continues to diminish in *relative importance* (as it must, unless its growth rate equals that of the entire metropolitan

[12] Alan Black, "An Examination of the Community Concept with Reference to the Study Area," Chicago Area Transportation Study, Chicago, 1961.

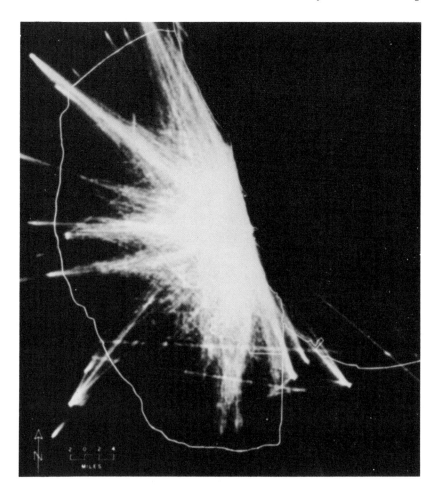

Figure 18.
Automobile trips ten miles in length or longer.

area), then circumferential travel will gradually increase in relative importance and we shall see that people must be provided with opportunities to go equally to all places in the metropolitan area, which is their field of opportunity.

Conclusion

The more travel is examined, the less it becomes an abstract, arbitrary, or capricious phenomenon, and the more it becomes the sum of the sensible and purposeful actions which people make in order to satisfy their wants within an urban environment. Everyone who looks at the tables and graphs which display the total trips of a metropolitan area, and studies the characteristics and locations of these trips, sees himself and his family or friends making these same kinds of journeys. Whether it is the mass movement to work which makes up the peak morning hour, or the very infrequent trip at two o'clock in the morning, others are doing the same thing; the quantities vary, as the time chart shows, but the happening is there.

It should be humbling to look at travel in this fashion. One sees oneself as a very small part of an enormous number of daily travelers. But more important, one must admit that if he is traveling and making intelligent decisions about whether to go, and where, and how, other people are probably acting equally intelligently on their parts. With this viewpoint one cannot afford to take a moralistic view or claim that other people are making decisions which are wrong or stupid. Planning for transportation facilities must be an action to help people who are doing important things and behaving reasonably intelligently as they go about their journeys.

III

URBAN TRAVEL: THEORY

In the various transportation studies that were undertaken up to 1955, very little work had been done to develop a theory or theories of travel. It was in the tradition of the early practitioners to look on data only as a means of solving very specific and immediate problems, such as the location of a new highway or transit line. The longer-range uses of data were subordinated to the immediate and practical; once the answers to certain specific questions were obtained, the data were filed. Considering the undoubted pressures which existed to find solutions to particular problems, and considering the limited finances and resources available in the 1930's and 1940's, this short-range viewpoint can be understood.

There were urgent reasons, however, for developing a theoretical understanding of travel, and these increased in importance as time went on. It was being seen more clearly that plans were needed for entire systems rather than individual projects. The larger the transportation system being planned, the longer the time period required to build it. The task of metropolitan transportation studies is to plan a network for an entire metropolitan area. Such a system generally will take a minimum of twenty years, and perhaps thirty or forty years, to complete. The longer the time period, the older is the data obtained by survey at the beginning of the planning process—and the planning process itself might take six years.

The purpose of developing theories of travel was to uncover and explain, in a reasoned fashion, those regularities in travel which would be likely to persist over a long time period and which would thereby make traffic forecasting sufficiently reliable to be used in long-range planning.

The kind of theory which was needed was quite simple to define, but being simply defined, was made harder to develop. Theory is a statement describing *how* something behaves. The statement could be verbal initially, but ultimately it had to be mathematical and hence quantitative; it had to be capable of being verified experimentally; and it had to be generalized rather than particular. Actually, this is the basic definition of theory used in science. Newton's law of gravity ($G = m_1 m_2/d^2$) and Einstein's theory of relativity ($e = mc^2$) are both exactly this kind of statement: a mathematical description of how certain phenomena behave.

The requirement of generalization distinguishes theory from empirical formulas. There are many formulas which describe, for example, how beams bend under loads or how trips are diverted from slower to faster roads. These are mathematical statements of how things happen, but they are intentionally limited and pragmatic descriptions, and they lack the wider applicability which characterizes theory.

The Travel Forecasting Problem

The critical problem facing the staff of the Chicago study in 1956 was to develop a reasoned theory which would enable estimates to be made of *where* trips would go in the future. The travel patterns of 1956 were known as well as any sample survey could determine. And it seemed certain that we could estimate, based on a land use plan or land use forecast, the locations and numbers of trip origins in 1980. But where would these trips go? Which origins would be linked to which destinations?[1]

---

[1] This was, of course, not the only area of need for improved theory. Trip generation, choice of mode of travel, and the time of travel (among other areas) were in need of theoretical bases. But it must be remembered that in 1956 we had just taken our first measurements of land use and one of the first travel surveys covering all modes of travel. It would take time to move into these new areas, whereas considerable work had been done previously in the area of trip distribution.

Related to this were questions like "Why are most trips short?" "Why does the trip length frequency distribution curve take its peculiar and regular shape?"

All these questions were important because unless they could be answered there was no solid basis for planning future transportation improvements. With ignorance about future travel movements, the planner would either have to guess, or simply build facilities to ease existing areas of congestion. On the other hand, with foreknowledge based on a theory demonstrably capable of reproducing or simulating travel patterns, plans could be prepared on a rational basis.

Estimating future patterns of travel had, of course, long been recognized as an important technical problem. This was one of the reasons why origin-destination surveys had been taken for so many years. One of the simplest ways of travel forecasting was to expand the known records of travel patterns in relation to the growth of the urban area being planned. This might be called the "factoring" approach to travel forecasting.

The outstanding example of the factoring approach is the Fratar method of averaging growth factors, developed for the Cleveland study in 1954.[2] In this technique, each of the zones comprising the Cleveland area was given an expansion factor to represent its probable growth in trip production for the target year. Known trips between every pair of zones were then expanded by the average of the factors of the zones of origin and destination. The resulting expanded trips were then balanced by an arithmetic procedure so that the sum of the trips leaving each zone equalled the sum expected to arrive at that zone.

One of the weaknesses of this method, as with all methods of factoring, was its inability to forecast travel in those zones which were so sparsely settled in the survey year that there was no adequate record of travel to expand. This was precisely where a method based on theory could prove superior.

[2] Thomas J. Fratar, "Vehicular Trip Distribution by Successive Approximations," *Traffic Quarterly* 8, no. 1 (January, 1954); 53–65. Also Thomas J. Fratar, "Forecasting Distribution of Interzonal Vehicular Trips by Successive Approximations," *Proceedings,* vol. 33, Highway Research Board, Washington, D.C., 1954.

The gravity model, on the other hand, provided a theory of travel which could deal with travel generated in new parts of cities. It was based on the well-known observation that many kinds of human interactions behave in a fashion which is strikingly similar to Newton's law of gravity. That is, trips (or messages) between groups of people occur, in number, proportionately to the products of the sizes of the two population groups and in inverse proportion to some power of the distance between.

The mathematical statement of the gravity model is as follows:[3]

$$T_{ij} = P_i \cfrac{\cfrac{A_j}{d_{ij}^{\,b}}}{\cfrac{A_1}{d_{i1}^{\,b}} + \cfrac{A_2}{d_{i2}^{\,b}} + \ldots \cfrac{A_n}{d_{in}^{\,b}}},$$

where T_{ij} = trips produced in zone i and attracted to zone j;

P_i = trips produced by zone i;

A_j = trips attracted by zone j (from all zones);

d_{ij} = spatial separation between zones i and j. This is generally expressed as total travel time (t_{ij}) between zones i and j.

b = an empirically determined exponent which expresses the *average areawide* effect of spatial separation between zones on trip interchange.

The gravity formula is probably the most widely used formula for estimating travel. However, it was and remains a theory of analogy, not explaining travel but merely saying "it appears that travel does behave in this fashion."

In the hope of developing a better understanding of travel, the staff of the Chicago study set out to develop a new theory of travel. It is worthwhile describing this theory in more detail, for two reasons. First, the "opportunity theory" is an integral part of the testing mech-

[3] *Calibrating and Testing a Gravity Model for Any Size Urban Area,* U.S. Department of Transportation, Federal Highway Administration, Bureau of Public Roads, Washington, D.C., 1968 (reprint).

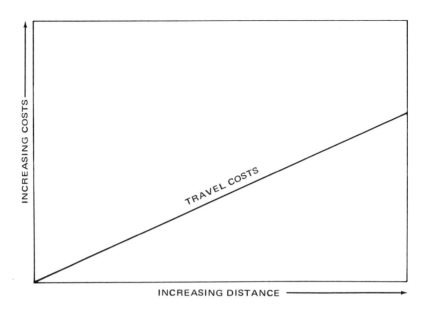

anism whose use is described in Chapter XI, and it later was adopted for use in a model to estimate urban growth. Second, study of the opportunity theory is helpful in increasing one's understanding of travel.

The Opportunity Theory of Travel

It is convenient to begin a discussion of the opportunity theory by describing four of the basic ideas which underlie it.

The first of these ideas is that people want to minimize the cost, time, danger, unpleasantness, and other adverse factors connected with travel. This assumption runs counter to many prevailing notions about travel which suggest that people tend to keep traveling more and more, without limit. But travel does have very real costs in time and money, and these increase with distance, as shown above.

In some fixed-fare systems (as in the New York City subway system) the out-of-pocket cost does not change with distance, but the time cost naturally continues to rise, and time is important to people. For the automobile driver, operating costs (excluding depreciation and insurance) range from 2.5 to 5 cents for every mile which he drives, depending upon driving speed and congestion. In addition, time costs increase with distance. It is quite reasonable to assume that people will consider these costs and will seek to keep their trips as short as possible.

The second idea is that every person who starts out to make a trip is surrounded by a field of opportunities—not all identical—from which he can select one which will meet the need which impelled him to make the trip in the first place. The traveler is selective. This selectivity of individuals can be expressed as a probability—the probability of accepting one of the opportunities available.

The third idea is that while the probability of finding greater rewards or satisfactions increases by traveling farther, the rate of increase declines with distance. As a person starts out from his home to satisfy some desire, the opportunities available to him increase very rapidly, because the land area containing these opportunities increases as the square of the radius outward where he is searching. Hence his probability of getting a greater reward increases. However, the traveler soon finds that the amount of extra satisfaction he gets by traveling a greater distance becomes less and less. Perhaps he comes up against the limits of his earning power—he can't find a better job—or perhaps his ability to find just the right kind of commodity to purchase is not being improved by traveling farther.

The position of the curves in the following diagram will vary depending upon the nature of the trip being made. A trip to buy milk or cigarettes will flatten out very quickly since these are standardized commodities. However, a trip to work or to visit a museum is much more specialized and selective, and people will travel farther for such rewards. (People will travel farther daily to work, and will also travel far, but very infrequently, to go to a museum.)

Fourth, there is an adjustment of the locations of people's activities or land uses to meet the realities of the costs of travel and of people's different needs. Chain store owners, for example, put their establishments at places which are very carefully considered to maxi-

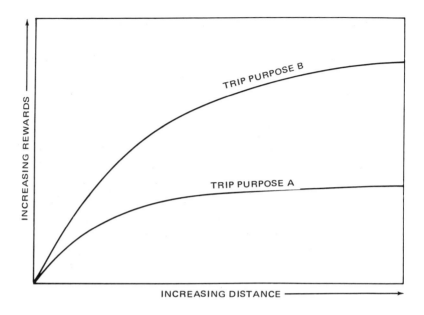

mize profits by getting close to the customer and yet not so close that each store is an uneconomic unit to run. Food store owners know how much the average family spends for food, and they know that trips to their stores have to be made fairly frequently because the average home is not a warehouse. Factories and offices have higher site costs to consider, and they can to a certain extent command people to come to them because the rewards for working are so great in relationship to daily journey costs.

The opportunity theory of trip distribution is a synthesis of ideas such as those described in the preceding paragraphs. In briefest terms, the opportunity theory states that a traveler, searching out from a zone of origin and looking for a suitable destination, has a definable probability of accepting each destination opportunity that he encounters, but that this probability is, in effect, modified so that it becomes lowered by each opportunity that is passed by in the outward search.[4]

[4] See Chicago Area Transportation Study, *Final Report,* II (1960), 79–97, 111. The opportunity theory was developed by Morton Schneider.

To make such a brief statement of the opportunity theory more meaningful, we can describe how a hypothetical person might search for a particular commodity that will give him satisfaction. Obviously, this is an unreal example, because people rarely if ever conduct blind searches for goods. They know by experience or through advertisements, directories, or by word of mouth the place they are going, or the two or three places which they may visit. But for purposes of illustration, the idea of a search is convenient.

The hypothetical person "inspects" every opportunity or set of opportunities which he encounters as he moves outward from his origin. Because he is discriminating about what he is doing—that is, he is shopping rather than inspecting every structure in the area, and is looking for a particular kind of commodity rather than just any commodity—he has a very low probability, perhaps one in 10,000 (that is, 0.0001) of finding what he wants at his first inspection.

The chance of his *not* being satisfied at the first stop, is, by the same token, very high. Mathematically, it is $(1 - 0.0001)$.

The chances of his *not* being satisfied at the first stop are exactly equal to his chances of reaching the second opportunity. They are, in this case $(1 - 0.0001)$.

When the searcher approaches the second opportunity, he still has a one in 10,000 probability of being satisfied, but this has been diminished by his lower chances of getting there. The over-all probability of making a "hit" at the second opportunity is therefore (0.0001) $(1 - 0.0001)$.

At every succeeding opportunity, the searcher has the same probability of stopping (0.0001), but his chances of reaching that opportunity are progressively diminished. The chance of getting to each new opportunity is $(1 - .0001)$, raised to the power of the number of opportunities which have been passed. This number of opportunities passed is conventionally called V. Hence the possibility of stopping at opportunity $V + 1$ is
$$(.0001) \ (1 - .0001)^V.$$
Or, if "*l*" is substituted as the basic probability (or discrimination of the searcher), then the probability of stopping at $V + 1$ is
$$l \ (1 - l)^V.$$
This formula becomes more complex when *groups* of searchers

are sent out from a zone (such as zone i) and when they inspect
groups of opportunities that are clustered together in other zones
(such as zone j). Under these circumstances, the preceding formula
is written

$$V_{ij} = V_i[(1 - l)^V - (1 - l)^{V+V_j}],$$

where V_{ij} are the trips going between zone i and zone j, V_i is the
number of trips searching outward from zone i, and V_j represents
the number of opportunities at zone j.

It is obvious that the probability of a searcher's terminating his
trip at any given opportunity is a function of the purpose of his trip.
A searcher looking for milk or a newspaper will find a suitable opportunity close at hand. This is because such commodities are standard and outlets are located for the convenience of people. A man
looking for a job, however, will be willing to search for a much
greater distance because the number of opportunities for his skills
may be quite limited and because the rewards are great in relationship to the cost of the journey. Therefore, different "*l*" values are
used to permit the better representation of those trips which are
likely to terminate close to home (as in convenience-goods shopping)
and those which persist for greater distances, as in work trips. In its
operational form, the opportunity theory is written

$$V_{ij} = V_i (e^{-lV} - e^{-l(V + V_j)}),$$

where V_{ij} = the number of trips going from zone i to zone j;

  e = the base of natural logarithms;

  l = probability per destination;

  V_i = number of trips being sent out from zone i;

  V_j = number of possible destinations at zone j;

  V = number of possible destinations lying between zone i
     and zone j.

The Use of the Theory

As will be seen often in this book, there is a steady use of data
on cities to develop theoretical and mathematical representations of
cities and travel within them, and a use of these representations to
reach planning decisions. The case of the opportunity theory of travel

is typical of the development of an idea in mathematical form which has utility in planning. It is, therefore, worthwhile to jump ahead of the main content of this part of the book (which is to present three views of the city) and to look briefly at the use of the opportunity theory in the transportation planning process.

The problem facing transportation planners in the mid-1950's, as pointed out earlier, was to develop the ability to estimate where trips would go in the future. Assuming that the numbers of trip origins and trip destinations could be determined reasonably well from estimates of the location of human activities, the remaining unknown was to know where trips from each zone of origin would go—or, in other words, how zones of origin and destination would link up.

This task of forecasting the distribution of trips for large numbers of zones and over complete networks of arterials and expressways became feasible with the advent of high-speed computers with large internal memories. These machines became available on a commercial basis in the mid-1950's, and it was only then that there was sufficient computational power available to estimate traffic flows on all streets in metropolitan areas.

The computers could be given data which represented all of the zones in a metropolitan area—on the order of five hundred or more zones. Each of these zones would have information representing the numbers of trips originating in it and the number of destination opportunities.

The computer would also be given data completely representing the highway or transit network serving the metropolitan area. How these networks were represented will be described in more detail in Chapter V.

The computer would then select a single zone of origin and search through the network outward from that zone, until the computer had arranged all the other zones in the network by their relative distance (in time, cost, or mileage) from the zone of origin. The searching technique will be described in more detail in Chapter XI; that technique was a major innovation without which traffic estimation as it is done today would not be possible.

Then, by using the opportunity theory of travel, the computer

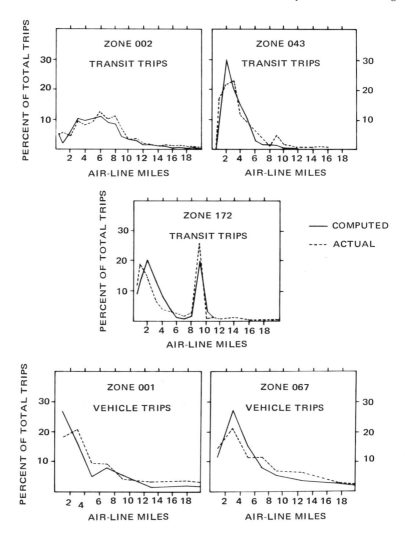

Figure 19.
Simulated and actual trips from selected zones, Chicago area, 1956.

would calculate how many trips would go from each origin to each destination.

Demonstration of how well the opportunity theory of travel simulates actual travel is given in Figure 19. A word of explanation is in order about these graphs. In each case the solid line represents the simulated trips while the dashed line represents actual trips. These lines show the percentages of trips (vertical axis) from the zone of origin that are distributed to destination zones at various distances (horizontal axis) from the origin zone. Two of these graphs show the distribution of vehicle trips over the road system, and three graphs show the distribution of person trips over the transit system. All graphs were prepared from data and estimates of the Chicago study.

It will be seen that the correspondence between the actual trips and those simulated by use of the opportunity model is by no means perfect, and yet, taken as a group, the correspondence is very good. The model allocates trips where the people and vehicles actually were reported as going and in the right orders of magnitude. These, it must be remembered, are very fine examinations of both the data and the simulation capability; the maximum number of trips distributed from any one of the zones of origin illustrated in Figure 19 to any one of the two-mile distance rings is less than 12,000 trips (the case of Zone 002), and in most cases is less than 5,000 trips. The trips to each two-mile ring beyond ten miles from the zone of origin are mostly less than 2,500 trips. The standard error, as a percentage of such reported trips, is 9.0 percent for 5,000 trips and 12.7 percent for 2,500 trips. Thus, we are comparing simulated trips with actual trips at a level where the trips are themselves subject to noticeable error because of sampling variability. When the actual and the simulated trips are aggregated for groups of zones, much closer correspondence can be found.

Conclusion

One of the critical problems facing transportation planners in the 1950's was to find some means of explaining the behavior of people's trip patterns. Until an adequate theory could be developed, planners were forced to rely too much upon data obtained from massive origin-destination surveys, and this data tended to become stale.

The gravity theory and the opportunity theory of travel eliminated this extreme dependence upon origin-destination data. With these theories, future patterns of travel could be predicted. This was a major breakthrough. How the opportunity model was used in simulating future travel, and its later use in 1964 in serving as the base for estimating future land use, will be described in forthcoming chapters.

IV

LAND USE

ALL the trips whose patterns were described in Chapter II take place because individual people undertake different kinds of activities during the day and, finding that they cannot do these things all at one site, they travel to reach the sites where the activities are. In the thinking of planners in the period 1955–60, it seemed essential to investigate the number and kinds of these activities.[1] By knowing more about human activities—at least by knowing their types, locations, and intensities as measured by the number of persons concentrated on each site—it was felt that plans could be prepared better. Certainly two prime estimates could be made with greater ease: first, the locations of future activities, and second, future trip generation.

In 1955 there was very little in the way of data or theory which could be very helpful in forecasting the locations of urban activities or trip generation. Consequently, the first step in studying activities had to be by a thorough survey, trusting that good data would at least provide insights which would be helpful in planning.

The first problem to overcome was how to measure the activities of people. This could have been done directly, through the process of counting trips going to each parcel of land and identifying the purposes for which they were made. In fact, this was done through the travel surveys. Trip purpose "to work" clearly identified a "working" activity. This might have been sufficient, but at that

---

[1] A book which initiated some of these investigations was Robert B. Mitchell and Chester Rapkin's *Urban Traffic—A Function of Land Use* (Columbia University Press, New York, 1954).

time it seemed too easy and lacking tangibility or stability. So it was passed over. Alternative measures were proposed: measuring activity by payrolls, by cash register receipts, and so on. These were discarded as being impossible data to obtain, and they were too indirect and too unstable an index of human presence and action.

The best index of human activity seemed to be land use. After all, what people did on land was what gave it its name, both in common parlance and in the technical terms of city planning and zoning. Moreover, the uses of land were given some kind of permanence by buildings and other improvements—often quite specialized and hence limited in what they could be used for. This stability suggested that trips could be related to land area, or to floor area, and that the number of trips and even the kind of trips would remain the same—being required to remain the same by the investment in land and building.

It seems difficult to believe, but measurement and detailed identification of land use for urban areas was quite rare in 1955. Most city planning agencies identified land uses at that time only within a dozen types, and practically never conducted surveys in which land uses were measured by type throughout their entire jurisdictions. The results of their surveys consisted almost entirely of colored maps. These were useful for zoning and general land use planning work, but were intractable for any kind of analysis. Bartholomew[2] had measured a number of central and satellite cities and 11 small urban areas (populations under 120,000). There had been some "real property" inventories conducted in the 1930's but since then largely forgotten. Outside of these and a few other efforts, there were no quantitative data on metropolitan land use.

There is no point in describing the survey methods used in Chicago or more recently by other transportation studies. These have been well documented[3] and are essentially mechanical tasks—

[2] Harland Bartholomew, *Land Uses in American Cities* (Harvard University Press, Cambridge, Mass., 1955).

[3] For example, see John R. Hamburg and Robert Sharkey, *Land Use Survey Manual* (Chicago Area Transportation Study, Chicago, 1956), and Robert Sharkey, *Suburban Land Use Survey Manual* (Chicago Area Transportation Study, Chicago, 1958).

although, like many mechanical tasks, they should not be under-estimated as to the amounts of ingenuity and care required. The data obtained included land area and floor area identified within 84 types of land uses. Like the travel surveys, the land use and floor area data were given geographic identification by block, and blocks were organized within a quarter square mile grid system. (Blocks were also numbered by census tract and political unit to permit summaries of those units.) The grid system allowed a fine-grained, mechanical presentation of the data to be made.

Survey Results

Selected data from the Chicago land use and floor area surveys are presented here and are compared with similar data from the Pittsburgh and Niagara Frontier studies, in order to accomplish three main objectives. First, we want to give some dimensions and proportions of land use and floor area so that general magnitudes of urban space needs are understood. Following the procedure of Chapter II, the major dimensions are presented first, followed by more detailed data, and then by the geographic distributions. Second, we want to show the kinds of measures which are useful for forecasting purposes—either for forecasting urban growth or for forecasting trip generation. Third, we want to use these data to present the city in a new light—a light which affects the way we think about cities when working in the fields of transportation or metropolitan land use planning.

Total Land Occupancy. Urban land uses are defined to include streets and residential, commercial, manufacturing, and transportation land uses, public and quasi-public land uses, and public open space. These terms, and especially the word "urban," are merely definitional conveniences, forced on us by our language-induced habits of classifying and categorizing. In Chicago all streets were "urban" even when passing through farming areas, and each farm house, no matter how big the farm, was credited with having an acre of "urban residential" land. With growing numbers of city dwellers living in rural nonfarm dwellings, these old distinctions should be disappearing.

In the Chicago area in 1956, out of 1,236 square miles measured in the study area, 562.8 square miles were devoted to these "urban" uses. The remainder was in agricultural use or vacant. With a 1956 population of 5,170,000 persons, this meant that there were about 3,000 square feet of land in urban uses per person residing in the study area.

By contrast, Detroit had 3,100 square feet per person in 1953, Pittsburgh had 3,500 square feet in 1958, and the Niagara Frontier had 4,500 square feet in 1962. Generally less land is used per capita in the larger and older urban areas because densities are higher.

As most people realize, the amount of land being brought into urban use per capita is increasing. Table 4 shows that the number of square feet in urban use, per person, rises with increasing distance from the center. Since distance from the center is a measure of newness (each ring in the Chicago area being the work of twenty years, approximately), we can see that the newer areas of the city are getting more land per capita.

Table 4. *Per Capita Land in Urban Uses in the Chicago Area, 1956, and in the Niagara Frontier, 1962*

Ring	Chicago Land Area in Urban Uses (square miles)	Chicago Resident Population	Chicago Urbanized Land per Capita (square feet)	Niagara Frontier Urbanized Land per Capita (square feet)
1	11.6	317,600	1,040	1,400
2	24.7	745,600	930	2,300
3	38.8	962,700	1,140	3,000
4	77.3	1,286,400	1,680	4,800
5	95.5	754,500	3,550	5,500
6	153.0	654,500	6,600	6,300
7	160.0	443,400	10,200	11,500

Source: CATS, *Final Report*, vol. I, Tables 19, 21.

The data for ring 7 in both the Chicago and the Niagara Frontier are not completely representative of urban land uses. In each case that ring was lightly developed, and the per capita measures include both a higher proportion of land in highways and also the acre lots which were assumed for each farm residence.

Space for Different Activities. In Table 5 the areas and percentages of land used for seven basic types of urban land uses in Chicago are compared to similar data obtained in Pittsburgh and the

Table 5. *Percentages of Major Land Use Types*

Land Use Type	Chicago (1956)		Pittsburgh (1958)		Niagara Frontier (1962)	
	Area (sq. miles)	*Per-centage*	*Area (sq. miles)*	*Per-centage*	*Area (sq. miles)*	*Per-centage*
Residential	180.6	40.3	80.9	50.2	86.7	47.0
Streets and Alleys	146.1	32.6	45.5	28.2	52.2	28.2
Transportation	50.7	11.3	10.5	6.5	18.2	9.9
Manufacturing	24.7	5.5	8.2	5.1	10.6	5.8
Public Buildings	23.1	5.2	9.7	6.0	7.0	3.8
Commercial and Parking	22.7	5.1	6.4	4.0	9.8	5.3
Subtotal	447.9	100.0	161.2	100.0	184.5	100.0
Public Open Space	114.9		20.7		31.8	
Total in Urban Use	562.8	—	181.9	—	216.3	—
Population (millions)	5.2	—	1.5	—	1.35	—
Population per Developed Square Mile	11,600	—	9,300	—	7,300	—

Niagara Frontier. The percentages devoted to each of the seven major types are strikingly similar across these three cities, despite their differences in gross population and in population density. Some differences do exist (Chicago's residential land, for example, is a lower percentage of its total), but these are almost variations of style and are not of an order of magnitude.

Residential land is the dominating use of land in these cities—between 40 and 50 percent is so used. People in their home-based activities seem to require a lot of space—much more than when shopping or exchanging goods or ideas.

The amount of land required for streets is surprisingly high— between 28 and 32 percent of the total (when parks and other public open spaces are excluded). Careful urban design could reduce this somewhat, but good urban design will often make streets more park-like, and this increases the area set aside for streets. Over-all, then, this percentage will not change much. Access, safety, and sheer need for a place for movement requires this much space.

It should be noted here that the amount of land used for streets increases as density rises, and as a result most central business districts have 40 percent or more of their areas reserved for moving people and vehicles. This is only about 10 percent more than the average for an entire metropolitan area. Knowing this, it is amusing to hear the shocked tones of those who exclaim, "Forty percent for streets and 20 percent for parking! More than half of the central business district's area used for motor vehicles!" What these people forget is that the street measurements are made between right-of-way lines and hence include sidewalks as well as streets. Actually, about 30 percent of the area reserved for the public right-of-way in a typical downtown area is used for sidewalks. If people are to be packed in at high densities, they must have both wider streets and wider sidewalks in order to be able to move about; the higher the densities, the more space must be used for movement—and for light and air.

Another 6–10 percent of land is used for all other types of transportation: airports, rail lines, yards, and terminals, and ports.

Hence the total amount of land (excluding public open space in the calculation) required for all forms of movement in urban areas is between 35 and 40 percent of the total land in urban use. This is a good index of the importance of transportation in a modern society.

The other major land use types—commercial, industrial, and public buildings—each take up about 5 percent of developed land. Variations occur, but that is the order of magnitude for these types.

Public open space fluctuates widely in amount, depending upon the size of the city and on the vision of its past and present leaders. The Chicago area has a proud history of men who got adequate land set aside for public open space—115 square miles in all, or 20 percent of all land in use in 1956. Other cities would do well to emulate this practice.

Floor Space. Along with land use, the Chicago study measured building floor space by type. This survey was not conducted in the whole 1,236–square mile study area, but only in the 295 square miles which included the City of Chicago (212 square miles) and the suburbs close to the city. The area measured included 80 percent of the study area's population and an estimated 86 percent of its floor area. Therefore, the data are fairly complete.

The floor area survey measured 2.2 billion square feet of floor space, or approximately 540 square feet per capita (see Table 6).

Table 6. *Floor Area by Type of Activity in the 295–Square Mile Inventory Area, Chicago, 1956*

Type of Activity	Floor Area (millions of square feet)	Percentage of Measured Floor Area
Residential	1,301.0	58.4
Commercial	351.9	15.8
Manufacturing	309.5	13.9
Transportation	103.5	4.6
Public Buildings	162.5	7.3
Total	2,228.4	100.0

Source: CATS, *Final Report,* I, 24, Table 2.

More than half of the floor area was residential; the remainder was divided between commercial, manufacturing, transportation (e.g., stations, truck terminals), and public buildings. The average dwelling unit in the surveyed area had 940 square feet of floor space, but this was based on external building measurements rather than useful floor space.

The intensity at which land is used can be given by the floor area ratio (FAR) index. This index is obtained by dividing floor space in a lot or block by the land area in that lot or block.

In Chicago's Loop district there were, in 1956, 92.3 million square feet of floor area. This same district (technically made up of four quarter square mile analysis zones) had 13.6 million square feet of usable land, excluding streets, public open spaces, and unusable land. Thus, in the Loop the floor area ratio was 6.8. This is very high, and to reach such a ratio, many of the buildings have to be twenty or more stories in height. In contrast, most of the remainder of the city of Chicago had floor area ratios averaging about 1.5, while in the suburbs the FAR's were generally below 0.5.

In the Niagara Frontier, floor space was measured only for the square mile containing the Buffalo central business district. That survey found 27.7 million square feet of floor area within the central square mile. The floor area ratio, calculated on the basis of a usable 0.6 square miles of land area, was 1.65, or substantially below the 6.8 FAR of Chicago's Loop.

The Distribution of Land Use and Floor Space

In this section two pieces of evidence are presented which had a profound effect upon the approach which transportation planners took in estimating future distribution of land uses. The first piece of evidence was the geographic distribution of land uses, and the second was the geographic distribution of floor space.

The geographic distribution of developed land in the Chicago area is shown in Figure 20. This is an isolined map in which quarter square miles of land having equal ranges of percentages of their gross land areas in "developed" uses are grouped together. Developed land is here defined to exclude public open spaces and certain large uses such as O'Hare Field, Glenview Naval Air Station, and the Argonne National Laboratories. Included within developed land are residential, transportation, manufacturing, public buildings, and commercial land uses, and streets.

There are two important things to note about this display of developed land. One is the shape or pattern of urban development— a highly organic form. The evolution of this form will be taken up later in this chapter.

The second is the correspondence between the pattern of de-

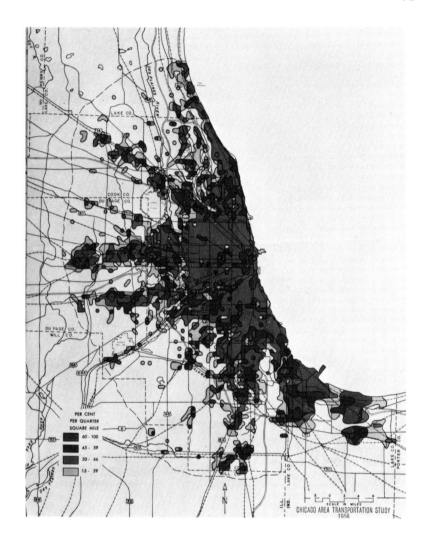

Figure 20.
Developed land, Chicago area, 1956.

veloped land and the patterns of travel which were displayed in Chapter II. The travel patterns shown in Figures 9, 11, and 13 co-exist with the pattern of developed land. This is a strong visual demonstration that travel and land use are related. They have to be: both

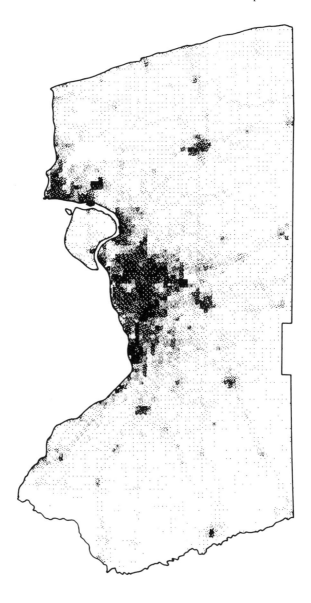

Figure 21.
Developed land in the Niagara Frontier, 1962. (Each dot equals
4 percent per quarter square mile.)

are simply different manifestations of human activity in cities. In one case people are in motion; in the other case, the same people are engaged in activities at particular sites. With most trips being short, there has to be a close correspondence.

A slightly different way of displaying urban development is shown in Figure 21, which shows developed land in the Niagara Frontier. Instead of using the isoline technique, dots have been printed on the map directly by computer. These dots allow a more continuous display of developed land, even though the same geographic unit, the quarter square mile, was used in both Chicago and the Niagara Frontier.

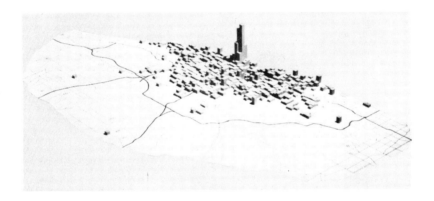

Figure 22.
Total floor area model.

The value of the Niagara Frontier display is that it shows the urbanized land not as a sharply defined unit but as the intensely developed end of a continuum of developed land. While there are some sharp edges in the display (not counting the edges along the waterfront, of course), most of the time the "urban" densities merely blur into the "rural" densities.

More dramatic than either of the foregoing displays is the model of floor space in the Chicago area shown in Figure 22. In this figure the height of each wooden block is proportional to the number of square feet of floor space in each quarter square mile. The highest block shown in Figure 22 represents 32,000,000 square feet of floor space, which is the equivalent of 1.14 square miles of building floor area. This amount of floor space occurs in a single quarter square mile of land area in Chicago's Loop. The lowest blocks in the model, in contrast, represent 1,000,000 square feet of floor area.

What is exciting about this model is the regularity and symmetry with which floor area is arrayed around the high-density Loop. The impersonal measures of the survey strip away the normal images we have of cities and hold up to view an organism that is as regular as a wasp's nest or an ant hill. This is in strong contrast with the claims which are made that the city is disorderly and unorganized. Here is evidence that in the aggregate there is orderliness and even symmetry in man's urban concentrations.

Here, then, is an insight. It deeply colored the thinking of the staff of the Chicago study, and of a number of subsequent studies. Cities were orderly rather than chaotic. The problem thereupon became one of discerning where the order was, why it existed, and how it could be turned to useful account in planning.

Distribution of Land Uses by Type. If the different types of land uses are studied by distance from the city center, a pattern emerges which has a great deal of consistency among the cities for which such data is available. This occurs despite variations in topography and shapes of the land masses on which these cities are built.

Figures 23, 24, and 25 give the percentage distribution of seven land uses in Chicago, Pittsburgh, and in the Niagara Frontier by distance from their central business districts. The similarities are quite obvious. Towards the center of the urban area, streets and commercial land uses make up very large proportions of all land in use, while residential land use is correspondingly small in proportion. Farther away from the center, residential land becomes a larger proportion of the whole, stabilizing at roughly 40 percent of all land in use.

About eight miles from Chicago's Loop and about four miles away from the centers of Buffalo and Pittsburgh, land uses appear to take on a kind of standard mix. In this mix streets take up 25

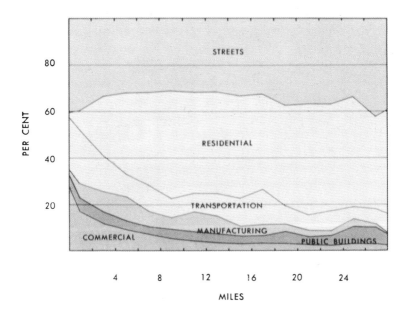

Figure 23.
Distribution of land uses, by distance from the Loop, Chicago area, 1956.

percent of the land, residences about 45 percent, and the remainder is divided between commercial, industrial, public buildings, public open space, and transportation. When seen from the street, of course, these land uses are not homogenized; zoning regulations separate residential, commercial, and industrial uses into districts which are intended to prevent one type from exerting harmful influences on the others. But within an area of a few square miles, it is surprising how these land uses approach an average mix. This mix will become less objectionable as industries become cleaner and less noisy. One of the forces leading toward the creation of an average mix is the desire of small governments to strengthen their tax bases by obtaining their share of commercial and manufacturing land uses.

This mixing of land uses in each ring is symptomatic of the layering on of growth to the city and is a result of changes in transportation. The high degree of specialization at the center of cities

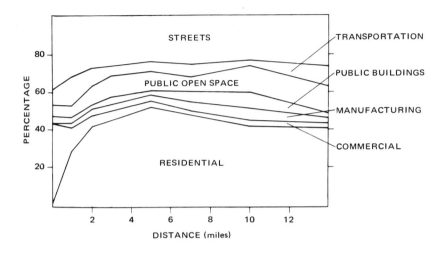

Figure 24.
Distribution of land uses, by distance from central business district,
Pittsburgh area, 1958.

which was shown in the preceding figures is partly a result of the strongly center-oriented mass transportation systems which dominated the growth of American cities from 1830 to 1930. That kind of transportation gave a monopoly of high access to the core; most activities which required assembly of large numbers of people had to locate there, as the evidence shows. However, the automobile and truck eroded the monopoly of the center; consequently subsequent growth has contained all the elements of land uses, more or less in constant proportion. (The pattern of heavier commercial use at the core is still partly responsible for the prevailing in-out character of travel.)

Density. Trip-making is determined not only by the kinds of land uses, but by the varying densities at which these lands are used. High-rise office buildings and apartments obviously place intense demands upon the transportation facilities in their immediate vicinities, whereas the more spacious (but not necessarily gracious) arrangements of buildings in the suburbs or in the country attract a smaller number of person trips per acre.

American cities have remarkably similar patterns of density. Very high densities exist at the core, with rapidly diminishing densities nearby and more slowly declining densities out to the fringe of the urban area. The pattern for the Chicago area is shown in Figure 26, and this same pattern can be seen in the photograph of the model of floor area in Chicago shown in Figure 22.

There is no complete theoretical explanation of why urban

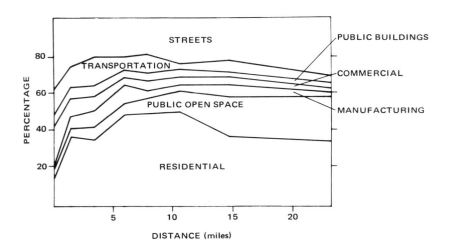

Figure 25.
Distribution of land uses, by distance from Buffalo
central business district, Niagara Frontier, 1962.

densities occur in this highly regular fashion.[4] This should not be surprising, because there has been until recently very little data on which such a theory could be based. Data on trip densities exist in abundance, but outside of Chicago, Philadelphia, and the New York

[4] Morton Schneider's recent theoretical work is probably the best exploration to date of the relationship between the density of land development and transportation. See his paper "Access and Land Development," in *Urban Development Models,* Highway Research Board, Special Report 97, Washington, D.C., 1968.

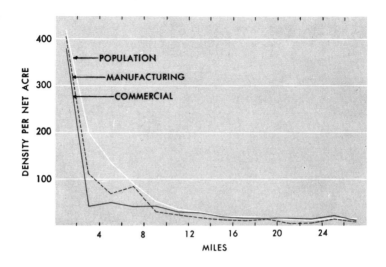

Figure 26.
Population and employment density per net acre,
by distance from the Loop, Chicago area, 1956.

metropolitan area there is very little quantified information on density of floor area per unit land area, to say nothing of related information on such things as historical land values and building costs.

We would like to know what forces are at work which will give
us future densities. The best explanation is that density as we see it
today is the record of the responses of builders to the forces of
their times, including means of transportation, the technology of
buildings, the processes used in the production of goods and services,
real wealth in terms of ability to command the purchase of goods
and services, and city size. What we see today is the record of decisions which were made in response to the conditions which appeared
or were anticipated at a particular time in history.

In colonial America, for example, densities were very low because towns and cities were small, and one could walk to work or
to the meeting house. The rewards of mutual association could be
obtained without crowding, and space was a real advantage from
the point of view of sanitation and water and food supply.

The colonial densities may be contrasted with the cities of the post–Civil War period. Railroads could bring in food, and water was now supplied by public piping systems. Factories were located in high-density, multi-story buildings. One of the reasons for high employment density in these factories was the limited distance which steam-generated power could be transmitted by belt or axles without excessive friction losses. Horse-drawn street railways permitted people to ride to work, but the range of transportation lines was still limited, and this kept the city packed close around the city center.

High densities got an even stronger boost in the 1890's. Steel-framed buildings equipped with elevators began to replace the old office buildings with their thick bearing walls; instead of an effective five-story limitation, office buildings could reach twenty and thirty stories. Electrically powered street cars and elevated lines had no technological limits to their lengths, and in Chicago could bring people in ten miles to the center of the city, which contained perhaps 30 percent of all the employment and most of the shopping facilities.

The technology of the twentieth century, however, began gradually to change these things. The assembly line required factories to be spread out, and it was cheaper to build them only one story high. Power could be transmitted to each machine by electrical wires. The automobile enabled travel to be made wherever there were roads. Supermarkets cut food prices, and were reinforced as efficient distributors of food by housewives who could drive. Communications began to chisel away the earlier absolute requirement that business be done face-to-face. And a wealthier society could command the additional space for living which formerly had been the prerogative of the nobility or the very wealthy.

It can be seen that changes in density are not simply functions of transportation, but are related to an entire matrix of conditions: a society's wealth, its building technology, and its manner of doing business as well as its transportation system. How these conditions will change in the future cannot be foreseen completely, but it does appear that with greater per capita wealth people will be able to afford space and the costs of longer-distance travel. Under these circumstances, it would appear that there will be a continued decline in average urban population densities.

Trip Generation

Ultimately, the uses and densities of land, taken together, define urban travel requirements. These have to be related, because the one quantity represents people in their different activities on the land, and the other quantity represents people in motion. In the Chicago study this relationship was calculated readily, since for the first time the travel questionnaires determined the type of land use to and from which people were going.

By inspecting the column averages in Tables 7 and 8, the different rates at which different types of land uses generate trips can be seen. Most of these are in line with everyone's expectations. Public open space is an extensive user of land, as its name implies; hence its rate of trip generation is very low. Commercial land is the modern market place where people congregate to trade and compare. Hence the trip generation rates are high. Between these extremes is residential land. It surprises many people that manufacturing land has a trip generation rate nearly identical to residential land, and public buildings also are of the same order of magnitude.

The difference between the trip generation rates of the various land uses is exceeded by the differences in trip generation rates within each type of land use which are caused by variations in density of land development. As shown in Tables 7 and 8 density-bred trip generation rates vary by factors of ten, twenty, and even greater, with the highest rates at the center and the lowest at the outside. Yet, each ring, representing the lamina of another generation, has the same relative differences between land use within it—commercial the highest, public open space the lowest, and residential, public buildings, and manufacturing in between.

Originally it had been thought that trip generation rates such as those shown in Tables 7 and 8 could be used, without much modification, as the basis for making estimates of future trip-making from any given plan or forecast of land use. Unfortunately this concept was too simple. The difficulty was that over time people make more trips. With more income and higher car ownership, people can afford to travel more, although this is not without limits. Hence

Table 7. Person Trips per Acre Generated by Land Use Type, by Ring, Chicago Area, 1956

Ring	Mean Distance from Loop (miles)	Commercial	Residential	Manufacturing	Public Buildings	Transportation	Public Open Space
0	0.0	2,132	2,228	3,545	2,014	273	98
1	1.5	189	224	243	256	37	29
2	3.5	122	127	80	124	16	26
3	5.5	143	106	87	101	11	28
4	8.5	212	68	51	78	13	14
5	11.5	179	43	27	58	6	6
6	16.0	132	31	16	47	3	2
7	24.0	132	21	18	14	6	2
Study Area Average		181	48	49	53	9	4

Source: CATS, *Final Report*, vol. I, Tables 9, 10.

Table 8. *Vehicle Trips per Acre Generated by Land Use Type, by Ring, Chicago Area, 1956*

Ring	Mean Distance from Loop (miles)	Commercial	Residential	Manufacturing	Public Buildings	Transportation	Public Open Space
0	0.0	728	1,337	1,081	461	103	62
1	1.5	194	93	162	116	55	26
2	3.5	117	54	64	51	31	23
3	5.5	132	50	66	46	15	18
4	8.5	165	36	44	34	12	12
5	11.5	150	25	23	30	7	4
6	16.0	112	19	15	24	3	2
7	24.0	115	13	16	7	6	1
Study Area Average		145	26	39	24	10	3

Source: CATS, *Final Report*, vol. I, Tables 9, 10.

an average family might increase its trip generation from six to eight or more person trips per day. When family trip generation rates increase, the purposes for which they make trips change also. A greater proportion of trips are made for shopping and social-recreation purposes, for example, and a smaller proportion (but not smaller absolutely) for work purposes. The trip generation rates of land uses, then, will vary over time.

For forecasting purposes the approach changed to one in which main attention was focused on people and their trip-making habits. Income and car ownership became important factors in estimating over-all rates. Land use became a control, useful in checking rates and useful in determining where people would locate.

Orderliness, Specialization, and Incremental Growth

Data have been presented which show a great deal of orderliness in urban settlement. This orderliness is contrary to many commonly held conceptions of the city. And yet it clearly exists, in the population density curves, in the consistent arrangements of land uses, in the symmetrical clustering of floor space around a central business district, and in the uniformly declining rates of trip generation for different types of land uses in relationship to distance from the central business district.

Why should things be orderly? Generally, when observing order in nature we associate the order with some economizing of effort. Is there such an economy of effort in urban development?

We have seen in the chapter on travel theory that there is a strong presumption that people tend to minimize their travel. The evidence shows that most trips are short. We know that travel has real monetary costs for people and that it takes time, which is definitely a fixed resource from our human viewpoint. Other things being equal, the desire to minimize travel will tend to keep urban settlements compact.

However, there are other forces of great strength operating here. One of these forces is specialization, which needs to be examined in some detail because it is the clue to the growth of cities and to the land use structure which we have been observing.

Specialization. Specialization, or the division of labor, is something which is associated most often with the industrial revolution; but we often fail to step back and see, in the larger sweep of time, that specialization is, in fact, a basic quality of human society from its beginning. This is implied in the dictionary definition of socety: "an enduring, cooperating social group so functioning as to maintain itself and perpetuate the species." A group whose members cooperate and who are not identical in ability is a group which inevitably must specialize in their activities and skills.

Specialization is, of course, not restricted to human societies; animals and insects have their own societies whose members specialize. But the degree of specialization in human society is enormously greater than in any other form of society. And it is from this high degree of specialization that man derives his power and his productivity.

Every distinct human activity, or specialty, requires some particular place to be set aside for it. The possession of these spaces, particularly within buildings but also in the open, with proper tools close at hand, invariably means that the person or society so equipped and specialized can be more productive than another without these facilities.

If one looks back in history, one can see how this is true. The stone-age hunting tribes were little specialized beyond the male-female duties: the hunter, and the keeper of the children; perhaps there was a tribal leader and shaman. The tribe was mobile and one place was very much like another. Much later, the agricultural societies were more specialized, and they invested more labor in buildings and land. They had houses instead of tents, villages instead of caves, and fixed market places instead of trading places which operated only at intervals. They generated surpluses of food and stored these surpluses in warehouses. And from all this they developed many of the specialities which persist to this day: lawyers, astronomers, judges, businessmen, and public administrators like Joseph and Daniel.

Still, outside of a few unusual buildings and places—like the market, the temple, the fort, and the theater or stadium—most cities simply contained houses which served simultaneously as living quarters, shops, and factories. Medieval and Renaissance European cities, and most Oriental cities up until World War II, had this characteristic of unspecialized land use and architectural appearance. One could not tell from the outside of a building what went on inside. Even the streets were not specialized, serving as markets, meeting places, and sewers as well as ways for travel. From the industrial revolution onward—and continuing today and beyond—the number of specialties was increasing. Further, greater productivity was being obtained by larger combinations of people, with more specialized equipment and greater capital investment in equipment and power available to them.

Accordingly, the number of different kinds of land uses multiplied—in effect, one for each new specialty. If land uses were classified by the kinds of specialized activity going on at a site, there now would be thousands of different types. In the manufacturing world there would be one for each kind of product. Fortunately or unfortunately, land uses have been categorized not by product but by process or generalized kind of activity—manufacturing, warehousing, and commercial, for example—and so there is a manageable number of types.

The immediate effect of the industrial revolution was to require daily urban travel to distances and at frequencies which had been unknown in the medieval and renaissance world. Activities became larger, required more space, more specialized equipment, and often emitted undesirable smoke, noise, or odors. Who could live in a brickyard or an iron-works? Travel was therefore made necessary to bring people together, flexibly, into larger and more productive combinations than had ever been known.[5]

---

[5] In the earlier years of the industrial revolution, even in the larger mill towns, people could walk to work. Residential densities were quite high, and housing was packed in close to the mills. After 1830, the capabilities of the mechanical age turned to the problem of urban transportation, and street railways of various types supported industrial progress by allowing even larger effective assemblages of workers.

Thus, specialization brought cities into being and increasingly within these cities created distinct types of land uses. At these places additional capital investment and productive combinations of labor brought about substantial increases in output and hence in the total wealth of the community.

Incremental Growth. Given some share in the rewards of specialization, people will move to cities and settle there. Unless famine or war drives masses of people suddenly to cities, they will come individually or in small groups. The growth of the city will therefore be by increments, by the accretion of these small particles. This is almost by definition.

Each person or family joining the urban mass must find a minimum of space in which to live and breathe. This minimum will include not only the space where he resides, but a share of space for movement and for the other activities in which he engages. This minimum amount will vary, depending upon the standards of the society in question and the ways in which wealth is distributed throughout that society. Earlier in this chapter some of these space requirements have been given dimension.

In a free society and in a society where land is held in small parcels and freely exchanged (and these two conditions are not synonymous), each person or family joining the urban mass can select where he will live. The newcomer may be able to afford new quarters, or he may be poor and fill old quarters, while a more affluent person builds a new residence or rents a new apartment. Either way, there is an increment of growth which is added to the urban mass. Generally, the middle and upper income groups are the ones who do the building, although in developing countries the newcomer may simply appropriate a site and build a shack on it.

Where will these increments of growth take place? Some will occur through the demolition of older structures and the erection of new buildings with more floor space on the same sites. But most new growth will take place at the periphery of an urban area, where building costs and land costs are lower and where transportation costs are kept low. This is the way most urban growth occurs and where at least two-thirds of the net increment of floor space is added.

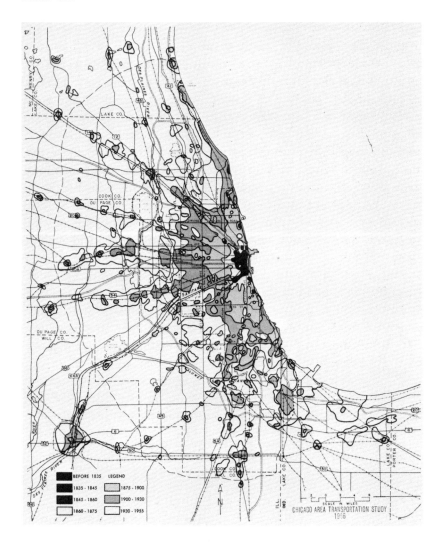

Figure 27.
Chicago growth patterns.

Evidence of this manner of growth is shown in Figure 27, which shows the successive rings of land which have been urbanized in the Chicago region from 1835 to 1955. Each ring represents the increment of growth of a generation of people.

Why do these laminae of growth take on an orderly and almost symmetrical form? Why are the concentrations of floor space shown in the model in Figure 22 so symmetrical? We can only assume at this time that the mass of urban development gains its symmetry because of the existence of certain important specialized functions which sooner or later touch the lives of all members of an urban society. These are the functions of leadership, communication, banking, and some key trading activities. New adherents to the urban mass want to minimize their travel to these specialized functions, even if they go there only rarely. These specialized activities, starting at the original place of settlement, rarely relocate. They have an increasing inertia of investment not only in their own buildings but in all the transportation and communication facilities which serve them. Because people want to settle close to the urban mass in order to minimize their travel or communication distances to these central functions, they build at the point on the periphery which is closest to the center. This produces the orderly and symmetrical appearance which has been disclosed by the land use and floor area measures.

If the foregoing hypothesis is correct and if travel were equally easy in all directions (that is, if the whole urban area were paved), cities would grow in circular form, as in the diagram below, left. If travel can only take place on a gridded system of streets, urban areas would be diamond-shaped, as in the diagram below, right.

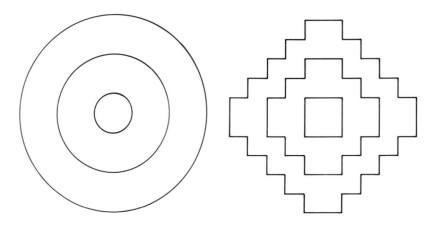

This latter shape is the form of Wichita, Kansas, as will be seen in Figure 40 in Chapter VIII.

The Chicago area, as illustrated in Figures 20 and 22 has a high degree of symmetry around its Loop district, although the symmetry is not perfect. The Gary, Indiana, area with its steel mills is a separate center which has merged with the main mass of Chicago development in recent years. The obstacle of the Chicago River (South Branch) has impeded development in the southwestern part of the region. The fingered development coming after 1900 is, of course, the result of the reductions in time-distance made possible by suburban rail commutation.

If buildings, once built, were never torn down, then all the increments of urban development would have to be at the periphery, and each new ring would contain all the kinds of activities required by an urban population. This situation, of course, does not exist, and transportation networks allow increasing specialization of activities as urban areas grow in size. In the nineteenth and early twentieth centuries, with mass transportation practically the only means of person transportation within cities, a much greater share of the specialized activities of the city existed at the center. That was the only place which had a substantial locational advantage. The result of that specialization has been shown in the higher concentrations of commercial and industrial land uses at the center as seen in Figures 23, 24, and 25.

More recently, however, the limitations of excessive concentration of specialized activities have begun to be apparent, especially in the larger cities. If everyone has to travel to the center each day, transportation costs build up. The automobile has allowed a more fluid travel pattern to exist in the outer rings of cities. Hence in the outer rings there is a more standard kind of land use mixture, as we have already observed.

It is quite possible in the future that with improved communications and a great wealth which reduces the relative costs of transportation, the power of city centers to organize growth in symmetrical fashion around themselves will be diminished. Under these circumstances we may see metropolitan areas and regions organized in quite different patterns than in the past.

The sum of these ideas is that urban areas exist because within them associations of people are made profitable by specialization of activities. The specialization of activities requires travel to be performed, and travel is a concomitant and extension of those activities. People will keep adding themselves to the urban mass as long as it is profitable for them to do so—that is, as long as the rewards exceed the costs, in their estimation. The bulk of the increments of urban growth occur at the periphery, because that is where land is less expensive and where travel costs are lower than they would be if settlement were made still farther out. The arrangements of land uses within the urban mass are the result of a continuing adjustment and compromising of the benefits of specialization, the costs of travel, and the economics of building and rebuilding.

Conclusion

The purpose behind a transportation study's investigation of land use is to establish knowledge which will be helpful in forecasting both where and how many trips will be made in the future. To make such forecasts, an understanding of urban structure and spatial needs is required, together with measured relationships between land uses and trip generation.

The data on land use and floor area collected by the Chicago study showed a degree of orderliness and symmetry in urban structure which had never been revealed before. It seems sensible to believe that this orderliness comes from forces which have operated consistently over many decades upon the increments of growth attaching themselves to the urban mass. Some of these forces are of an economic nature—operating to reduce effort. A desire to reduce travel costs is certainly one of these forces which might be expressed in reverse as a desire for mutual proximity, or the desire to have proximity to a center.

The amounts and kinds of land uses found within the urban structure were consistent with data obtained from subsequent studies. The arrangements of these land uses were also consistent and orderly to a surprising degree. How these facts and ideas were incorporated in methods for forecasting land use will be taken up in a later chapter.

V

TRANSPORTATION NETWORKS: THE LIMITATIONS
OF CONVENTIONAL THOUGHT FORMS

IN THE preceding chapters we have seen how data were collected which described urban travel and land use. Increased understanding of these phenomena, and particularly of their regularities, allows better forecasts to be made of future travel and of urban growth. These forecasting operations have to be followed, in the steps of the planning process, by planning and testing operations. But before these latter operations can be started, a complete inventory has to be made of transportation facilities serving the urban area being planned. Clearly, if a planner is given the task of drawing plans and testing them, he has to have at his fingertips complete, measured representations of the stock of transportation facilities which it is his task to modify and improve. And just as surely, these representations have to be in such form as to be useful to him in his thinking or calculating operations.

These inventories of transportation facilities had been made for many years, and extensive descriptions and analyses had been made of different types and characteristics of transportation facilities and of their abilities to move people, vehicles, and freight. Unfortunately, these inventories and descriptions had, in varying degree, remained outside the main stream of the planning process. It became one of the major contributions of the Chicago study to make transportation facilities data a vital and integral part of the processes of planning and testing, to take this subject out of the conventional thought forms, and by employing new representations, to establish the capability of a true testing of networks. How this was done is told partly in this chapter and partly in Chapter XI.

Before getting into the newer ways of dealing with networks, however, it is necessary to look briefly at the inventory of transportation facilities itself, and then to examine some of the more conventional findings which can be produced as the result of a thorough inventory. These conventional descriptions are important because they provide insights into the workings and limitations of transportation facilities of several types.

The Survey

In the Chicago study the inventory of transportation facilities was the last of the three major surveys to be undertaken. All arterial streets, parkways, and expressways serving the 1,236–square mile study area were included within the scope of the survey, as were all bus lines, subway and elevated lines, and suburban railroads. Local streets, primarily serving residential land, were excluded because their principal function was land service, not traffic service. Although these local streets made up 72 percent of all the street mileage in the area, they carried only a sixth of the vehicle miles of travel.[1]

Most of the data on transportation facilities was available from the records of the highway engineers and mass transportation companies in the area. As a result, this inventory was conducted almost entirely within the office and was neither expensive nor time-consuming. The main outline of this survey work is described in Chapter VII. Data obtained in the survey included, for each segment of street, its length, width, speed limit, parking restrictions (if any), one- or two-way operation, and direction. For each mass transportation segment, data on length, scheduled speed, headways, and seating capacity were gathered, among other data.

Of all the data obtained by a transportation organization, the records on transportation facilities were undoubtedly the most accurate: street widths, for example, were measured to the nearest foot, lengths to the nearest fifty feet, speed limits exactly as signed, and

---

[1] Actually, they should carry less, but in Chicago the pressures of traffic on arterials were sufficiently great that some through traffic "backed up" into the local street system.

transit headways to the nearest minute. And the survey was complete; *all* transit lines and *all* roads (except local streets) were identified, and thus, all the principal ways by which people and rubber-tired vehicles could move within the survey area were represented.

Conventionally, the survey and its results were organized along the lines of what seemed to be a logical set of categories. All transportation facilities were typed according to these categories before the survey was started. This was done with the help of local officials and so, although some of the decisions were hard to make (for example, it is difficult to decide whether a street carrying 2,500 vehicles is a heavily loaded local street or a lightly loaded arterial), there were few disagreements afterwards.

Roadways, to start with, were divided into three major categories:

1. *Local streets:* those minor streets whose chief function it is to provide access to land, and mainly to residential land. These streets carry light volumes—rarely more than 1,000 vehicles per day—and should be laid out so as to discourage through traffic. Pavements are mainly two lanes in width, although four-lane pavements are common in high-density areas where off-street parking is not available.

2. *Arterial streets:* the main channels for movement in an urban area, averaging 9,700 vehicles per day in the Chicago area with many individual roads carrying in excess of 20,000 vehicles per day. Arterials are generally wider than local streets and are given preference in signing and signalization over local streets. Arterials have a dual function: to move traffic and to provide access to land uses, particularly the high trip-generating commercial activities. The traffic and access functions of arterials conflict with each other and this is one of the major problems of planning.

3. *Expressways:* divided roadways having no direct land access and no intersections with other streets at grade. Expressways (also called freeways) and those parkways that are built to expressway standards allow vehicles to move continuously. Continuous movement, with opposing traffic separated by wide medians, allows travel on expressways to be between two and three times as fast and safe as travel on urban arterials.

Mass transportation facilities were divided by the Chicago study into three categories:

1. *Bus systems.* Operating chiefly on the arterial road system, buses provided the most nearly ubiquitous form of mass transportation service. In suburban areas this bus service diminished rapidly as densities declined, both in frequency of service and in proximity to population.

2. *Subway and elevated lines.* These were electrified rapid transit lines, operating variously above and below the streets, within their own rights-of-way.[2]

3. *Suburban railroads.* This service differed only in degree and ownership from the subway and elevated lines. Partly electrified, partly diesel, the suburban railroads provided service to suburbs between ten and thirty or more miles from the Loop, with only a few stops nearer than ten miles from the Loop.

The Supply of Transportation Facilities: A Conventional Analysis

The supply of transportation facilities in any city has many dimensions—some, like length and width, are purely quantitative, and some, like street capacity, contain qualitative elements. The following short descriptive passages cover first the key quantitative dimensions of length, width, and distribution of the various types, and then look at the subject of carrying ability or capacity. Subsequently the subjects of speed, safety, and cost of travel are taken up.

Length. Table 9 gives the lengths of the types of transportation facilities measured in the Chicago survey and, in a parallel column, the lengths of transportation facilities in the Niagara Frontier. Reasons for differences, as well as similarities, will be given below.

The dominating fact, of course, is the very large mileage of local streets. In the Chicago aera, 72 percent of all street mileage

---

[2] Excepting certain places, such as along the outer part of the Lake Street elevated line, where grade intersections with streets existed in 1956. The Lake Street tracks have since been elevated and so this problem has ceased to exist on that line.

was in local streets, and in the Niagara Frontier, 56 percent. The smaller percentage in the Niagara Frontier is partly due to the greater proportion of land in that study area which was rural, where arterials form a higher proportion of all street length, and partly due to the smaller population needing the services of local streets. In Chicago there were about 1.4 miles of local streets per 1,000 population, in the Niagara Frontier, 2.2 miles, but again the greater mileage relationship to population is offset by the smaller total population and the larger, predominately rural land area.

Although local streets were most numerous, they carried in both study areas very small proportions of the total vehicle miles of

Table 9. *Miles of Transportation Facilities in Chicago and the Niagara Frontier, by Type*

Type of Transportation Facility	Chicago[a] (1956) (miles)	Percent	Niagara[b] Frontier (1962) (miles)	Percent
Local Streets	7,400	72.2	2,940	55.7
Arterial Streets	2,796	27.2	2,261	42.8
Expressways	66	0.6	82	1.5
Total	10,262	100.0	5,283	100.0
Buses	1,561	81.7	356[c]	100.0
Subway-Elevated	70	3.6		
Suburban Railroads	283	14.7		
Total	1,914	100.0	356	100.0

[a] Source: CATS, *Final Report,* vol. I, Table 13.
[b] Source: NFTS, *Final Report,* vol. I, Tables 9 and 11.
[c] Street miles of urban bus service.

travel. In Chicago 72 percent of the total streets carried only 17 percent of the vehicle miles of travel. In the Niagara Frontier, 56 percent of all streets carried only an estimated 10 percent of vehicle miles.

The arterials, a minority as far as length goes, and the expressways, which in Chicago in 1956 were less than 1 percent of total roadway length, carried together more than 83 percent of all the vehicle miles of travel. In the Niagara Frontier, arterials and expressways, with 44 percent of the street length, carried about 90 percent of all vehicle miles of travel. In these cases the expressways carried respectively 8 and 14 percent of the vehicle miles of travel although they were each less than 1.5 percent of total street length.

These data demonstrate very clearly that from the point of view of metropolitan transportation planning, local streets have no real significance, and that attention can be focused on a smaller number of larger facilities. If the larger facilities can be laid out in an efficient manner, then transportation problems can be reduced in their impact. Prime attention in the world of planning for automobiles and trucks can be devoted to the expressways—a tiny but very efficient part of the whole, which as will be shown, should ultimately carry 35, 40, or higher percentages of all vehicular travel.

In the world of mass transportation, buses provide the most extensive portion of service. In Chicago in 1956 buses provided 82 percent of the mileage of the mass transportation system. In the Niagara Frontier, buses provided all mass transportation service.

The higher speed and higher capacity transit systems in the Chicago area (subway-elevated trains and suburban railroads) together made up just over 18 percent of the total system mileage. Yet with that minority of the mileage, they carried almost half of the person miles of travel using mass transportation. Table 10 gives the vehicle miles and the person miles of travel for Chicago and the Niagara Frontier as measured by various surveys in each area. By dividing the total vehicle or person miles of travel by the number of miles of transportation facilities of each type, the average loading on each side is obtained. These are data for the average weekday.

On the street systems progressively heavier loads are carried by the larger street types. In both Chicago and the Niagara Frontier, arterial streets carry about ten times the traffic volume of local streets, and expressways carry about five times the volume carried on arterials.

An unusual feature of this table is that vehicle volumes have been translated into average person volumes on the street types. This is done by subtracting a percentage to reduce traffic volumes by the appropriate number of trucks, and then multiplying the estimated

Table 10. Percentage Distribution of Daily Vehicle and Person Miles of Travel (Air-line), by Type of Transportation Facility, and Average Volumes of Vehicles and Persons, by Type of Transportation Facility, for the Chicago Area (1956) and the Niagara Frontier (1962)

Type of Transportation Facility	Chicago (1956)				Niagara Frontier (1962)			
	Vehicle Miles of Travel[a]	Average Volume	Person Miles of Travel[b]	Average Volume	Vehicle Miles of Travel	Average Volume	Person Miles of Travel	Average Volume
Local Streets	6,000,000	810	7,900,000	1,060	1,150,000[c]	390	1,500,000	510
Arterials	27,200,000	9,700	35,600,000	12,700	8,744,000[d]	3,900	11,500,000	5,100
Expressways	3,000,000	45,500	3,950,000	60,000	1,606,000[d]	19,600	2,100,000	25,600
All Streets	36,200,000		47,450,000		11,500,000		15,100,000	
Buses			7,950,000	5,100				
Subway-Elevated			3,444,000	49,000				
Suburban Railroads			4,127,000	14,600				
All Mass Transportation			15,521,000		712,000		712,000[e]	2,000
Total	36,200,000		62,971,000		11,500,000		15,712,000	

a CATS, *Final Report*, I, 81 (unweighted VMT over the road).   b 12.3 percent trucks, 1.5 average vehicle loading factor.
c Assumed 10 percent.   d NFTS, *Final Report*, vol. II, Table 28.   e Excludes school children on school buses.

number of automobiles by their known average loading of 1.5 persons per car. The resulting figure is the same as would be obtained if a person were to stand by the roadside and count the number of persons in all automobiles passing by. This feature permits comparisons to be made between the number of persons carried by streets and by mass transportation systems of various types.

The average mile of bus line in Chicago carried 5,100 persons per weekday. The higher capacity subway-elevated lines carried nearly ten times as many, or an average of 49,000 persons per mile per day. Suburban railroads, on the other hand, had 14,600 persons per mile per day. Surprisingly, expressways carried the largest average number of persons per day—about 60,000 persons on the average mile.

Distribution of the Supply of Streets: Spacing and Width. It has already been shown that population density and travel demand occur in regular patterns, with the highest densities of population and trip generation at the core of a city. Moving away from the core, these densities decline quickly at first and then more gradually until they become asymptotic with the population densities of the rural areas surrounding the city.

If one were to observe these densities knowing that they had existed for many decades, and if one were to assume further that intelligent beings were reacting to these pressures, one would deduce quickly enough that there would be some adjustment of street space to accommodate the pressures for movement. And this in fact is what the evidence shows. The adjustment is far from perfect because new streets in built-up areas are very expensive to build because of land costs, and because automobile and truck travel was never imagined by the surveyors of the nineteenth century. Nevertheless, the attempts are clearly visible in the records.

One way of seeing the regularity in the distribution of street service is in the average spacing of arterial streets. Spacing is defined as the distance between parallel arterials, assuming that all arterials in a certain area lie in a uniform grid. This assumption is often untrue, but even so, the measure is an extremely useful indicator of average supply of streets.

Spacing is given by the formula:

$$S = \frac{2A}{l},$$

where $S =$ spacing in miles;
  $A =$ land area in square miles;
  $l =$ length of arterials, in miles, for any defined area.
Using this formula, the average spacings of existing arterials in the Chicago area and the Niagara Frontier were calculated and are given in Table 11.

In each case, the spacing of arterials at the center is one-tenth mile, which is about 500 feet apart. Then, steadily, the spacing in-

Table 11. *Mean Spacing of Arterials in the Chicago Area and the Niagara Frontier*

	Chicago Area (1956)		Niagara Frontier (1962)	
Ring	*Mean Distance from CBD[a] (miles)*	*Mean Spacing of Arterials[b] (miles)*	*Mean Distance from CBD[c] (miles)*	*Mean Spacing of Arterials[c] (miles)*
0	0.0	0.1	0.0	0.1
1	1.5	0.3	1.5	0.3
2	3.5	0.4	3.0	0.5
3	5.5	0.4	6.0	0.7
4	8.5	0.5	8.0	0.7
5	11.5	0.7	10.5	0.9
6	16.0	0.9	15.0	1.2
7	24.0	1.2	23.0	1.9

[a] Source: CATS, *Final Report,* vol. II, Table 9.
[b] Source: CATS, *Final Report,* vol. III, Table 14.
[c] Source: NFTS, *Final Report,* vol. I, Tables, 13, 14.

creases to 1.2 miles in Chicago's ring 7 and 1.9 miles in the Niagara Frontier's ring 7. The average spacing is less in Chicago because of the greater density of population there, especially in rings 1–4.

This is the clearest kind of evidence that in the denser areas, over many years, more and more streets have had to be assigned the role of carrying heavy traffic volumes and as a result have had to be

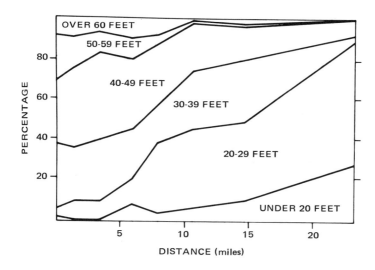

Figure 28.
Distribution of primary arterials, by pavement width and distance
from Buffalo central business district, Niagara Frontier, 1962.

signed, signalized, regulated as to parking and stopping, and even
physically altered in order to fulfill their new role adequately. Sometimes new streets are built, but more often an existing street is given
a new task, and thereafter is modified as conditions and finances
permit.

One of the actions taken to modify existing arterials is to widen
their pavements. The data available on street widths in the Niagara
Frontier suggests that street widening, viewed over an entire metropolitan area, is a process which is a gradual adjustment to the
requirements of vehicular traffic dictated by the density of human
settlement.

In Figure 28 is shown the percentage distribution of street
widths by distance from the center of Buffalo. At the center, the percentage of streets forty feet in width or greater is quite high—over
60 percent. But this percentage gradually falls off until at ten miles
from the center less than 30 percent of major arterials have pavements more than forty feet in width, and the proportion continues to

decline with increasing distance. (The foregoing data are for "primary arterials," which are the principal arterials or major streets and which tend to include most of the wider streets.)

It should not be thought, because there are larger proportions of arterials with wider pavements close to the center, that these wider streets necessarily form a coherent, connected system of wide streets. In some cases, of course, they do; but in many cases wide streets suddenly become narrow ones, or are placed at right angles to the prevailing directions of traffic. It is as if they were built because they could be built there. This is not always a loss of investment, but the lack of continuity of these wider pavements reduces their ability to move traffic.

Carrying Ability. The ability of a street system to carry traffic is a function of many factors, of which width, length (as a surrogate of number), and street type are the most important. Obviously, the more lanes, the more vehicles that can be moved past a point in any given time period. The more streets there are (that is, the greater the sum of lengths in any given area), the more vehicles can generally be moved. And finally, type of street is important: for example, an expressway can carry, lane for lane, more than three times the number of vehicles that a regular surface arterial can. The main reason for this is that vehicles on expressways flow continuously, whereas arterials are stopped for approximately 50 percent of the time while crossing traffic moves through signalized intersections.

The traffic-carrying ability of streets is of substantial interest to engineers, planners, and public administrators, since it is their task to provide a supply of street service which will be closer to the level of demand created by present and future populations. A measure of carrying ability is therefore needed, and so for many years "capacities" have been calculated for streets in a road network, using street width, type, and other data from the inventory of transportation facilities.

In the traffic-engineering sense of the word, "capacity" is the number of vehicles that can pass a point on a road *under certain carefully specified conditions.* Thus, a road's capacity is not a fixed quantity, but a variable. This variable is dependent not only upon width and geometrics (types of intersections, separation of opposing traffic, turning bays, shoulder widths, and other built-in elements of the roadway) and not only upon percentages of trucks, percentages of turning movements, and other characteristics of the stream of vehicles, but also upon the conditions of relative congestion under which the traffic is expected to flow. More vehicles, up to a certain point, can move past a point under conditions of slower speeds and tighter spacing between vehicles, and under these conditions the roadway is said to have a higher "capacity." Thus capacity has a strong element of judgment in its definition, and it can vary depending upon the quality of service desired by its user. This has been recognized in the latest *Highway Capacity Manual*.[3]

The Chicago study employed a "design capacity" definition which was conservative; that is, it was set at a high volume of vehicles, and hence did not tend to overstate the need for new facilities. It was appropriate to the size and density of the country's third largest metropolitan area, a place where one simply could not afford to provide that ease of movement which one expects in a city of 50,000 population. In numeric terms, arterial design capacity was defined as 70 percent of "maximum capacity" (about the maximum number of vehicles ever observed to use a roadway of the given type) and expressway capacities were defined as 85 percent of "maximum capacity."

Table 12 shows the design capacities used by the Chicago study. The lower capacities of arterial streets in the downtown and intermediate parts of the city reflect the presence of more pedestrians, greater interference from parking and unparking vehicles, greater numbers of buses, and similar frictions. The table also shows that, lane for lane, expressways can carry about three and a half times as many vehicles as surface arterial streets.

It must be pointed out that these capacities are expressed in terms of 24-hour periods and are based upon the assumption that the peak hour's capacity is 11 percent of daily capacity. This assumption

[3] *Highway Capacity Manual*, Highway Research Board, Washington, D.C., 1965.

Table 12. *Design Capacities Employed by the Chicago Area Transportation Study Expressed as 24-Hour Traffic Volumes*[a]

Facility and Area Type	20-Foot Pavement	40-Foot Pavement	60-Foot Pavement
Arterials[b]			
Downtown	5,100	11,400	19,100
Intermediate	6,400	14,000	23,000
Outlying and Rural	7,000	15,300	23,000
Expressways[c]	*4 Lanes*	*6 Lanes*	*8 Lanes*
All Areas	54,000	81,000	108,000

[a] Volumes are in automobile equivalents; i.e., trucks are weighted so that comparable volume counts on roads would be about 10 percent less.
[b] Assuming no parking, 50 percent green time, 10 percent left turns, 10 percent right turns, 60–40 directional split, and 11 percent of daily travel in peak hour.
[c] Assuming 60–40 directional split and 11 percent of daily travel in peak hour.
Source: CATS, *Final Report,* vol. I, Table 15.

is made simply in order that capacity can be related readily to average daily travel, which, as was earlier shown in Chapter II, follows a regular cycle.

Table 13 shows the "practical capacities" used in the Niagara Frontier. In all cases, these capacities are lower than those used in

Table 13. *Practical Capacities Employed by the Niagara Frontier Transportation Study Expressed as 24-Hour Traffic Volumes*[a]

Facility and Area Type	20-Foot Pavement	40-Foot Pavement	60-Foot Pavement
Arterials[b]			
Downtown	3,840	7,680	11,520
Other Areas	5,520	11,040	16,560
Expressways[c]	*4 Lanes*	*6 Lanes*	*8 Lanes*
All Areas	47,070	68,100	94,130

[a] Traffic volumes include 10 percent trucks, unweighted.
[b] Assuming no parking, 10 percent left turns, 10 percent right turns, 60–40 directional split, sixty-second signal cycle, 11 percent of daily traffic in peak hour, and 50 percent green time.
[c] Assuming 60–40 directional split and 11 percent of daily traffic in peak hour.
Source: NFTS, *Final Report,* vol. I, Table 8.

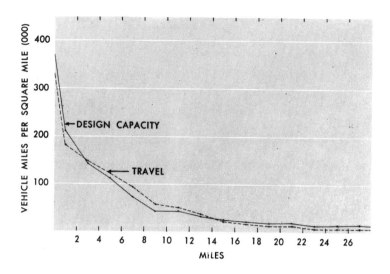

Figure 29.
Design capacity and vehicle miles of travel, by distance from the Loop,
Chicago area, 1956.

Chicago. They reflect a higher standard of service which is more readily obtainable in a metropolitan area of 1,350,000 persons.

Reverting to the Chicago data, the design capacity of each street in the entire study area was multiplied by its length, and the result was the vehicle miles of capacity of all the streets in the area. "Vehicle miles of capacity" exactly expresses the ability of a street— or an area—to carry vehicle miles of travel. It conveys not only the width, geometrics, and quality of service of a street's cross-section, but the length of each street and through this, the quantity, that is, the number and spacing, of streets in an area. For the entire Chicago area, there were 36,473,000 vehicle miles of arterial and expressway capacity in 1956. Eighty-five percent of this was provided by arterials and 15 percent by expressways. At the same time, there were 36,200,000 vehicle miles of travel (unweighted) in the same area. Unfortunately, the supply and the demand were not both distributed in the same way throughout the region.

The difference between vehicle miles of capacity (VMC) and

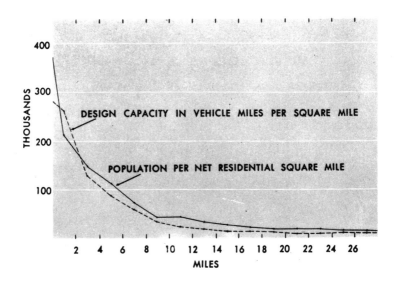

Figure 30.
Design capacity and population density, by distance from the Loop,
Chicago area, 1956.

vehicle miles of travel (VMT) are shown in Figure 29, related to
distance from the Chicago Loop. As can be seen in that area lying
between three and fourteen miles from the Loop there was in 1956 a
broad band of congestion where travel exceeded capacity. Closer to
the center and farther out, street capacity exceeded travel demand.
These are, of course, averages over many streets, and cannot show
isolated points of congestion which may exist even in areas with an
over-all surplus of capacity.

Figure 30 shows that capacity and population density follow
the same pattern, and very closely. This is another demonstration
of the gradual adjustment of supply to demand—and of demand to
supply, since it is probable that some inhibition on high densities of
settlement and on trip generation is exercised by the congestion
brought about by an inadequate street system.

Distribution of the Supply of Mass Transportation Facilities.
The miles of mass transportation routes for Chicago and the Niagara

Frontier were shown in Table 9, but that table gives only a limited idea of the service rendered to the public over these routes. Service is not only a function of the length of routes but also of the frequency with which buses, subway or elevated trains, or suburban trains pass over those routes, and, of course, the number of seats available.

Seat miles is probably the best measure of service to employ in dealing with mass transportation. The concept of capacity, which is a troublesome enough concept to use for road service, is meaningless when applied to mass transportation. Rail transit vehicles do have the highest capacities for moving people; in a space twelve feet wide they *can* move 72,000 persons in an hour.[4] But in only a few places in the world have such volumes been recorded. Capacity is not an advantage to be claimed; it is, in fact, irrelevant if people are not likely to use it. The actual service that is provided by transit companies is what is really of interest.

Table 14. *Weekday Supply and Use of Mass Transportation Services in the Chicago Area, 1956*

Type	Scheduled Seat Miles of Service	Percent	Person Miles of Travel	Percent	Ratio of Supply to Use
Bus	20,060,000	62	7,950,000	51	2.5
Subway and Elevated	7,244,000	22	3,444,000	22	2.1
Suburban Railroad	5,048,000	16	4,127,000	27	1.2
Total	32,352,000	100	15,521,000	100	2.1

Source: Chicago Area Transportation Study, *Final Report,* I (1959), Table 17.

As shown in Table 14, buses provided 62 percent of the seat miles of service, although as shown in Table 9, they had nearly 82 percent of the route miles. Subway and elevated lines, with less than 4 percent of the route miles, provided 22 percent of the seat miles

---

[4] "Capacities and Limitations of Urban Transportation Modes," Institute of Traffic Engineers, Information Report, Washington, D.C., 1965.

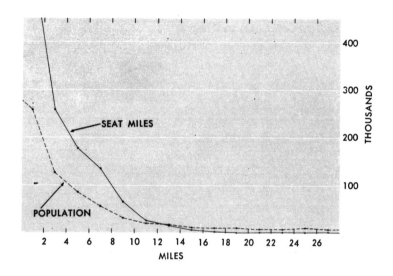

Figure 31.
Seat miles of mass transportation service and population density,
by distance from the Loop, Chicago area, 1956.

of service. And suburban railroads, with nearly 15 percent of the route miles, provided 16 percent of the service.

This service was utilized by the public in quite different ways, as shown in the column of Table 14 which relates supply to use. Buses had 2.5 times as many seat miles as passenger miles; subway-elevated trains had 2.1 times as much service as use. These inefficiencies result from two major factors: vehicles having to travel nearly empty when moving against the prevailing peak-hour traffic direction, and vehicles moving with light loads in the off-peak hours. The suburban railroads appear to be much more efficient, but this is explained by their practice of storing trains downtown during the day—in effect using their vehicles mainly in the peak hour and mainly in the peak direction.

As might be expected, the geographic distribution of the seat miles of transit service in the Chicago area is closely aligned to demand. The best way of showing this is in graphic form, because both demand and supply change continuously. Figure 31 shows seat miles of transit service per square mile in the Chicago study area compared to population density per net residential square mile. The level of service drops off faster than population density as distance from the Loop increases; this is because transit lines focus on the core of the city, bringing passengers in and out in a predominantly radial pattern. As the Chicago study noted, "beyond 12 miles from the Loop the level of mass transportation service is very low—of the order of three or four thousand seat miles of service per square mile. This is about the amount of service provided by one bus route with 15 minute headways." Beyond twelve miles from the Loop, the average population density is less than 15,000 persons per net residential square mile.

The same kind of situation was found later in the Niagara Frontier. There, also, seat miles of bus service drop off more rapidly than population density, and service reaches a low level (about 3,000 seat miles per square mile) when population density falls below 15,000 persons per net residential square mile.

One can readily observe from these data that there is a kind of equilibrium or balance between supply and demand. This is not an equilibrium which is achieved in a free market, because public service commissions require service to be provided in accordance with political and social demands, not just in terms of the unit profitability of each line. Nevertheless, these data suggest the existence of powerful economic forces which have to be recognized in the development of mass transportation policy.

Speed of Travel. The kind of service produced by any given mode of travel can be measured by a number of factors, such as speed, safety, cost, and the more elusive comfort-convenience group. In this section, speed of travel is analyzed, using data both from the inventory of transportation facilities and from the travel surveys.

The effective speed of travel provided by any given mode is not its line-haul speed or the legal speed limit possible under ideal conditions, but the speed of travel from door to door. This is affected by the time it takes to walk to an automobile or transit vehicle, waits (if any), transfer times, parking times, and the walk at the destination.

Effective speeds of the various modes of travel were measured in Chicago through the home interview survey. Times of departure and arrival were known, and air-line distance could be calculated. All modes could thus be treated equally. The results of this process are shown in Table 15.

Table 15. *Mean Journey Speed and Time in Transit, by Mode of Travel, Chicago Area, 1956*

Mode of Travel	Mean Journey Speed[a] (miles per hour)	Mean Journey Time[a] (minutes)
Suburban Railroad	14.4	56
Automobile (Driver)	11.1	22
Elevated Subway[b]	8.9	48
Bus	6.2	35

[a] Computed on a door-to-door basis.
[b] All trips using elevated-subway lines. Trips using elevated-subway lines without using any other mode, such as a bus, in the same journey averaged 10.0 miles per hour. Those trips which did employ another mode averaged 8.4 miles per hour.
Source: CATS, *Final Report*, vol. II, Table 47.

Suburban railroad trains provided the fastest journey speed; this was attained by a long journey (as indicated by the mean journey time of fifty-six minutes), by high-speed equipment, and by infrequent stops within ten miles of Chicago's Loop. Automobile travel was the next fastest. Subway-elevated service was third in speed; like the suburban railroad, this was attained by a longer than average journey, with stops averaging one-half mile apart.[5] Buses provided the slowest travel, averaging 6.3 miles per hour.

What are the limiting influences on the speeds of urban travel? For transit vehicles (setting aside the effects of street congestion or slow-downs caused by other transit vehicles operating on the same track) speeds are controlled by five factors. These are acceleration rate, deceleration rate, cruising speed, average times stopped at stations, and distances between stations. Average transit vehicle

[5] This is the average number of stops per mile over the whole Chicago subway-elevated system; in many places, stations are one mile or more apart.

speed (including station stops) is what people are effectively judging and it is given by the following formula:

$$S = \frac{D}{T + D/C + C\,(1/2a + 1/2d)}$$

where   S = average transit vehicle speed;
        T = stop time at stations or stops;
        C = cruising speed;
        a = rate of acceleration;
        d = rate of deceleration;
        D = average distance between stations.

The preceding formula is only valid for cases where cruising speed is actually attained, and it assumes continuous acceleration and deceleration at the stated rates. If anything, this formula over-states average speeds.

Acceleration and deceleration rates in transit vehicles are limited not so much by power or mechanical factors as by the comfort and safety of passengers within the vehicles themselves. Acceleration and deceleration rates of more than three miles per hour per second are not only uncomfortable for passengers standing or seated sideways, but are likely to cause accidents.

Equally as limiting as acceleration and deceleration rates are the distances between stations or stops. No matter what the cruising speed of a transit vehicle may be, average speed is most directly a function of station spacing. The closer together the stations are, the lower the speed. With stops one-quarter mile apart or less, it is almost impossible to get average speeds of more than fifteen miles per hour. With stops of a mile apart, it is very difficult to get average speeds of more than thirty-five miles per hour. With two-mile station spacing, average speeds of forty-eight miles per hour can be obtained (see Table 16).

These physical constraints show the futility of talking about "high-speed" transit within cities, at least insofar as "high speed" is taken to mean average speeds of sixty-seventy miles per hour. Except for long-haul suburban railroad trains, the speeds of urban transit are severely limited by factors which cannot be changed by mechanical improvements.

Table 16. *Calculated Transit Speeds as a Function of Station Spacing*[a]

	Mean Speed (miles per hour)	
Station Spacing	*With Top Speed 50 mph*	*With Top Speed 60 mph*
2 miles	38	46
1 mile	30	35
½ mile	22	24
¼ mile	14	14

[a] Assuming average station stop of thirty seconds and acceleration and deceleration rates of three miles per hour per second.

Average automobile speeds, on the other hand, are limited by two principal factors. These are the geometric design of roadways and the volume or density of other vehicles using the same roadway. Basically, the class of arterial streets, which allows for intersections with other streets at grade, permits free-flow speeds of fifteen-forty miles per hour, depending upon the number of intersecting streets, signing, and signalization.[6] Expressways, on the other hand, permit free-flow speeds of fifty and sixty miles per hour in urban areas, except in cases of the earliest expressways, which had very short turning radii.

Greater density of vehicles on any road, however, can reduce speeds drastically, as every driver knows. These relationships can be graphed in a variety of ways; Figure 32 indicates the relationships used by the Chicago study.

Safety. Safety of travel is one of the important qualities of service provided by transportation facilities—and there are substantial differences in performance between the different types. Data which were obtained by the Chicago study and shown in Table 17 illustrate this point clearly.

[6] Measured free-flow speeds in the Niagara Frontier ranged from 18.0 miles per hour in the center of Buffalo to 29.1 miles per hour in the near-in suburbs and to 41.5 miles per hour in rural areas. Free-flow speeds were measured in the very early morning hours.

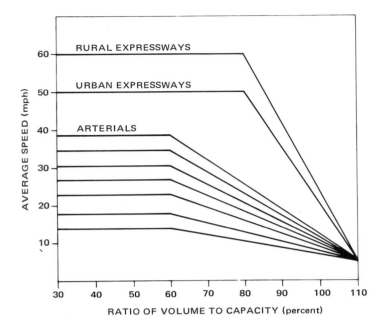

Figure 32.
Relationship between speed and the ratio of volume to capacity.

The least safe street to drive on, mile for mile, is the local residential street. The number of accidents on local streets is small, but the proportion of vehicle miles driven there is still smaller, so that the rate per mile driven is quite high. In direct costs alone—which include property damage, medical expenses for injuries, and awards for fatalities, but not indirect costs such as value of time lost due to injury—the accident costs on local streets were equal to 3 cents per vehicle mile in 1958.

In contrast, arterial accident costs were estimated at about 1 cent per vehicle mile, while expressways had the lowest rate of any street type, at 0.3 cent per vehicle mile.

Transit vehicles provide travel which is generally safer than automobile travel. Based on the amounts budgeted by the Chicago Transit Authority to pay for claims against the Authority, the costs

Table 17. *Direct Costs of Accidents, by Type of Transportation, Chicago Area, 1958*

Type of Transportation	Costs in Cents per Vehicle Mile
Local Streets	3.09
Arterial Streets	1.07
Expressways	0.31
All Streets	1.32

	Costs in Cents per Passenger Mile
Buses	0.4
Subway and Elevated Trains	0.1
All Transit	0.3

Source: Dayton P. Jorgenson, "Accident Costs and Rates on Chicago Area Streets and Highways," *CATS Research News*, 4, no. 4. Transit costs are estimated from budget data of the Chicago Transit Authority. Both sources are reported in Chicago Area Transportation Study, *Final Report*, III, 11.

of accidents in 1958 were 0.4 cent per passenger mile on buses and 0.1 cent per passenger mile on subway-elevated trains. Even though these figures are rates for passenger miles and not for vehicle miles, there is still no escaping the conclusion that transit travel is substantially safer than automobile travel.

A Language for Networks

Up to this point, we have been dealing with transportation facilities in fairly conventional terms. The conventional descriptions are ones in which a single attribute of a transportation facility—or perhaps two or three in combination—has been extracted from the universe of data on these facilities and held up for examination. Length, width, carrying ability, speed, and safety are examples of such characteristics.

The examination of these kinds of data produces knowledge and some understanding, but of a limited scope. These are essentially descriptive processes; they are static; they deal with small parts and aspects rather than the whole. Only very limited and

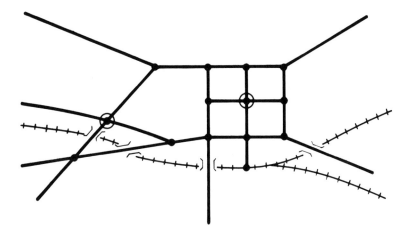

clumsy use could be made of these facts. The data did not flow into, and become a part of, the main stream of the planning process.

What was desperately needed was a language which would permit a transportation system to be dealt with as a complete entity, and furthermore as a working, operational entity. In other words, a language was needed which would permit the planner to deal with the network as a network. This is the opposite of trying to dissect a network so that it can be dealt with in traditional verbal thought patterns.

To illustrate this point, let us see what a transportation network actually is. It may be defined as a collection or set of individual links—not necessarily all of the same type—which are connected together to form a system for the movement of people and goods through a given area. A diagram illustrating a very small portion of an urban network is shown above. An actual urban network will typically be several hundred times larger than this example.

If this network, or one several hundred times larger, is to be dealt with, it must first be represented in some fashion. However, transportation networks have certain special characteristics which make them hard to describe.

1. Transportation networks occur in space and their spatial arrangements and interconnections are a vital part of their existence.

2. Transportation networks as they now exist are composed of links which differ by small degrees, thus forming a continuum of types.

3. Transportation networks provide varying service to the vehicles or persons using them, and these variations are determined not only by the nature of each segment of the transportation facility but by the number of vehicles using that facility.

Compare the foregoing characteristics with the conventional, English-language way of describing transportation facilities. A conventional study of transportation networks, as has been shown, begins by classifying facilities into major categories. Roads are separated from mass transportation facilities; each of these two major categories is broken down into smaller groups—expressways, arterials, and local streets on one hand and subways, elevated trains, and buses on the other. Each of these types is then described in terms of speed, physical characteristics, capacity, and so on.

These conventional classifications, however, perform very poorly when they are compared with the requirements which need to be met in describing a transportation system. The spatial aspects of even small networks cannot be dealt with except by the static device of the map. Small variations in the links forming a transportation system cannot be dealt with explicitly. And the varying performance levels of different kinds of transportation facilities under different loads cannot be dealt with at the network level.

This inadequacy of language as a means for dealing with networks may seem to be a labored point, but actually it is not; it is an extremely important point. People often make serious attempts to use conventional reasoning as a means to deal "rationally" with complex transportation problems. But the foregoing section indicates how far ordinary language misses the mark when it comes to dealing with descriptions of present networks; and networks, present and planned, are at the heart of the whole transportation problem. Missing this important area, language must largely fail as a means for dealing rationally with the problems of transportation.

More than this, language is intimately tied to a form of reasoning which works through equalities and inequalities of categories.

By means of a kind of verbal trigonometry, the classically trained thinker (and this is most of us) attempts to triangulate his way into the unknown to extend his knowledge. He reasons by equating or denying the equality of classes.

This kind of thinking, however, is not useful when dealing with multiple particulars such as the links of a network, especially when these particulars are spread out across space. Under such circumstances, conventional thinking is both inaccurate and harmful. Language encourages oversimplification in order that things may be stuffed into classes which can then be dealt with in the conventional reasoning processes. Further, language invites comparison and (unless one is very careful) conflict. A prime example of this kind of comparison and conflict is the situation of mass transportation *versus* the highway—a ridiculous competition! By comparing categories and creating conflict, language in this fashion distracts attention from much more important issues such as service to the people and economy of resource.

It is interesting to trace the development of a language suitable for dealing with networks. Inventories of roads had been made for many years; most inventories of statewide systems were made after 1934, using funds authorized by the Hayden-Cartwright Act of that year.[7] These recorded the lengths, widths, type, construction, condition, traffic, and sometimes the accident facts about individual links. The location of links was typically within counties, and the numbering system followed the engineering practice of distance measures from some initial point, such as a county boundary. Thus, a road segment might be numbered 12.25–15.45, meaning that it lies between 12.25 and 15.45 miles from a county boundary. This form of inventory provided exact descriptions of each link, but only very rudimentary identification of location.

Between 1945 and 1955, transportation studies in California, Detroit, and Wichita identified shorter urban segments and recorded not only their exact measurements but their geographic position as well. Location was identified by the coordinate (that is, x and y) location of one end of the transportation link. Using such data, the

[7] H. S. Fairbanks, "Planning for Future Highways," U.S. Bureau of Public Roads, Washington, D.C. (unpublished speech made about 1936).

Detroit study prepared maps of the geographic distribution of arterial capacities. This was a major advance because street capacity
could then be compared with the geographic distribution of demand
for travel, and those areas with inadequate capacity could be identified: a necessary input for the preparation of trial plans.

The preceding studies thus added precision of geographic location to the basic measurements which described each part of the
network. Still, all that could be produced from such data were lists,
maps, or summary tables: the static characteristics of an existing
supply of transportation facilities. Such materials still could not be
employed directly in the planning process. One more breakthrough
was needed, and this was to find a system which would define how
the parts of a system interconnected with one another. This breakthrough was supplied by a very simple numbering system which was
developed in the Chicago study. This system can be described in
three sentences.

1. The entire metropolitan area was divided into zones (512)
and each zone was given a three-digit number.

2. Each intersection between links in the street network was
identified by a five-digit number, the first three digits being the number of the zone in which the intersection was located, and the last
two digits identifying intersections within the zone.

3. Each link, or segment, of a transportation system was identified by the numbers of the intersections at its beginning and end—
a ten-digit number.[8]

An illustration below shows how this numbering system worked
in practice, for a road system. Transit numbering was similar.

With this numbering system, all the links within a transportation system are *interconnected numerically*, just as they are interconnected physically on the ground. In the foregoing illustration,
the numbering of link 34102–34206 is such that its eastern terminus

[8] Actually, the first system used in Chicago used a four-digit node number,
with a consequent eight-digit link number; that system saved two digits, which was
an important saving for computer calculation. Subsequently the five-digit system
described here was used, and a computer conversion program was developed for
reducing the node numbers to four and the link numbers to eight.

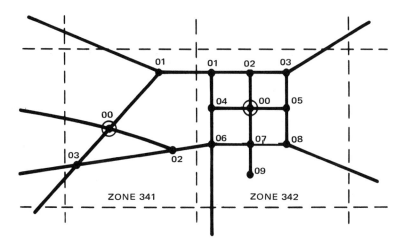

(intersection 34206) is the beginning number of all three links emanating from that intersection. And all of these links, in turn, are numbered so that their other terminals are the beginning points of still other links. Thus a driver on one link can find his way to any part of the network, providing that he knows the correct sequence of numbered links to use.

This system of notation satisfied the requirements for describing the first two important characteristics of networks. First, the spatial arrangements and interconnections of the networks were fully described, because knowing the length of each link and how it connected with other links implied a complete identification of network geometry, at least as far as any driver would want to know, which was after all the crucial test. If more specific geographic identification were required for drawing maps mechanically or electronically, the x and y positions of each node could be added, as was done later in the Niagara Frontier study.

Second, the Chicago study's numbering system continued to supply all the descriptive capability in the same fashion as previous network descriptions: by strings of digits added to the link identification number. Length, speed, width, geometric type, and number of lanes were the more important road characteristics which were measured; and length, speed, number of tracks, headways, and seating capacities described the mass transportation links.[9]

With this network coding convention, it became possible to represent an entire transportation system within a computer, with its essential quality of being an interconnected whole. This in turn opened the door to techniques which allowed the minimum time paths through the network to be found, and this led to the simulation of vehicle flows over the network. But the story of traffic simulation and how it was developed for use in testing alternative transportation plans must be reserved for a later chapter.

Conclusion

Although much space has been given to the elementary facts on transportation networks, the real purpose of this chapter has been to show that specialized systems of notation are needed to describe transportation networks in urban areas. Without these special notational systems, one simply cannot deal effectively with network problems. For many years, despite the fact that extensive surveys of transportation facilities had been taken, the data on roads and mass transportation lines stood outside of the planning process. Under such circumstances, planning practitioners could only use their intuition or their experience in making decisions.

With the numbering system described in this chapter any transportation system can be described completely and accurately, with its essential interconnective character fully represented. Further, the behavior of vehicles within the network can be similarly represented, so that increases in volume of traffic will result in reductions of speed, as happens in the real world. These numbering systems became part of the machinery for completely representing urban travel over transportation networks, and this in turn provided the means by which plans could be judged against the goals of an urban community.

---

[9] The details of network surveys and coding are well described in a large number of manuals, examples of which are furnished in Chapter VII.

PART TWO

THE TRANSPORTATION PLANNING PROCESS

The urban transportation planning process has developed steadily over more than two and a half decades, but most rapidly since 1955. The core of this process is a series of steps involving data collection, forecasting, stating goals, planning, testing, and evaluating. Although there are substantial variations in the detailed techniques which are used by different transportation planners, the basic sequence of operations is very nearly alike.

In the following ten chapters, the major steps of the transportation planning process are described. To illustrate the very difficult problems which arise when real cities are being planned, examples of the process in action are given, using the plans and data of the Chicago and Niagara Frontier studies.

VI

THE URBAN TRANSPORTATION PLANNING PROCESS

WHILE the urban transportation planning process which is the subject of this book evolved mainly within the past twenty-five years, its roots go back well beyond that point. It is worthwhile, therefore, to take a quick look at the development of surface transportation in the United States. A historical view shows how investments were made successively in different modes of travel and how these modes competed with and complemented one another, gradually building up more and more complex networks. As the problems and complexities of transportation increased, the urban transportation planning process developed to meet the needs of the times.

The Evolution of the Planning Process

As soon as the first settlements on the American continent began to expand and move inland, investments began to be made in transportation improvements over land. For many years, with lack of capital funds, these improvements were obtained by the required giving of the people's labor to the making and maintenance of dirt or corduroy roads. This was the "labor system." Such roads were vital if the country was to be opened up for development and if trade and communication (other than by river or coastal waterway) were to take place.

After the Revolution, the hesitant beginning of heavier investments in transportation began to occur. The first macadamized road built in the United States (1792–93) was the Lancaster Turnpike in

Pennsylvania; this road was not only the first all-weather road, but it was the start of the era of privately financed (but often publicly subsidized) toll roads. The Cumberland Road, from Washington to Wheeling and later to Illinois, was started into construction in 1811 as a federal road, but this effort at federal direct intervention in transportation was abandoned to the states in 1830. The toll road era ended about 1835.

Canals and canalized rivers offered much greater potential for the movement of heavy freight than the roads of that time; a few horses could readily pull barges containing more material than a hundred animals could haul in wagons. With this kind of advantage, a canal such as the Erie Canal (1825) could afford an investment averaging $20,000 per mile[1] in contrast to the Lancaster Turnpike's $7,500 per mile.

However, railroads, which were ushered into the United States by Peter Cooper's steam locomotive (1830), offered even greater advantages: both mechanical power and speed. Putting a steam engine on steel rails, which provided a low-friction way for all-weather travel, was sufficient to force both the canals and the nation's long-distance roads into obscurity for sixty years. The railroads were thus the prime cause of what has been called the "dark ages of road-building," lasting from about 1830 to 1890.

Meanwhile, within cities the era of mass transportation began when Abraham Brower started in 1825 to provide service in a public coach called an "accommodation." For a shilling, one could travel any distance in this horse-drawn vehicle along Broadway in New York City. Horse-drawn omnibuses and street railways were introduced to New York City in 1831 and 1832 respectively.

The improvement of mass transportation within cities continued throughout the nineteenth century. The steam-powered elevated transit line was introduced in New York in 1868, the cable car in San Francisco in 1873, the electric streetcar in Montgomery, Alabama, in 1886, and the subway in Boston in 1897. In 1905 a double-decker motor bus began to operate in New York. As of that date all the types of conveyances (except the helicopter) that we

[1] Archer B. Hulbert, *The Great American Canals—The Erie Canal* (Arthur Clark Co., Cleveland, 1904).

know today for moving groups of people in public vehicles within cities had been invented and brought into use.

Practically all transportation inventions and developments in the United States, from 1825 to the advent of Duryea's motor car in 1893, were for the transportation of groups of people rather than individuals. Prior to 1825 all transportation within cities had been individual transportation—foot travel, horseback, or horse and carriage. But the nineteenth century, and even the first two decades of the twentieth, were dominated by group transportation. It is only within the past fifty or sixty years that individualized transport has become available again for city dwellers.

Most of the mass transportation facilities that were built in the nineteenth century, both between and within cities, were planned and built as single facilities without consideration of how they would link up and work together as parts of a total transportation system. Even the terminals were, many of them, in separate places. Sometimes the single lines were directly competitive with one another; in other cases franchises were handed out which gave a single company a monopoly in a certain territory. In planning these facilities, profit was the main criterion while the hard practicalities of grade, subsoil, river crossings, and (in the case of canals) water supply acted as the chief constraints.

About the turn of the century, it began to be apparent that the separately built transit companies operating in the major cities were not providing the total service that they might be able to give if they were unified. In Chicago, Bion J. Arnold drew up a plan for an entire, unified transit system in 1905. The slogan was "one city, one fare." This was followed by other plans, to much the same effect, by Burnham in 1909 and by others in 1916, 1923, and 1927. The early plans called for substantial extensions of transit, but as time went on and the automobile became more widely used, the transit plans became more and more conservative.

The renaissance of road-building started about 1890; some credit for this goes to the League of American Wheelmen, who represented the bicycle enthusiasts that wanted good roads for their pleasure. About this same time the "labor system" of constructing town roads throughout the country was abandoned, and taxes were

raised which permitted local public works departments or contract
construction companies to bring heavy equipment into play for the
construction and maintenance of roads. New Jersey began to provide state aid for the construction of roads in 1891, New York followed suit, and by 1921 all the states had highway departments.

In 1916 federal aid for highway construction purposes was
granted to the states, but within a few years there began to be a
reaction among the engineers of the Office of Public Roads, and some
highway departments, against the way in which federal road investments were being spattered around. In the words of Fairbanks,

> Federal aid began in 1916 and the idea of the limited system wasn't
> strong enough then to get itself into the first Federal law; but it did get
> into the Federal Highway Act of 1921. In fact, it was the principal
> requirement of the amended Act, and we began at once to designate
> the Federal-aid highway system. A main system of interstate and
> inter-county highways, limited in extent to 7 per cent of the total
> mileage of highways of record in the country at the time of passage
> of the Act. That was what the Act said it was to be; and that was
> what we tried to make it. And when we had in that way selected the
> roads that we thought were really important and had joined them
> together into connected systems, can you imagine what we found out
> about the roads we had built with Federal aid during the previous
> five years? Yes, *we found that about three-fourths of all those roads
> we had built before we had a plan were so unimportant and so scat-
> tered that they couldn't by the longest possible stretch be made to fit
> into the new system.*[2]

So, from 1921 to 1934 the greater part of the national road-
building effort went into building a defined system of more important roads which would carry, despite its small total mileage, the
largest single proportion of vehicle miles of travel. Here was a policy
laid down and followed, and it meant that for the money expended,
more service was given than if investments had been scattered.

As a planning technique, the process which led to the designa-
tion of the federal aid system in 1921 must have been heavily dependent upon judgment and experience. The total size of the system

[2] H. S. Fairbanks, "Planning for Future Highways," U.S. Bureau of Public
Roads, Washington, D.C., 1935 (italics supplied).

was given, the sizes of the principal cities were known, and topography and the more frequently traveled routes were known. Undoubtedly, the combination of these factors was by a hand-designed layout on maps and by mutual agreement. Within the limits of mileage available (7 percent of rural road mileage) and the other basic constraints, there could not have been much leeway. Once the system was designated (and it was an intercity system, with no federal funds to be spent within cities of more than 2,500 'population), the process of precise location and construction design became a matter of engineering.

From other directions, however, other forces were at work which began to bring new skills and ideas into transportation planning. In 1893 the Chicago World's Fair had given to many Americans an idea of civic grandeur and magnificence which they felt appropriate for the growing wealth of the country. In 1909 Burnham, one of the leading architects of that exposition, continued this tradition of magnificence and optimism and presented his Plan for Chicago. From a transportation viewpoint the plan was not outstanding; Burnham merely superimposed a system of diagonal avenues onto the prevailing grid system in order to shorten travel distances. The terminals of these diagonals offered convenient and dramatic sites for public buildings as well as a legacy of very difficult traffic intersection points. Burnham saw the need for grandeur, for recreational spaces, and for the preservation of the lake front. In these things he was successful, and his work helped to expand the City Beautiful Movement, which was for a long time the heart of the city planning profession.

Burnham also gave rebirth to the concept of a fixed "master plan"—a plan which by its own force of logic would outlast its maker and influence the course of the future. This fixed master plan contained as one of its chief elements a plan for streets and boulevards. The notion of a plan for the totality of all streets was at least better than the practice of planning and building streets one or a few at a time. The drawbacks were the limited knowledge and number of factors which one man could bring to bear, and the danger inherent in following one man's ideas—no matter how bold in area coverage—for any length of time.

Opposed to this single-minded and intuitive approach we can begin to see how, from 1916 onwards, extensive surveys of travel were beginning to be made. In that year an unusual survey was made in Chicago, containing many elements which are used in today's transportation studies.[3] Employees working in establishments with more than 100 workers in the city of Chicago were interviewed about their work trips; origin and destination data were therefore available. These facts were then used to prepare a transit plan for Chicago, but like Burnham's plan, this plan failed to recognize the dynamic growth of the automobile.

However, in the 1920's increasing congestion began to be felt in many cities, and technicians began to respond to this problem. The traffic engineering profession obtained its start in this decade. And a succession of surveys began to measure the size of the traffic problem. In 1923 a massive one-day counting of traffic was undertaken in Los Angeles, using Boy Scouts for personnel. In 1927 the Detroit police made a survey which featured a cordon count, a parking survey, and an accident study. In 1932 the roadside interview technique was used in a Washington, D.C., traffic study.

The Hayden-Cartwright Act of 1934 provided definite incentives for planning. Up to 1.5 percent of federal highway funds given to each state could be spent for research and planning purposes. Using these moneys, state highway departments undertook statewide traffic counting surveys, inventories of road systems, mapping programs, and truck weight studies. It is significant, however, that these funds were used for rural and intercity planning purposes, not for urban studies.

The great change in road planning came during World War II. Here was an opportunity—when lack of men and materials forced slow-downs of construction—for rethinking the direction of road construction. The cities up to this time had received very little aid, yet vehicular congestion was greatest in cities. City finances were incapable of paying for anything significant in the way of road improvements. The states and the federal government had to intervene and bring both the powers of superior tax resources and their much

[3] Report of the Chicago Traction and Subway Commission on a Unified System of Surface, Elevated, and Subway Lines, Chicago, 1916.

larger engineering and highway-building organizations to bear if anything significant was to be accomplished. This policy change was passed in the Federal Aid Highway Act of 1944.

But where were the news roads to go? Which ones should be improved? The cordon-line surveys of the 1930's had demonstrated that in large cities external traffic was not important enough to determine internal improvement locations. A new survey technique was needed and—probably not coincidentally—was available. Influenced perhaps by the success of the Gallup poll, and certainly by methods of the Bureau of the Census, comparatively small-sample (5–10 percent) home interview travel surveys were carried out. By catching people at home, a representative proportion of all travel by all modes within a metropolitan area could be obtained. This became the basis for a series of 115 comprehensive transportation studies which were made in United States cities between 1944 and 1957.[4]

In this way, the pattern of planning for urban transportation systems got its birth. A steady flow of funds from the federal government and the states permitted substantial research and planning efforts to be undertaken. These urban area studies cost generally between $1.00 and $1.50 per capita of population in the urban area being studied.

The legacy of the earlier planning operations remained: extensive surveys of transportation networks and of traffic volumes. Cordon counts were combined with home interview surveys and with sample surveys of the trips made by trucks and taxis. And new techniques were being developed. In the Salt Lake City study (1947), for example, the first traffic assignment was made; this was a procedure in which trips whose origins and destinations had been recorded in the travel survey were assigned to a planned expressway, and estimates of traffic volumes which would have used the expressway, had it been in existence at the time of the survey, were thus obtained.

But along with the gains made by these early transportation studies there were important failures. Some of these may be listed:

1. The area within which data were obtained was often too

---

[4] E. H. Holmes and J. T. Lynch, "Highway Planning—Past, Present and Future," *Journal of the Highway Division, American Society of Civil Engineers* (July, 1957), Paper 1298.

small; the cordon line was drawn in too tight around the urbanized area, and even around the central city, leaving unstudied the growing parts of the metropolitan area.

2. Often the data which were gathered were not used when it came to draw up the plan. The plan was justified by judgment alone.

3. Traffic estimates were incomplete, being made only for the express roads. Sometimes, when more traffic was found to use an expressway than it could possibly hold, the excess was simply assumed to use existing streets.

4. The use of transit was often inadequately studied.

5. Sometimes only a few highway improvements were suggested when a superior planning process would have shown the need for many.

6. Very frequently, the plan was not demonstrably tied into any specific set of goals—even economic goals.

7. The plans were frequently limited only to traffic and transportation considerations and were often unrelated to plans for other elements of urban growth and change.

These failures do not mean that the plans which were drawn and the highway improvements which were made were wrong. The lack of adequate, logical bridges between data and goals on one hand and the plan on the other hand simply meant that there was no proof that the plan was right. Often the plans were quite good ones, but the studies did not demonstrate this; there was simply little connection between data, goals, and the plan.

The real failure of most of the plans, and it did stem from this lack of connection between goals, data, and plans, was that the plans were simply not big enough. Those who did the planning were too limited in their outlook, and the years of depression and of wartime restrictions on construction can be held partly accountable for this shortsightedness. Single facilities were being planned, but not systems.

But systems were being built! Every piece of new road which went down on the ground became part of a new and larger system. Every piece of new road circumscribed the choices which could be made for all following pieces of road. And all too soon the difficulties of adding new pieces, the embarrassments of having to parallel one fine new expressway with another, and the need to acquire space for interchanges which had not been foreseen—these things became apparent.

It is to the credit of J. Douglas Carroll, Jr., that in the 1953–55 Detroit study he recognized that something substantially different was needed to cope with the difficulties and conflicts which had arisen in urban transportation in the preceding two decades. He was convinced that the only way to plan transportation facilities for urban areas was to plan them *as systems.* Each facility was known to affect traffic loads on its neighboring facilities;[5] therefore an entire system had to be planned as a unit. This became the philosophy which pervaded the Chicago study.

The First Major Ad Hoc *Transportation Studies*

As we have shown, urban transportation planning came of age not as a fortuitous happening but as the result of long-standing, well-supported, and deliberate policy on the part of the states and the federal government. Ever since World War II, the Bureau of Public Roads encouraged the states to engage in extensive transportation planning efforts for their major metropolitan areas. In the Highway Act of 1962 this became a declared national policy, and this act actually set a deadline of July 1, 1965, by which time all metropolitan areas with central cities having more than 50,000 persons were required to have a completed comprehensive transportation plan embracing all modes of travel and taking land use plans into consideration.

As a result of this policy a number of the larger states created *ad hoc* organizations, separate from their highway departments, to develop the desired metropolitan plans. The first of these special organizations was the Detroit Metropolitan Area Traffic Study (1953–55). This was followed by the Chicago study in 1955, the Pittsburgh study in 1958, the Penn-Jersey study in 1959, and others in smaller cities. New York State, with seven metropolitan areas, set

---

[5] For example, an expressway will decrease traffic on parallel arterials but increase traffic on those arterials which connect to its interchanges.

up the Upstate New York Transportation Studies[6] (1962) to prepare plans for the six major upstate areas and cooperated with New
Jersey and Connecticut to create the Tri-State Transportation Committee (1962).[7]

These special-purpose organizations were found to be extremely useful devices where (as was frequently the case) the existing
state highway organization was not adequately staffed to undertake
such work. Not all states, of course, set up separate organizations;
some did their planning work in-house and others employed consultants to prepare their plans. In fact, a bewildering variety of organizational combinations was created in order to respond to "local
conditions," a euphemism describing the prevailing balance of power
between local organizations.

Of all these types, however, the major *ad hoc* studies, and particularly the Chicago study, were the shapers of today's transportation planning process. In fact, it might be said that the work of these
studies was one of the bases on which the Highway Act of 1962 was
written, and was the basis for its supporting administrative provisions. It is to these special-purpose organizations that we look for
major influences on the transportation planning process.

These major transportation studies were like large polar or
Himalayan expeditions. They had an objective to reach—a plan had
to be prepared. But the route by which this plan was to be obtained
lay across largely unknown territory. So in order to reach their
objective these studies had to survey the course, learn the nature of
the terrain, and build bridges across the chasms. In effect, these expeditions had two major drives: planning, and research to make that
planning possible.

It would be a mistake not to recognize at the outset the effect
of size. The *ad hoc* transportation studies were among the largest
efforts ever mounted to prepare long-range plans for man's environment. The scale of the problem was immense, dealing as it had to

---

[6] The UNYTS group was, to be precise, the successor to the Niagara Frontier Transportation Study (1961). In 1964 UNYTS was merged with the Department of Public Works' Bureau of Highway Planning to create the Subdivision of
Transportation Planning and Programming.

[7] Since 1965 the Tri-State Transportation Commission.

with thousands of miles of facilities lying across hundreds of square miles of territory and serving millions of people. In order to deal with this size problem, suitably large resources had to be assembled. These large resources then made possible an approach quite different in kind than would otherwise have been the case.

1. *Multi-Discipline Approach.* The major transportation studies in the United States found it rewarding to employ persons with a broad range of training and skills. The Chicago study, for example, employed persons from the following professions: traffic engineering, city planning, transit engineering, census taking, data processing, demography, sociology, economics, and geography. The same could be said of the Penn-Jersey Transportation Study, the Upstate New York Studies, and other major studies.

The specialists, quite literally forced to work together, helped and influenced one another substantially. The result was not just a breaking down of professional chauvinism but an enlargement of the views and skills of each professional. Many of the advances which were scored in these studies resulted from the combination of two or more disciplines. For example, the optimum spacing technique resulted from the application of mathematics and economics to a spatial problem in planning. The land use forecasting models were developed by the combination of mathematical, planning, statistical, and network techniques.

2. *Group Effort.* The transportation studies used group power to tackle urban problems—not just a few people, but teams of twenty or more professionals working full time for periods generally exceeding three years. A quick review of the number of distinct operations which are described in this book will explain why this is so. Not only the number of operations but the sheer size of many of them demanded teamwork. It takes a group's strength to deal with urban areas which cover hundreds of square miles of land, thousands of miles of roads and transit lines, and millions of people.

Team play is one reason why the transportation study has been so productive in inventing new techniques and so much a discoverer of new knowledge about urban phenomena. The academic world, so renowned for research and discovery in science, has performed less well in this world of urban affairs than the transportation studies. One reason is that universities do not have the financial resources for major, long-term, group efforts. But there are two other reasons for their doing less well than the *ad hoc* transportation studies. First, universities are peculiarly slanted toward individual work, toward the production of individual publications by which individuals gain academic recognition. Second, university faculty members have a teaching obligation, and this substantially reduces time available for effective research.

3. *Strength of Computers.* The transportation studies depended to an unusual degree upon data processing equipment and computers. There are two reasons for this dependence. First, the transportation studies have always gathered enormous quantities of data, amounting literally to millions of bits of data. The Niagara Frontier Transportation Study—not a particularly large one—had files of original records exceeding 125,000, containing in excess of 6,000,000 pieces of information. The only way to refine this mound of data was with the use of automatic data processing equipment.

Second, the *only* means of assigning travel to large networks and of simulating interzonal travel in medium-sized or large cities was with the use of computers. It was no coincidence, of course, that computer programs for traffic distribution and assignment, for projecting land use, for estimating economic growth, and for many other operations were developed at the same time that computers were becoming commercially available (1955 and later).

4. *Large-Scale Financial Support.* Few of the advances in understanding and technique made by the transportation studies could have been achieved without large-scale financial support. Typically, transportation studies have cost, over the three-year (or longer) periods necessary to obtain data, prepare and test plans, and produce a final report, an amount equal to $1.00–$1.50 per capita. The large studies generally cost less than this (the Chicago study cost less than $1.00 per capita for a six-year initial effort) and the smaller studies sometimes more.

The sources of these funds have varied. Most of the early studies were financed by state highway departments, with the Bureau of Public Roads contributing up to 70 percent of the total cost. Counties and cities sometimes contributed a share. More recently the Department of Housing and Urban Development has been financing studies, in cooperation with the Bureau of Public Roads. The Bureau's contributions have been through the "research and planning" funds which were originally set up under the Hayden-Cartwright Act of 1934, in amount equalling up to 1.5 percent of all the federal aid funds for primary, secondary, and (after 1956) interstate construction. This dedication of a small percentage of construction funds, so that year after year planning and research in highway and urban transportation could go forward steadily, is a fine example of statesmanlike vision. We must also be grateful that these funds have been administered with a noteworthy lack of red tape, and this has allowed research workers to put higher percentages of their time into the kind of work they do best.

5. *Work Pressure.* An unusual feature of the work done by the major transportation studies was the fact that it was done under the great pressure of having to produce a product by a given deadline.

As systems for larger and larger cities were planned, the impossibility of using older, hand techniques created a substantial force toward invention. Typical was the work done in upstate New York. There we were faced with having to do not one but six major studies. Both the composite network technique and the computer plotting technique were deliberately invented through the sheer necessity of having to test plans many times as fast as before. We knew where we were slow, and we had to invent in order to speed things up.

All this pressure created a sense of urgency which was genuinely exciting for most of the people involved. Everybody was caught up in the mood. One man who worked with us said that he had never worked so hard in all his life—and he liked it. Part of this mood may have resulted from the idea that we were playing the master designers for networks of the largest scale. After all, what

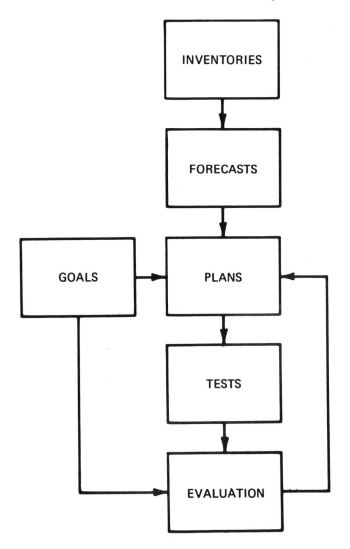

Figure 33.
The metropolitan transportation planning process.

could be bigger than a transportation system requiring twenty years
to build and embracing a whole metropolis? This may have been
naive or too courageous; certainly we did not see all the pitfalls which
lay in our way. But it was and continues to be fun.

The Metropolitan Transportation Planning Process

The basic procedure used by the major transportation studies since the mid-1950's was a sequence of six steps. These were: data collection, forecasting, stating goals, preparing network proposals, testing, and evaluating. Figure 33 shows the basic relationship between these steps.

The six-step planning process is one degree less generalized than the five-step process described in the Introduction. In the five-step process the forecasting and testing steps are combined in a single step called "simulating" which incorporates models simulating both urban growth and daily travel, whereas in Figure 33 these steps are shown separately. Actually, the transportation planning process can be diagrammed in a number of ways, all of which tell much the same story.

The following brief description of each of the six steps is intended to give the reader a quick overview of the process of transportation planning, a framework whose steps will be described in more detail in subsequent chapters.

1. *Inventories.* Any planning which concludes with recommendations for the expenditure of public funds must obviously be based upon fact. To obtain a measured understanding of the subject, inventories are taken as the first operation in the transportation planning process.

Three major inventories are generally undertaken, plus a number of minor ones. The major inventories cover travel (trips made wholly or partially within an urban area), land uses, and the transportation facilities over which vehicles, people, or goods must move. (The travel inventory in a metropolitan area is actually a special kind of census, since interviews conducted at the home collect population and employment data as well as data on trips by all modes of travel.) The minor inventories vary in number, but may include speed-volume-density studies of travel behavior on streets, traffic volume counts, transit passenger volume counts, parking surveys, a central business district floor area survey, and similar studies.

Data obtained in these surveys are reduced to numeric form and constitute a complete representation—even if only on a sampled basis—of the major transportation-related aspects of the city. The surveys are selected to provide those particular kinds of information which are essential for carrying out the planning process.

2. *Forecasts.* While inventories describe a city[8] as it is, forecasts are needed to estimate what it will be like in the future, since plans are intended to meet future as well as present problems. There are two types of such forecasts: aggregate and distributed.

The aggregate forecasts are estimates, based on historical data, of what certain totals will be for a particular urban area. Population forecasts are examples of aggregate forecasts, as are economic projections. All the forecaster is interested in doing in such cases is to establish how many people and jobs, and how much income and consumption, will exist within an entire metropolitan area.

These totals must then be distributed geographically; that is, location within the metropolitan area must be estimated. There are two ways to make these distributions: one is by planning, in which values are imposed to indicate a desired pattern of location; the other is by forecasting, which assumes that some (at least) of the items being distributed behave in an orderly or at least predictable fashion.

Based on the distributed forecast of population, other forecasts —both distributed and aggregate—can be made. The automobile ownership forecast, for example, can only be made sensibly when the location of the population is known. Similarly, forecasts of trip-making (which are the principal output of the forecasting operation and the principal input to the testing stage) depend upon a distributed population.

3. *Goals.* In a systematic planning process, stating objectives is an essential step. The objectives become the criteria against which

---

[8] Throughout this book, "city" and "urban area" will be used interchangeably simply for variety, except where modified by a name to denote the land area of a municipal corporation, as in the City of Chicago. "City" is never used here to mean a central city.

all plans are measured. An explicit statement is made and formal processes are created to connect the plan with these goals and objectives. In a democracy the objectives used in governmental planning must be those of the people.

The objectives may fall into several groups. Some are quantifiable; others have to be related to the plan subjectively. Some objectives can be measured in the same units as others, and consequently the trade-offs between opposing objectives can be estimated. Some objectives relate to things at the regional scale in the transportation planning process, while others relate to things which can only be accomplished through detailed design after the general location of a new transportation facility has been settled.

Whatever plan is selected must be demonstrated as being best in the light of the explicitly stated objectives. How such a demonstration can be made is described later in this book.

4. *Preparing Network Proposals.* The fourth step in the planning process is the preparation of a number of network proposals. In an urban area these should include proposals for transit as well as highway facilities. The proposals must be for complete systems, not increments of one or two facilities, but complete systems serving an entire urban area at its expected size at the time of the target year. Target years for transportation planning are generally twenty to twenty-five years from the year of the survey work.

The preparation of network proposals will involve consideration of trip density, trip length, land use, network planning principles, investment cost, and network characteristics among other things. A methodical procedure is used to bring these factors together, and a number of network proposals are prepared for testing purposes. Always in the background, as proposals are prepared, are the goals which the plan is expected to achieve.

5. *Testing.* The purpose of the testing phase in the planning process is to determine how well any given network proposal will perform at some prescribed future time.

It is impossible for an individual to appraise correctly how well a transportation system consisting of hundreds of different segments of streets and transit lines will perform under either present or future conditions. Therefore the testing must be done by a computer. The essence of the testing process is the representation of trips and networks by the use of numbers within the computer, and the use of the computer to estimate where the trips will go, what kinds of transportation facilities will be used, and what path each trip will take through the network. This is all done by rules prescribed to the computer, rules whose results are verified by comparing simulated with actual volumes of travel on the links of the present system.

6. *Evaluation.* The results of each test of a separate transportation network are evaluated in terms of the objectives which have previously been specified. If the objectives are primarily economic ones, direct outputs from the computer can give the time, accident, and travel costs associated with each network plan. The capital costs of the plan are also known. These two sets of costs can be accumulated to give the total transportation cost of the plan.

By comparing the test results of different plans, it is possible to determine which types, configurations, and quantities of transportation facilities provide greater reductions of the costs of transportation in return for additional investment. A series of tests and evaluations gradually permits planners to "zero in" upon a best plan, or at least a plan which cannot reasonably be bettered. This plan is then recommended for adoption.

Comparisons with Other Planning Processes

The preceding major steps of the urban transportation planning process are similar, in many respects, to the steps used in other kinds of planning. Yet there are also important differences. It is worth comparing various planning processes not only because the comparisons heighten understanding, but because if at some future time it is desired to extend that kind of work done by transportation planners into other fields, it will be helpful to know that we are dealing with a process which is basic.

In his book *The Corporate Planning Process*,[9] Melville C. Branch describes the procedure of corporate planning as a series of four inter-related work phases. The following excerpts from his book (pp. 41ff.) convey the main ideas of this procedure.

The method of corporate planning reflects the continuous nature of the process. Its four phases—objectives, plans, integration-decision, and implementation—comprise a procedural circle of interdependence. Modifications are made as analysis, action, or results in one of these phases call for compensating adjustments in any one or all of the others. Both feedback and feedforward are involved. An unexpected operating decision may require a change of objectives and plan; a sound plan anticipates insofar as possible the problems of implementation. Were it feasible and desirable, all things considered, the procedural system would allow constant adjustment. . . .

Objectives. Since the purpose of planning is to provide a rational direction of activities toward established goals, a plan cannot be drawn without objectives. . . .

Plans. In accordance with corporate objectives, each component of the business prepares a plan for the ensuing year, with extensions for each of several additional years. . . .

Integration-Decision. Corporate management performs the final integration and makes the final decisions. . . . The result of corporate integration may call for modification of the component plans. When this is accomplished, they are combined into a comprehensive plan for the business as a whole which is the performance target for the ensuing fiscal year and the official reference for an additional two to four years. . . .

Implementation. Plans are of little value if they are not followed and carried out to the extent practicable. Because of the widespread participation in planning and formal approval of plans already discussed, there is general recognition throughout the company of the operational commitment they represent. Plans are developed and accepted as a basis for the measurement of performance. . . .

In the corporate planning process, a form of simulation is employed which Branch calls "corporate representation." He writes (pp. 161ff.):

[9] Melville C. Branch, *The Corporate Planning Process* (American Management Association, New York, 1962).

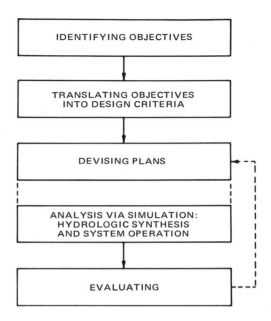

The corporate representation shows past trends and is projected into successive stages in future time. It is used to simulate the results of alternative courses of action, project the cumulative effects of present commitments and trends, and identify the probable consequences of a major decision or event. . . .

The function of the corporate representation strongly favors its establishment as a room. . . . Within this space, different ways of maintaining information can be employed, ranging from manual posting to the type of mechanical recording used in automatic stock-quotation boards. . . .

The text, *The Design of Water-Resource Systems*, by Maas *et al.*[10] describes a planning process which is shown above.

Note that this diagram includes a step called "translating objectives into design criteria." This is a step in which broad objectives are stated more precisely and as many as possible are expressed in terms of benefits and costs. This step in the transportation planning process was included within the goal-setting operation.

[10] Arthur Maas *et al., The Design of Water-Resource Systems* (Harvard University Press, Cambridge, Mass., 1962).

In *The Design of Water-Resource Systems*, Maas incorporates the planning and testing-by-simulation operations into one major activity under the heading of "devising plans." In the planning of water-resource systems, design and testing is a back-and-forth operation, with many adjustments made and tested to see if this or that alteration in design produces gains in over-all performance. Hence the combination of these two operations appears reasonable. I have, however, identified them separately in the diagram to stress the basic similarity of this approach to transportation planning.

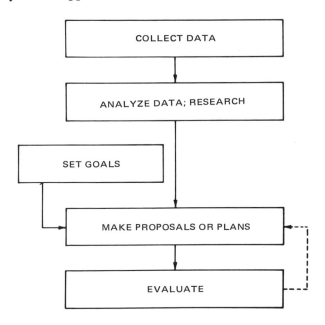

Turning to the urban land use planning process, we find a different picture. The process inherited from the physical design parents of city planning was a simple sequence of research, analysis, and design. Some called this research, analysis-synthesis, and design. In both cases the heart of the process was the absorption of facts in the mind of the designer and his genesis of a creative solution. However, this is a process which, while containing that vital feature of creative design rarely present in the analytic disciplines, is completely inadequate for dealing with the complexities of a large urban area.

A more formal and analytic land use planning process can be diagrammed as shown above.

This process is very much like the transportation planning process, except that it lacks an adequate basis of data and theory and includes no formal simulation or testing operation.

At the neighborhood scale, or in certain types of planning (such as school planning), the data base is fairly good and there is little need for formal theory or simulation. Here the design tradition of planning, or basic reasoning ability, is adequate.

However, at the metropolitan scale the lack of adequate data, the absence of formal theories which can be used to explain in quantitative terms such phenomena as growth, decay, and migration, and the absence of simulation capability prevent the testing of alternative governmental policies. Consequently, while alternative urban development policies have been proposed, their true meaning and their consequences have not been adequately measured. The metropolitan or regional transportation planning process, if it is to become real and effective, is going to have to add the simulation element and also is going to have to get the data which will permit a tightly organized process to be constructed in at least the degree of detail and refinement which will be shown in the ensuing chapters.

In general, there is a high degree of similarity between these different planning processes, despite the differences in subject matter and despite the inevitable differences in terminology which reflect varying professional approaches. Whether directly stated or implied, each process uses data, makes forecasts, establishes objectives, prepares plans, evaluates the plans, and modifies plans as may be required. Undoubtedly, the biggest difference lies in the way in which simulation is used in testing the consequences of plans.

Features of the Transportation Planning Process

Certain features of the transportation planning process need to be stressed because these features produce the strength and capability needed to deal with large-scale problems.

1. *Dependence upon Simulation.* As a process, transportation planning is unusually dependent upon simulation as its means of testing plans. Other kinds of planning may employ intuition or "conventional" reasoning or a series of simple calculations. But these are not adequate in a situation where the mutual interdependence of facilities is so great, and where changes in facilities can so easily cause a redirection of travel, a change in habitual origins and destinations or even in choice of mode of travel. No means other than simulation offers the ability to determine the ramifications of the kinds of actions proposed to be taken in urban systems.

Water resource planning of the type described by Maas *et al.* relies heavily upon simulation also. It is curious that water resource planning simulates a random phenomenon (rainfall) whereas transportation planning simulates a regular phenomenon (average daily travel). Both planning processes in effect mimic the behavior of the phenomena and observe what happens when different kinds of physical things (channels, dams, roads, etc.) are erected to alter the previous patterns of flow. If the transportation planning process is to be extended, we shall need to employ this idea of simulation extensively.

2. *Inclusiveness.* It should be trite to say so by this time, but a basic feature of the transportation planning process is its inclusiveness, both in terms of area covered and in terms of dealing with all forms of transportation. Too many planning studies are only partial: they cover a small area or only one mode of travel. Such a limited scope generally leads to biased results. A study which deals with transit alone, for example, will often ignore the fact that road improvements are constantly being made. Or a study of a central business district may not see how the access differential, which gave it a monopolistic position in former years, is being eroded.

Inclusiveness based upon a measured understanding of the whole is therefore an extremely desirable quality.

3. *Formality of Process.* Because the transportation planning process involves so many different steps, cuts across so many kinds

of data, and employs so many different kinds of operations, it has been necessary to set up formal procedures by which these steps could be linked. This is not to say that planning needs to be done with military efficiency, but a definite procedure is necessary to make the parts contribute their full share to the whole.

4. *Scientific Method; Objectivity.* In great part due to the influence of Carroll, the transportation studies adopted the scientific method as the standard for their work. The features of observation, advancement of hypotheses, testing of hypotheses, and replicability of calculations were considered to be the proper guidelines for all the analysis and development of theory which were done by transportation studies. Although the preparation of plans necessarily included the subjective element of human goals, even this part of the planning operation was treated with extreme objectivity once the list of goals was adopted. And even in selecting goals, attempts were made to deduce goals from an observation of what people actually choose to do. In short, judgment was out and the rules of evidence and demonstration were in as the standards by which decisions were made.

5. *Data Base.* One of the great strengths of the transportation planning process has been its extraordinarily rich data base. In this book the surveys of land use, transportation facilities, and travel are described. We have seen how in each case these files of data have provided the understanding which enabled the planner to do a better job, and that without such information he would be utterly without the reference points by which to navigate.

6. *The Bridge between Goals and Plans.* In sharp contrast with more intuitive kinds of planning, the transportation planning process has built a bridge of logic between the shadowy realm of goals and the world of physical plans. This bridge, although not broad and certainly not rigid, was still fashioned with care, and provides the means for bringing the worlds of desire and action together.

Conclusion

In this chapter we have sketched out the growth of complex transportation systems in the United States and the development of methods for planning systems within urban areas.

The transportation planning process has been displayed as a highly generalized series of steps. The basic concepts of this process are reasonable, but it is obviously not at this level that plans are prepared or tested. To plan, we have to go into more detail. The following chapters describe the kinds of work which have to be done to prepare transportation plans and illustrate the steps, where appropriate, with examples drawn from actual practice.

VII

DATA COLLECTION FOR TRANSPORTATION PLANNING

IN THIS chapter, we look at data collection for transportation planning—why data are needed, what kinds are collected, how they are collected and processed, and what precautions should be taken to insure a reliable data base. The material presented in this chapter does not constitute a manual; it is, rather, a survey of certain fairly standard data collection practices.[1]

There are two basic reasons for collecting data for transportation planning. There is, first, the immediate and practical need for getting raw material for planning; second, there is the need to obtain information for learning more about cities and their travel functions.

Planning in itself requires data for several purposes. One of these is the "stock-taking" or "mapping" purpose: to find out what exists right now in the way of travel, land use, and transportation facilities. Knowing what exists is a necessary condition for planning changes. Second, data are needed to provide the basis for making projections of future growth and change in travel demand, since

[1] Manuals on data collection include: National Committee on Urban Transportation, *Better Transportation for Your City* (Public Administration Service, 1313 E. 65th St., Chicago, 1958). This book is supplemented by a series of procedural manuals printed in the same year, including: (1A) *Determining Street Use*; (2A) *Origin-Destination and Land Use*; (2B) *Conducting a Home Interview Origin-Destination Survey*; (3A) *Measuring Traffic Volumes*; (3B) *Determining Travel Time*; (3C) *Conducting a Limited Parking Study*; (3D) *Conducting a Comprehensive Parking Study*; (4A) *Measuring Transit Service*; and (5A) *Inventory of the Physical Street System.* John A. Baerwald (ed.), *Traffic Engineering Handbook* (Institute of Traffic Engineers, Washington, D.C., 1965), Chapter 7. Donald E. Cleveland (ed.), *Manual of Traffic Engineering Studies,* 3rd ed. (Institute of Traffic Engineers, Washington, D.C., 1964).

transportation facilities must meet future needs as well as present crises. And third, facts have a public relations value: they demonstrate to officials and the public that a careful job has been done in preparing transportation plans.

The task of research in transportation planning has been historically more operational than "pure" or "basic," and this has been in response to the pressing need to develop better tools for planning. Studies, for example, of speed, volume, and density on highways have been made so that estimates can be made of the impact of changing volumes upon the levels of service provided by roadways. Nevertheless, the transportation research worker in meeting this need has also obtained data about the city which satisfy the requirements of basic research. Measures of *all* land use and *all* travel across a metropolitan area, for example, have given the "basic" research worker a quantitative understanding of cities.

The improvements in planning techniques invented by research workers have gradually merged the data collection requirements of both planning and research. Data requirements for planning have moved away from the immediately practical, as we have seen in the case of the inventories of transportation facilities in Chapter V. Data are now used to develop operational representations of cities and of people and vehicles in motion.

There are, therefore, certain requirements for data collection which are in common for both planning and research. Obviously, both activities depend upon quantitative information; without measurements there would be no transportation planning or research as we know them today. Second, both activities require complete coverage of metropolitan areas. Third, both activities require information covering a wide set of related data, for example, on all modes of travel, not just one. And finally, both activities require that the data be to fine units of detail—geographical, temporal, and so on. This is what is needed to open up a subject for examination.

The data collection practices described in this chapter have evolved over many years. Origin-destination surveys were taken as early as 1916,[2] and there have been a succession of expansions and

[2] Report of the Chicago Traction and Subway Commission on a Unified System of Surface, Elevated, and Subway Lines, Chicago, 1916.

improvements in data collection techniques since that time. Large-scale manual counting of traffic volumes occurred in the Los Angeles area in 1923.[3] Traffic counts on a cordon line surrounding the Detroit central business district were taken in 1927.[4] One of the first roadside interview surveys was conducted in Washington, D.C., in 1932.[5] Highway inventory studies appear to have had their genesis in 1934–35 when statewide highway planning was initiated.[6] Home interview travel surveys, beginning in 1944 and 1945, gained widespread use in the first ten years after World War II.[7] One of the first measured land use surveys covering an entire metropolitan area was taken in 1956 in Chicago. In 1958 the first coding of complete arterial, expressway, and transit networks for computer traffic assignments was undertaken in Chicago and in the same year a survey of vehicle miles of travel on all road types was completed. In 1958 a survey of person miles of travel on buses was made in Pittsburgh. In 1962 a simultaneous survey of passengers departing from a metropolitan area by air, rail, and bus was taken in the Niagara Frontier.

Data collection practices will continue to evolve, especially as planners gain greater assurance through widespread and continuous measurements of travel and other related phenomena. The practices which are reported in this chapter had widespread use during the decade 1955–65, and will continue to be employed to provide the information which is required for urban transportation planning. In the future, smaller samples may be taken and some of the massive surveys which were required in exploratory phases of urban transportation planning may be reduced in scale. Nevertheless, it seems certain that basic data on travel, on transportation networks, and on

[3] *Major Traffic Street Plan*, Los Angeles Traffic Commission, Los Angeles, 1923.

[4] *Traffic Survey Bureau Report*, Department of Police, Detroit, 1927.

[5] *Report of a Survey of Traffic in the Washington Regional Area*, U.S. Bureau of Public Roads *et al.*, Washington, D.C., 1932.

[6] H. S. Fairbanks, "Planning for Future Highways," U.S. Bureau of Public Roads, Washington, D.C., 1935. Also John T. Lynch, "Highway Planning in the United States," Public Roads Administration, Washington, D.C., 1941.

[7] E. H. Holmes and John T. Lynch, "Highway Planning—Past, Present and Future," *Journal of the Highway Division, American Society of Civil Engineers* (July, 1957).

the locations of activities which generate trips must be obtained if transportation plans are to be prepared and maintained.

Data collection for transportation planning is always a compromise. The planner and research worker would like to have complete detail on everything that can possibly have a bearing upon decisions in transportation matters. The director of a transportation study, on the other hand, recognizes the need to keep costs low and to produce results in time. Greater reliability can be purchased, but at an increasingly high price. Over time, greater confidence has been built up in the reliability of smaller samples. Also, greater familiarity and experience in metropolitan planning has indicated which data are essential and which are less essential. It takes substantial experience to know at what point to draw the line of compromise.

All data which are gathered for urban transportation planning should have the same degree of geographic detail so that meaningful comparisons and relationships can be developed. And these data should be coded to a fine unit of geographic detail, such as a block or a quarter square mile. Fine geographic detail permits closer checking and more precise research work, whereas coarse geographic coding (e.g., to an analysis zone of several square miles) prevents adequate checking and permanently restricts the amount of research work which can be done. The basis for most detailed geographic coding for transportation studies is the x-y grid or Cartesian coordinate system. This system is perfectly adapted to computer processing.

It is desirable that data collected for transportation planning be collected during a single time period. In this way travel and transportation facilities can be meaningfully related to each other and trip generation can be studied.

It is impossible to convey adequately the arduous nature of the work of collecting data for transportation planning. Even metropolitan areas of moderate size—in the 500,000 to 1,000,000 population class—are tremendous organisms. They cover hundreds of square miles of land, contain thousands of miles of roadways and hundreds of miles of bus and transit lines, and each day will see the production of from one to two million trips.

To measure a city, even on a sample basis, will involve the expenditure of from fifty cents to one dollar per capita. Large crews of people must be assembled, trained, and deployed in activities which are new to them and often new to their leaders. Supervision of surveys requires a combination of great administrative skill and, at the same time, a scientific watchfulness on the quality of the product. Failure in either of these two latter requirements can result in a product whose quality is substantially below that needed.

Generally, as a rule of thumb, as much money has to be set aside for coding, keypunching, contingency checking, and processing the data after they have come in from the field as is spent on the field work itself. Without the most painstaking care in processing and checking for accuracy, substantial errors may persist through the file. While certain errors may not in fact be critical to the final result of the plan, they are always embarrassing to the transportation planner and can cause a lack of confidence in his product.

This is not to say that perfect information can ever be produced from the surveys taken for transportation planning purposes. There will always be mistakes in transportation data files just as there are errors in even the most precise scientific measurements of the physical universe. The scientist uses instruments which, while very precise, have known limits of resolution and known aberrations; the social scientist must use crews of people as his sensing instruments, and these have their own obvious limits. It calls for a high degree of critical judgment to know what level of mistakes can be tolerated and what cannot.

There are three main categories of data which need to be collected for urban transportation planning. The major surveys include inventories of travel, of land use which is an index of the human activities which generate travel, and of the networks over which trips move. These major surveys are described in the following sections.

The Travel Surveys

Travel surveys should be designed to catch all possible kinds of movements of persons and vehicles which traverse any part of a metropolitan area. Some small categories of trips need not be surveyed, but such gaps should be clearly identified. For example, trips by motorcycle, by bicycle, and by individual watercraft or aircraft are generally ignored because the volumes of such movements are minuscule and have no material effect on transportation planning.

The diagram shown below indicates one way of categorizing trips which are made within a metropolitan area. "Internal" trips are those whose origins and destinations are both within the survey area; "external" trips have at least one end of each trip outside the survey area. External trips are subdivided into two classes, one having one end inside the survey area and one end outside, while the other category, "through" trips, has both origin and destination

Table 18. *Person and Vehicle Trips, by Type of Survey, Chicago Area, 1956*

Survey Type	Completed Sample Interviews	Expanded Weekday Person Trips	Expanded Weekday Vehicle Trips
Internal Surveys			
Home Interview	49,591	9,931,638	4,824,773
Truck Interview	7,346	—	801,951
Taxi Interview	147	—	171,478
External Surveys			
Roadside Survey	73,078	555,143	337,286
Railroad Survey	5,239	33,446	—
Total	135,401	10,520,227	6,135,488

Source: Chicago Area Transportation Study, *Final Report,* vol. I, Table 3.

outside the survey area. Table 18 shows the relative magnitudes of internal and external surveys of the Chicago Area Transportation Study.

In the study design phase of each metropolitan transportation study, a decision has to be made as to how these kinds of trips can be intercepted most efficiently for interviewing purposes. The design of the survey and the selection of the interviewing techniques will depend upon the size of the city, upon budget constraints, and upon the philosophy of the organization that is doing the work. There are no set rules nor would the establishment of rules be desirable. If the metropolitan area is very large and if mass transportation planning is an integral part of the over-all transportation planning operation, then the home interview technique will generally be employed. For cities under 50,000 population, external traffic may be the most important influence on planning and the only travel surveys that are taken may be roadside interviews.

There are a variety of techniques for obtaining information on trips within an urban area. These include the home interview tech-

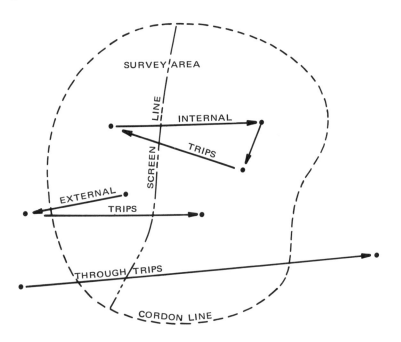

nique, telephone surveys, postcard or mail-back surveys, and interviews taken at the place of employment. There are proponents for each of these methods. The work place inventory is attractive to many because the person being interviewed will presumably cooperate on the instructions of his employer, and because this kind of interviewing concentrates on work travel which makes up the bulk of peak-hour travel. The difficulty with work place inventories is that not all workers are easily located; many men and women work for themselves or for very small organizations which are not regis-

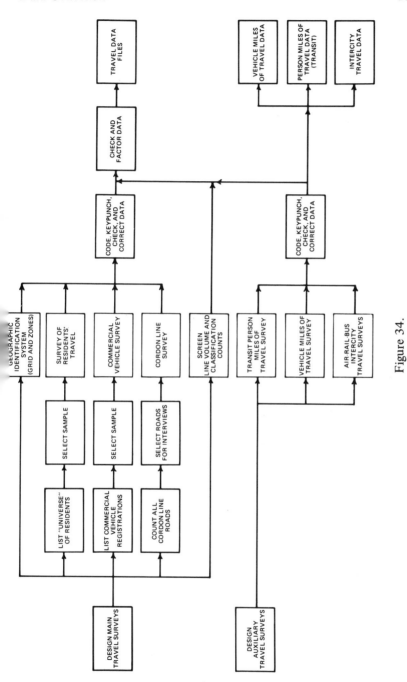

Figure 34.
Generalized travel survey procedure.

tered with the Labor Department; and as many as 10 percent of those who are employed are likely to be absent on any given day. Postcard surveys are inexpensive as field collection devices but produce results which are difficult to control from a statistical viewpoint. Furthermore, the volume of returns from postcard or mail-back surveys can be so large that coding costs become very high. The telephone survey produces good results in some cities but must be patched with home interviews to tap persons who do not have telephones. The home interview survey is the most expensive kind of survey but produces results which are controlled and which contain data on trips by all modes of travel. A trained interviewer working with the adults in the household can insure that all the questions on the form will be answered.

In the following pages, the steps of a typical travel survey are described. These same steps are shown in flow chart form in Figure 34 in their arrangement with respect to each other.

Home Interview Survey. The home interview survey is an inventory of travel taken by contacting a sample of urban households. The sample is selected by listing all the dwelling places within the metropolitan area. Every nth household is drawn from this list in such a fashion that there is an even distribution of interviews, geographically speaking, each day of the week over the entire metropolitan area.

There is a variety of sources from which samples may be taken. These include census lists, street directories, electric utility meter listings, or special field lists[8] of the metropolitan area made especially for the transportation study. Selection from among these sources may depend upon such factors as budget, reliability and currency of existing sources, and whether or not a field list taken for travel survey purposes may also be used to generate other material such as data on land use.

The information which is collected at the home interview in-

---

[8] For example, see Frederick W. Memmott III, *Field List Manual* (Upstate New York Transportation Studies, Albany, 1963), 74 pp.

cludes data on the characteristics of the household as well as information on trips made by members of the household.[9] Characteristics of the household which are determined include number and ages of residents, occupation, industry, car ownership, and sometimes income. Income data, although harder to get than other information, have been found to be very useful for studies of trip generation and car ownership.

Travel data gathered at the home include information on such items as the origin and destination address of each trip, trip purpose, land use at origin and destination, mode of travel, time of day, and car loading. Travel data are obtained for every person five years of age or older on the theory that persons five and over have purposeful trips (e.g., trips to school) which may have an impact upon the planning of future transportation systems. Children under five are considered simply as accompanying adults.

The basic interviewing technique calls for letters to be mailed to each potential interviewee the day before the interviewer arrives. This letter together with the interviewer's identification card and sometimes newspaper clippings describing the survey are generally adequate to help the interviewer get a favorable reception at each household. The interviewer attempts to talk to all persons sixteen years of age and older in each household and can normally complete his interview in twenty minutes. Six to eight interviews per day per interviewer are a normal load. It is essential in the management of the survey for the survey supervisor to take all precautions to insure the safety of the interviewer and a favorable reception for him in the area where he is working. Police officials must be notified. Generally, ethnic groups are interviewed by persons of their own background.

To check on the work of interviewers, telephone follow-up calls are made from the office and a very small number of sample households are reinterviewed to see whether the interviewer has taken the pains necessary to secure information about all trips made by a

[9] For example, see Charles R. Guinn and Frederick W. Memmott III, *Home Interview Survey Manual* (Upstate New York Transportation Studies, Albany, 1963), 94 pp.

family. These techniques, together with immediate postinterview edits by a competent editing crew, will generally insure a high-quality product and will quickly catch that very small percentage of interviewers who try to invent data in local bars.

The size of sample for interviewing for transportation studies has been decreasing. Home interview sample rates have run from 1 percent in the New York metropolitan area to 10 percent in small cities.[10]

The Truck-Taxi Survey. The sample source for the truck survey is generally the registration lists that are maintained by a state and recorded in the county in which the registration is made. Selecting every nth registration for a county is therefore fairly easy and at this time the address of the individual or firm registering the vehicle can be recorded. A difficult problem with truck sampling is the fact that trucks may be registered in counties where they are not operated and operated in counties where they are not registered. It may be necessary to run a check on a sample of trucks registered in neighboring counties to determine whether any of the vehicles so registered are actually operated in the urban area which is being studied.

Taxis may be sampled either from state registration lists or from a list of local taxi permits. While taxis produce a very small amount of the total vehicle miles of travel in an urban area, their use is concentrated in the downtown areas and it is worthwhile to obtain a sampling of their trips.

In an interview of commercial vehicles, drivers of vehicles or dispatchers are contacted to obtain information on the trips made by a given vehicle on a particular date. The interview form generally calls for data on the origin and destination of each trip, the purpose of the trip, the number of passengers in the vehicle, and, in the case of a truck, data on the industry of ownership and truck loading. Truck loading information, unfortunately, is not highly reliable.

---

[10] Somewhat higher rates are recommended in "Manual of Procedures for Home Interview Traffic Study," Appendix 34 of the *Highway Planning Program Manual*, Bureau of Public Roads, Washington, D.C., 1957.

Addresses of origin and destination of taxi trips are readily obtained when the driver keeps a log of his trips.[11]

It is essential in making truck-taxi interviews to obtain broad industry support of the purposes of the survey. This may be done by working with the local chamber of commerce and truck owners' and operators' associations.

The Roadside Interview Survey. Where the home interview and commercial surveys contact the trip-maker at the home base from which a large proportion of the trips are made, the roadside interview surveys intercept the driver as he is moving. This interception is done at a cordon line which surrounds and defines the study area. All roads which cross this cordon line are identified and traffic volumes on these roads are counted by portable mechanical counters. The cordon line is located at some distance from the built-up portion of the study area, where the density of roads is not too high.

After these roads have been counted, they are arrayed in order from largest to smallest. The most heavily traveled roads may be interviewed around the clock, less heavily traveled roads for sixteen hours, and minor roads for twelve or eight hours. Generally, a sufficient volume must pass through the interviewing stations to equal about 90 to 95 percent of the total average daily traffic crossing into the study area.

Interview stations are set up on the roadside. Warning signs, cones, flags, and at night, lights warn the motorist of the presence of an interviewing station. Vehicles are stopped and in less than a minute information is obtained on origin, destination, trip purpose, land use at the trip end inside the survey area, and number of occupants in the vehicle. Trucks are similarly interviewed, but buses and emergency vehicles of all types are not stopped.

The location and design of the interviewing stations themselves are matters requiring skill. Standard layouts for interviewing stations on different types of roads have been developed by the traffic engi-

[11] For example, see Frederick W. Memmott III, *Truck and Taxi Survey Manual* (New York State Department of Public Works, Albany, 1966), 56 pp.

neering profession. Great care must be exercised in location and layout of stations in order to reduce the risk of accident. It is always necessary to have police protection during the course of the interviewing operation.[12]

Miscellaneous Travel Surveys. In addition to the foregoing standard kinds of travel surveys, it may be necessary in any given metropolitan area to undertake additional surveys either to close a gap which is not covered by the home interview, commercial vehicle, or roadside interview survey, or to obtain information on a particular type of travel for which planning decisions need to be made.

In the case of the Chicago Area Transportation Study, for example, about 33,000 commuters crossed into the Chicago area each day on suburban railroads in 1956. These trips could not be picked up in any way except by a special survey. Therefore, a survey was designed in which postcards were handed out to boarding passengers at suburban railroad stations outside the cordon line. By this simple device, which could readily be controlled by counting the number of boarding passengers and by precoding the postcards, it was possible to get an accurate picture of this particular kind of movement.[13]

Questions are raised often about walking trips. Do walking trips reduce the need for vehicular transportation? It is possible to conduct walking trip surveys along with regular home interview surveys. In the course of the Chicago survey a sub-sample of one in every eight interviews in the last month of the survey was interviewed using a form nearly identical with that of the home interview survey itself.[14]

Surveys of long-distance passenger movements by intercity modes of travel (such as airplane, railroad, and intercity bus) can

[12] For example, see Charles R. Guinn and Frederick W. Memmott III, *External Survey Manual* (New York State Department of Public Works, Albany, 1966), 43 pp.

[13] John Howe, *Mass Transit External Survey* (Chicago Area Transportation Study, Chicago, 1957).

[14] Roger L. Creighton, "Report on the Walking Trip Survey," Chicago Area Transportation Study, Chicago, 1961.

be readily conducted at terminals which are within an urban area.[15] The number of departing flights, railroad trains, or intercity buses is known from schedules. Boarding passengers can be counted or records can be obtained from the transportation company. Interviews can be taken at the terminal just prior to departure or on the vehicle itself. Alternatively, interview forms can be printed on postcards to be mailed back.

Processing of Travel Survey Data. Inventorying is only half of a travel survey. The remaining half starts when the interviews have been completed and received in the field offices. There these forms start through a long series of editing, coding, keypunching, checking, and factoring operations which must be completed successfully before the data can be tabulated and used for planning and research.

Even before the interview forms go out into the field they are arranged in batches by interviewing district. One batch constitutes one day's work for one interviewer. In order to maintain control, the interview forms are preaddressed with the address of the interviewee and all of one day's addresses are printed on a batch control form. Record-keeping is made easier if the interview and batch control forms are filed in an envelope whose cover is printed with a record of all the steps of interviewing, editing, and coding. To maintain control of the batches, log books are kept so that at any given instant the location of a batch is known. This control becomes increasingly important as data on each piece of paper increases its value. A completely coded interview form may be worth $10.00.

As soon as interviews have been completed, the forms are brought into the field office where the entries are checked by an experienced editor. The editor will have had some field experience at the beginning of the survey. By reviewing the work of the interviewer, he will be able to catch errors and omissions which may be corrected by a telephone call or by consultation with the interviewer.

---

[15] David R. McCullough and Robert S. Scott, *Findings of the Survey of Intercity Travelers Using Air, Rail and Bus Modes in the Niagara Frontier* (New York State Office of Transportation, Albany, November, 1964).

The feedback from the editor to the interviewer is an extremely important part of improving quality.

When completed batches of interviews are transferred from the field office to the main office, they are ready for coding. Coding is the translation of written material on the form into numeric form so that the data can be keypunched. Coding is generally classified into two categories: nongeographic and geographic.

Nongeographic coding is simply the translation of data on trip purpose or land uses into numbers. The only material needed by the coder for this operation is a coding manual.[16]

Geographic coding is much more difficult and time-consuming. The objective of geographic coding is to translate every street address or building named by the interviewee as the origin or destination of a trip into a set of numbers which uniquely describes a block within a Cartesian coordinate (x-y) system. To do this, the geographic coder is given a variety of information sources. One of these is a street address guide that directly converts street name and number into x-y and block numbers. The geographic coder will also have a "major generator file" which gives the geographic codes for schools, shopping centers, churches, hospitals, office buildings, and other major buildings whose names are used as the origins or destinations of trips. If the preceding sources fail, the geographic coder can use maps or the telephone to hunt down difficult addresses.

After all the data have been coded, the records are sent to keypunching stations where they are punched, verified, and converted either into card or magnetic tape records. These records are then subjected to a series of contingency checks which examine each record to see whether the code numbers are legitimate or not. For example, there may be only five allowable modes of transportation in the home interview survey and these are coded one through five; if the machine finds that there is a zero or six through nine in the mode column, then an error has been found. After 1960 the widespread availability of computers with increasingly large internal memories made it possible not only to check individual fields for impossible

---

[16] For an example of a coding manual, see David I. Gooding and Carl Swerdloff, *Coding Manual* (Niagara Frontier Transportation Study, New York State Department of Public Works, Albany, 1963), 80 pp.

codes, but also to check whether responses in one field were illogical with respect to another field. For example, it became possible to make certain that no person arrived at his destination at a time which was earlier than the time of his departure. With these computers it also became possible to print out tables indicating the exact location of errors which could then be corrected.[17]

After the data have been contingency checked and corrected, they can be factored. The purpose of factoring is to give each record a number which represents that record's proportion of the entire universe of travel. For example, if one in twenty-five homes are interviewed, then theoretically every completed interview should have a factor of twenty-five since that record stands for twenty-five homes and their trips.

Interviews obtained on the roadside at the cordon line surrounding the survey area are readily factored. Within each hour, the number of completed interviews is known for each vehicle type (e.g., automobile or light, medium, or heavy truck), and the number of vehicles which have been interviewed can be divided into the known total of vehicles of that type which were counted passing through that cordon station at that hour. Manual classification counts of vehicles passing through each interview station are kept for this purpose. Under this procedure, records of interviews of two heavy trucks would each be given a factor of five if ten heavy trucks were counted going through that station at that hour.[18]

Records of home interviews and truck-taxi interviews have a more complex factoring program. Each record must be weighted in accordance with its known sample rate, but also to take account of those interviews where the interviewer could not contact the householder but where trips could have been made by him.

After this preliminary factoring, the records of home interviews and truck-taxi interviews are then processed to sort out those trips which, in accordance with the known location of origin and

[17] Frederick W. Memmott III and John R. Hamburg, *Contingency Check Manual for the Home Interview, Truck-Taxi, and External Surveys* (Upstate New York Transportation Studies, Albany, 1963), 40 pp.

[18] Roger L. Creighton, *Factoring the External Survey* (Upstate New York Transportation Studies, Albany, 1964).

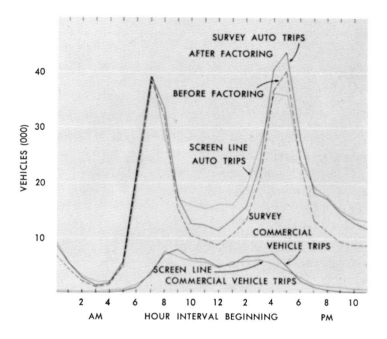

Figure 35.
Hourly distribution of automobile and commercial vehicle trips
compared with screen line counts, Chicago area, 1956.

destination, must have passed a line dividing the study area in two
parts. This line, generally running along a river or other natural bar-
rier, is known as the screen line. During the course of the travel
survey, careful counts are made of the number of vehicles of each
type crossing the screen line, by hour of the day. It is therefore possible (see Figure 35) to compare the preliminary expanded results
of the home interview and truck-taxi surveys with the screen line
count. (External trips which cross the screen line are in effect subtracted from the screen line counts and so play no part in this phase
of the factoring of the home interview and truck-taxi records.)

If the home interview and truck-taxi surveys have been good
ones, the number of vehicles which they record as crossing the screen
line should be 85 percent or more of the number counted crossing the

screen line by the ground counts. An excellent survey conducted in a small city may check out at 95 percent or more of the screen line counts. Larger cities generally do not have as good results as those in smaller ones. At this point, a decision must be made whether or not to expand the home interview and truck-taxi surveys again so that they more closely approach the ground count at the screen line. It is desirable also to check the travel data against whatever independent data are available in order to establish their over-all accuracy.[19]

The Vehicle Miles of Travel Survey. Traffic counting and the preparation of volume flow maps have long been used to provide background data for the preparation for traffic plans for urban areas. Until recently, however, traffic volume data have rarely been integrated fully with other surveys and processes, to play their part in the preparation of comprehensive transportation plans.

In Chicago in 1956 and later in Pittsburgh and in the Niagara Frontier, the vehicle miles of travel survey assumed an important role, providing controls which were used to check other data and defining areas of congestion. This came about because the obvious gradually became clear: the street network was a beautifully fixed universe which could be sampled with comparative ease. The presence of vehicles in this network, both in space and in time, could be counted with no objections from the respondents.

The basic procedure for conducting the vehicle miles of travel survey is as follows.[20] The network of roads in an urban area must first be mapped and classified into convenient categories such as expressways and parkways, major and secondary arterials, and local streets. The streets so identified are sampled, with the sample rate being in direct relationship to the volume on the class of streets. Expressways may be sampled at a rate running between 30 and 100 percent of all links. Arterial streets may be sampled at rates of be-

[19] Roger L. Creighton, *Report on Accuracy Checks* (Chicago Area Transportation Study, Chicago, 1958), 25 pp.

[20] Kenneth W. Shiatte, C. W. Ockert, and Joseph H. Winkler, *Vehicle Miles of Travel Survey Manual* (New York State Department of Public Works, Albany, 1966), 49 pp.

tween 20 and 25 percent. Very small samples are taken of local streets, since these streets carry such small volumes that great reliability is not warranted. The samples of arterials and expressways are selected in such a fashion that there is a regular geographic distribution of counts throughout the urban area.

On expressways counts are generally taken with portable machine counters for periods of 24 hours or more. The arterial streets may be counted manually for short periods of time (two hours) and these short counts may then be expanded to 24-hour counts on the basis of a 24-hour mechanical count taken on a sub-sample of these same streets. In similar fashion the very small sample of local streets is counted manually for two-hour periods, and the results are factored to represent 24-hour volumes.[21]

To conclude the survey, the estimates of 24-hour volumes on the sampled streets are applied to other streets of similar type in each part of the study area. These data can then be mapped. The traffic volumes are multiplied, for each part of the study area, by the length of streets of each type in that area. This produces the estimate of vehicle miles of travel.

Person Miles of Travel Survey. While public and private transit systems normally have good statistics on average numbers of revenue passengers per weekday and per year, information on passenger volumes on the different bus or rail transit routes is often meager. As a basis for planning and as a means for checking the computer simulation programs used to test alternative transit plans, therefore, it is desirable to obtain data on passenger volumes and on person miles of travel within the transit systems.

A person-miles-of-travel survey may be taken in two ways. One technique is to place observers at stations or at bus stops where they can estimate the number of passengers on each bus or rail rapid transit car. A second technique is to place observers in buses or rail transit vehicles where they can maintain records of the number of

21 John R. Hamburg and Kenneth W. Shiatte, "A Short-Count Method for Estimating Vehicle Miles of Travel on a Transportation Network," paper presented at the Forty-third Meeting of the Highway Research Board, Washington, D.C., 1964.

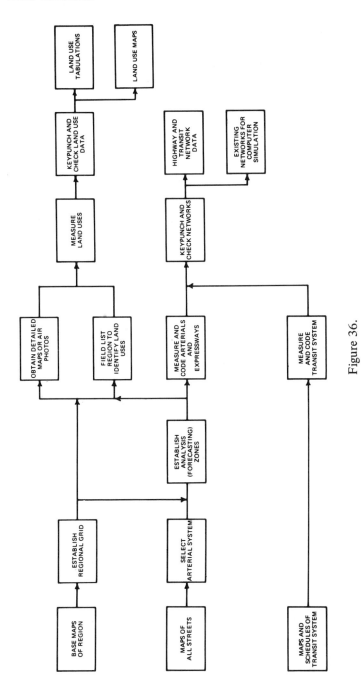

Figure 36.
Generalized land use and network survey procedures.

persons entering and leaving the vehicle on each segment of the transit journey.[22] Numbers of passengers on each route segment can then be multiplied by the length of the segment to produce the number of person miles of transit travel.

Land Use and Floor Area Surveys

The purpose of the land use and floor area surveys is to obtain a measured indication of the location and density of activities within an urban area and to determine the location and extent of land which is ready for future urban development. While not as expensive as the travel surveys, a land use survey is a costly undertaking because it involves a great deal of hand measurement and calculations (see Figure 36). A land use survey may take six months to a year or more to complete.

While it is possible to identify the kinds of activities on each parcel of land from electric utility meter cards, zoning occupancy permits, and even assessors' records, the best source for land use data is a field list. If a field list of dwellings has to be taken for a home interview study, the same survey can obtain data on land uses. For measurements of land area, maps or air photos are used.

The basic data which a land use survey seeks to obtain are the type of land use, the area of land devoted to that activity, and the location of the parcel by block number and x-y location. Auxiliary data such as parking, street access, railroad siding availability, and zoning may also be obtained.

The process of the survey requires the convergence of information on the kind of activity taking place on a parcel of land with information on the location and area of that parcel.[23] Bringing these two types of data together is a time-consuming process; errors in addresses can cause delays.

Once a parcel has been identified and located, its land area must

---

[22] Cleveland, *Manual of Traffic Engineering Studies*, Chapter 5.

[23] For example, see George Ferguson, *Land Use Measurement Manual* (Niagara Frontier Transportation Study, Albany, N.Y., June, 1962).

be measured. This can be done by reading areas off maps (assessors' maps often have land areas noted on each parcel) or by scaling. If parcels are regular rectangles, equal-area templates can be used for direct reading of areas.

An essential part of the land use survey is the checking of parcel measurements within each block so that they correctly add up to a control total obtained by measuring the area of the entire block. From a practical viewpoint, the best present technique is to record the areas of all parcels on a form where they can be summed and compared manually with the total area of the block which is also placed on that form.

The density at which land is used can be measured effectively through the use of a floor area survey. Floor area surveys are expensive per square mile and consequently are most often taken only for central business districts.[24] The floor area survey, like the land use survey, requires convergence of information on location of activity within a building and a map which gives the exact dimensions of all parts of that building. Commercial insurance atlases are the most common source for measuring floor area.

The Network Inventory

Inventories of the networks of transportation facilities in urban areas—both road and mass transportation networks—are obtained for several purposes. The network inventories give the status of the supply of transportation services both in amount and (when combined with travel data) in quality. The network inventories identify the major streets, expressways, and bus and rapid transit lines which are to be altered by planning. However, the main purpose of surveys of transportation facilities is to provide complete representations of road and mass transportation systems which can be used within computers to simulate traffic flow in testing alternative plans.

The procedure for conducting the road inventory (see Figure

[24] Robert Sharkey, *Land Use Survey Manual—CBD* (Chicago Area Transportation Study, Chicago, 1957).

36) requires maps of an urban area which show all streets.[25] All streets are then classified by type. The types which are used by different transportation studies vary somewhat, but the significant distinctions are between expressways, major streets, and local streets. Dividing streets between the latter two categories is at times an arbitrary process. The selection is normally done by transportation study personnel in cooperation with local engineering officials. Upon the completion of the selection process, all local streets are excluded from further consideration and the inventory proceeds for arterial streets and expressways alone.

The system of geographic identification used for the transportation study is superimposed over the maps of arterial systems and expressways, and network coding begins. Working directly from a map, a coder completes a form which stores data such as link location, link length, pavement width, speed limit, parking restrictions, and area type (downtown, intermediate, or outlying). The numbering system which is used to identify the beginning and ending nodes of each link in the road network also identifies the location of the link and its interconnection with neighboring links (see Chapter V for a description of this numbering system).

The inventory of mass transportation facilities uses different sources but the same basic technique.[26] Maps are obtained on which the location of each bus line, subway-elevated line, suburban railroad, or other type of mass transportation facility is noted. Data on link location, speeds and headways, the number of seats per car or bus, and the number of cars per train in the case of subway-elevated and suburban railroad trains are obtained from schedules or from the transit or suburban railroad company itself.

A notation system similar to that used in the street network inventory is employed when the mass transportation network data are coded on forms for keypunching. In the case of the mass transportation system, false links have to be included within the network to represent the potential for transfers between bus lines and rapid transit lines.

[25] For example, see *Transportation System Inventory Coding Manual*, Chicago Area Transportation Study, Chicago, 1959.

[26] For example, see John Howe, *Designing and Coding the Transit Network* (Chicago Area Transportation Study, Chicago, 1960).

Conclusion

In this chapter we have outlined the basic mechanics of survey work for transportation planning. This is a kind of activity which is highly specialized and often foreign to the skills of planners. Yet it is to planning what laboratory work is to the scientist: the essential measurements providing observations from which hypotheses can be verified or from which generalizations can be inferred. Thus, although this data-gathering work is often dull as well as arduous, it is vital to the success of planning.

It has been said that current understanding of national economics is based to a considerable extent upon the massive and continuous statistical data series which have been collected since 1930. In the same way, the heavy expenditures for data collection which have been made since 1945 have provided the bases for the advances in transportation planning made since that time. Future transportation data collection will probably be more selective and use smaller samples. It will also have the virtue of continuity, monitoring the functions of the urban organism at regular intervals.

VIII

FORECASTING LAND USE

IT WAS shown earlier in this text that cities grow by the addition of buildings in small increments, most of which are placed at the periphery of developed land. Most of these new structures are built by individuals or by small builders, and these structures reflect individuals' appraisals of opportunities that are available to them in the short run. Nearness to the mass of population as represented by previously erected buildings assures those who live in the new structures a share in the wealth of the highly profitable urban group.

Regions change in the same incremental fashion. Individuals in a free society move to and build in places where they conceive they will be better off. In the pioneer days of the United States this meant moving west to find good land. For the past hundred years this has meant a gradual movement of people from rural areas to the cities, and particularly to the larger urban areas.

The basic principle that governs these migrations and settlements is a very simple one: each person seeks to maximize his own net benefits to the best of his ability and knowledge. In a fundamental way the migration and settlement of people are like the actions of travelers within an urban transportation network. In both cases each individual moves to maximize his own advantage. The traveler chooses the best path for himself. He is aware of the transportation system and of the others using that system. He may be polite to individuals, but he still tries to find the least-cost or least-time path from O to D, regardless of his impact upon the mass of other vehicles. As long as all obey certain rules and as long as there is adequate room in the system (for motion or for improvement), people can move and better themselves.

Freedom to migrate and to build is a basic right in a democratic society. In the United States, especially, the right to build where and when one chooses is a strong tradition which has its sources in the pioneers who came to this country to obtain land. They disliked the European system of large land-holdings and rents and wanted absolute control of their own land. This absolute control and absolute freedom has been reduced by common consent, especially in higher-density areas, through zoning ordinances, subdivision regulations, and other police power regulations which prevent landholders from harming their neighbors. However, these regulations have always tended to be local in nature, since the harmful impact of one man's activities on a piece of land does not extend very far—perhaps a mile or two at the most, and usually only a few hundred feet. From the metropolitan viewpoint, the basic right to build or not to build has not been abridged.[1]

Any kind of planning for metropolitan areas or regions has to take into account the principle of incremental growth by the actions of individuals intent on maximizing their own benefits. This is a basic condition of regional growth and change, at least in the United States. We do not tell people where to go or when to build or not to build any more than we tell them which mode of travel to use or which route to select in going from origin to destination.

Transportation planning for metropolitan areas depends upon having a good idea, in advance, of where this growth will occur. To have a good idea of where people will be is as important as knowing how many there will be, since the location of people in their various activities determines where within the region loads will be imposed on the different parts of the transportation network. Furthermore, the time span for which a transportation system is planned is a long one—twenty or thirty years—and this system has to take into account as well as possible the transportation problems of the future city and not simply the existing city.

[1] We are coming to the point in time when uncontrolled growth may damage people and society to such an extent that new controls may have to be imposed.

There are two basic approaches which can be taken to determine the location of future growth. The first is *to plan* the metropolitan area or region, that is, to decide where people should live, where they should build their factories and shopping areas, where locate their parks and cemeteries, and equally important, where they should never build.

In Great Britain and in certain other countries, the planning approach has been followed. Stringent rules have been set up, "green belt" areas have been effectively sterilized against development at urban densities, and new towns have been built where and when planned. While there have undoubtedly been adjustments in the face of growth pressures so that the plans have not been adhered to completely, the basic conception has been bold and the actions decisive. From the viewpoint of a transportation planner, nothing could be better than this kind of planning because the placement and density of population and human activities can be considered as given, and the only remaining task (although not an easy one) is to devise the best possible transportation system to serve the planned land use pattern.

However, in the United States this planning approach is not currently possible at the metropolitan or regional level. Successful planning implies the existence of controls to carry the plans out; without controls, planning is a meaningless activity. Transportation planning, corporate planning, military planning, and water resource planning all have the potential of controls to carry out plans. This is not to say that the controls are always exercised or the plans carried out to the last detail, but the potential is there which makes planning a realistic activity. But land use planning presently does not, at the metropolitan level, have such controls. Land ownership is atomized and governments are fragmented. The local governments are democratic and reflect the will of the people. The people build when and where they want to, and the result is that the metropolitan area expands incrementally and organically, the summation of the actions of thousands of people.

These paragraphs are not meant to deny the desirability of metropolitan land use planning. On the contrary, one can be quite certain that, given real controls, planners could do a far better job of designing urban areas than is happening under the circumstances of incremental growth. The purpose of this argument is simply to note that in the United States, at least, the methods of estimating the location of future growth must be based on a realistic appraisal of what metropolitan planning can currently accomplish.

The second approach to determining the location of future growth is *to forecast* growth, not only in amount but in location within a metropolitan area or region. Forecasting land use and population location is one of the two major simulation operations which is used in transportation planning—the other being the traffic simulation model which will be described in Chapter XI. The balance of this chapter is devoted to land use forecasting.

Outline of the Land Use Forecasting Process

Estimating the growth of an urban area must start with long-range forecasts of population and economic growth, as illustrated in Figure 37. These are forecasts of the total number of persons and of employment, production, income, and consumption expected to exist within the area being planned at the time of the target year.

The target year is generally twenty years in the future. A planning period of five or ten years would be too short, since major transportation facilities frequently take five years to complete once a decision to build is made, and commitments often exist for a decade's worth of construction. A forecasting period of more than twenty-five years becomes increasingly uncertain, since technological changes and unforeseen events are likely to have greater and greater impact. The twenty-year forecast is a compromise figure and one which generally sees sufficient growth that major trends can be anticipated. Revisions of the long-range plans should be made every five years, so that plans are continually updated. A long-range forecast with revisions every five years constantly stretches the community's vision and makes certain that provisions are made for system interconnections, for example, that could not be foreseen with a lesser planning term.

There is no need here to describe the methods which can be

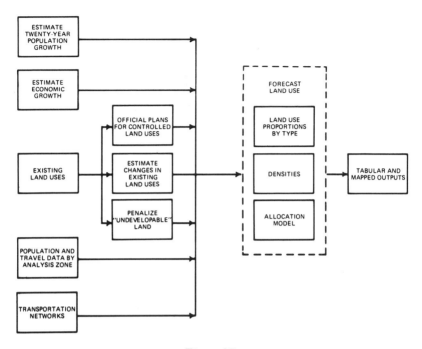

Figure 37.
Generalized land use forecasting procedure.

used to make long-range forecasts of total population and economic growth. Various techniques have been described in other texts.[2] It is important, however, to produce a single estimate rather than a range of estimates. Transportation plans are prepared for a single, expanded city; whether the city reaches that size two or three years sooner or later is unimportant, since administrators can accelerate the pace of transportation construction to suit actual growth rates.

In addition to the aggregate population and economic forecasts, land use forecasting requires data files describing the present city. These include a complete land use file, a file of population by residence place, and a file of employment by location. Employment location is readily obtainable by identifying the locations of the

[2] For example, see Stuart Chapin's *Urban Land Use Planning* (University of Illinois Press, Urbana, 1965), Chapters 3, 4, and 5.

destinations of work trips as recorded in the origin-destination travel surveys. Both population and employment data are needed to measure the densities at which land is used.

Data describing the transportation network(s) serving a metropolitan area are necessary for some forecasting procedures which are sensitive to changes in accessibility. One such model is described later in this chapter.

It must be emphasized that forecasting land use is not done completely by simulation, but can profitably employ the outputs of certain planning operations. Certain extensive uses of land, such as major airports, seaports or lake or river harbors, large public open spaces, and major institutions such as colleges, universities, and hospitals are under the control of organizations which can make —and may carry out—long-range plans. Each of these land uses has special requirements for location, for transportation services, for space, and/or for particular kinds of topography. It is far more efficient to obtain the plans of such organizations, or even to approximate what their plans are likely to be, than it is to try to construct a computer model to simulate the decision processes by which such land uses are planned.

Most cities have some areas around or within them which are considered "undevelopable." These may be water or lake areas, areas of steep hillside, swampy areas, or areas subjected to some kind of pollution. Experience suggests, however, that when economic pressures become great enough, such lands are often brought into use. Examples include portions of the Hudson River adjoining Manhattan Island, the "Jersey Meadows," and the hills behind Honolulu. In the forecasting process, these "undevelopable" lands must either be extracted as being irrevocably unavailable for development, or penalized in some fashion so that they become developed only at a higher cost.

The preceding steps are preliminary to the main work of land use forecasting; they only define 15–25 percent of the land requirements of an urban population. The main work of forecasting consists of estimating where dwellings and industrial activities will be located and where the streets, schools, small parks, churches, municipal buildings, and shopping centers will be located that serve people.

Altogether, these uses will occupy 75–85 percent of the new lands that are brought into urban use.

As Figure 37 suggests, there are three major operations which have to be carried out to do the main work of a land use forecast. First is the determination of the proportions of land in each small part of the city (generally called a "forecasting zone" or "analysis zone") that will need to be set aside for housing, streets, schools, industry, and other uses. This is a kind of land accounting. Second is the determination of the density at which certain land uses (mainly residential and industrial) will be used. Third is the determination of how much of the land available for a particular use will, in fact, be used.

There is a wide variety of ways of making these forecasts. For a listing and criticism of most of the more prominent methods, the reader is referred to Special Report 97 of the Highway Research Board entitled *Urban Development Models*.[3] The available methods vary substantially in approach, in complexity, and even in whether or not they have been made operational. In the following pages, two of these methods are described. These were used in Chicago and in the Niagara Frontier. The Chicago model was the first land use forecasting procedure. The Niagara Frontier model was the first which explicitly took accessibility into account.

The Chicago Procedure

Land use forecasting as an overt part of a transportation planning process may properly be said to have started in Chicago.[4] The forecasting approach was partly adopted out of conviction that this was the best approach and partly as a result of circumstances. At that time, the Northeastern Illinois Metropolitan Area Planning Commission was just being established, and there was no prospect

---

[3] *Urban Development Models,* Highway Research Board Special Report 97, Publication 1628, Washington, D.C., 1968.

[4] For a complete description of the Chicago land use forecasting process, see John R. Hamburg and Robert H. Sharkey, *Land Use Forecast* (Chicago Area Transportation Study, Chicago, 1961). See also Chicago Area Transportation Study, *Final Report,* vol. II (1960).

that it could complete a regional land use plan in time to meet the needs of the study's transportation planning process. The City of Chicago had a plan, but this was being revised and, even if finished in time, would cover only one-sixth of the land area within the study's cordon line. Unless the study were to have prepared a plan for itself, which it was reluctant to do, the forecasting approach had to be adopted.

The process started with the examination of existing, developed land for evidence of possible change. The evidence at hand consisted of a 1940 land use survey covering the city of Chicago and 1940 population densities. Both could readily be compared with 1956 surveys. These data showed that, over a sixteen-year time span, there was little change in either density or kind of land use.[5] Once an area is built up, there is a tendency for it to remain stable, mainly because the investment in buildings has a long useful life. Only a limited number of the oldest and most dilapidated buildings are cleared by public urban renewal, and these are generally replaced by land uses at densities close to those of the preceding uses.

Since the Loop and its environs were heavy generators of trips, the City of Chicago's plans for its Central Area were examined. The City's plans indicated a 5 percent increase in floor area, and this was used as the basis for estimating future trip-making to the Central Area.[6]

Such a review of existing land uses indicated that practically all of the future population and their new activities would have to be located on land that was vacant in 1956. The procedure for estimating the location of future activities was based upon the assumption that a rough priority system existed *de facto*.

It was assumed that large public open spaces—major parks and forest preserves—would be set aside by public action from the stock of vacant land. Accordingly, park and forest preserve agencies were contacted for their long-range plans. These plans, and the study's own estimates of other park and forest preserve acquisitions, were carefully mapped and measured, and the required areas were subtracted from the supply of available public open space.

[5] See Chicago Area Transportation Study, *Final Report,* II, 22–23.
[6] *Ibid.,* p. 24.

In similar manner, areas zoned for industry were set aside. It was assumed that such areas would be available only for industrial purposes, with residences being excluded. While a few unzoned areas listed by a major utility as available for industrial development were added, for the most part lands set aside for industry were based upon expressed public policies. Generally, these lands met functional requirements by being accessible to good transportation facilities.

Land was set aside for a third major airport, and this constituted most of the area which had to be reserved for new transportation facilities.

A proportion of all the remaining land—about 25 percent—was reserved for future streets. This was based on the evidence of existing areas in streets required, in each ring, to provide access to land as that land is brought into use.

The remaining land—still a very large proportion of all vacant land—was then considered as available for residential development and for a fixed proportion of other activities which serve residential population. These other activities include public buildings such as schools, city halls, and firehouses; quasi-public buildings such as churches; small parks; and local commercial activities.

Nearly the last, and certainly the most important, land use forecasting question was how to allocate dwelling units to the available residential land. This was considered to be a question of two parts. First, at what density would residential land be used? Second, how many of the available opportunities for residential siting (residential acres times dwelling units per acre) would be used?

Density was fixed very pragmatically on the basis of 1956 densities and studies of current land subdivision practices, but the usage of available opportunities or capacity for residential location required more work. To identify the 1956 pattern, the usage of the opportunities for residential siting was plotted in relationship to distance from the Loop (see solid line, Figure 38). This showed a regular pattern, highest near the Loop (although dropping down below 90 percent in the Central Area itself) and then declining rapidly and regularly with increasing distance from the Loop.

As noted on page 29 of Volume II of the Chicago Area Transportation Study's report,

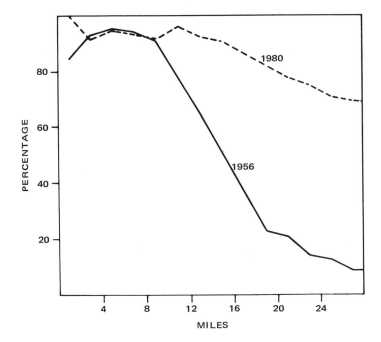

Figure 38.
1956 and estimated 1980 use of residential land,
by distance from the Loop, Chicago area.

This shows the tendency to have progressively lesser percentages of total measured residential capacity in use at ever greater distances from the core of the city. This figure is a way of describing the transition from city to country—a transition which is becoming less and less abrupt. The most abrupt transition known was typified by the twelfth century walled city—all urban development had to be within the walls. Today, with fewer restrictions on personal choice and with flexible transportation, this transition is becoming gradual and less easily defined. Close in, some land may remain vacant because its price has increased and developers have a wider range of nearly equal choices. But the farther removed the site, the greater the chance it will not be used.

. . . the 1980 curve represents the summarized results of the distribution of residential land according to the enumerated considera-

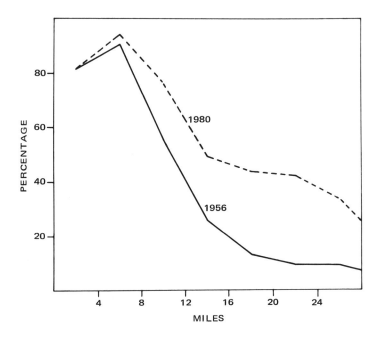

Figure 39.
1956 and estimated 1980 use of designated manufacturing land,
by distance from the Loop, Chicago area.

tions. Many detailed studies were made as each zone was separately estimated and reviewed. At common distances out, those zones lying nearer to existing suburbs were given higher priorities on utilization because of the attractions of existing community services and utilities. But, taken all in all and plotted only by distance, the results . . . illustrate the more gradual transition from city towards country expected in 1980. This is the natural consequence of assuming both higher speeds of travel and more uniform level of access to transportation facilities.

This same kind of procedure was used to allocate manufacturing employment to available industrial land. As in the case of residences, a more complete use of available industrial sites was found near the center of the city, with lower utilization farther out. The 1980 forecast assumed a flatter "percent capacity" slope than that of 1956 (see Figure 39).

In retrospect, we can see how much the Chicago land use forecasting procedure was a hand-tailored operation. Many land uses were forecast using methods identical to those employed in planning operations. However, at each step along the way evidence of past and present land occupancy practice was obtained and used. The biggest improvement was in the employment of a "percent capacity" curve to allocate residences and manufacturing employment to available land. The simplicity of this device should not detract from its merit as a first step toward improved land use forecasting procedures.

The Niagara Frontier Model

As we have seen, the Chicago land use model allocated residential population and manufacturing employment to land available for those purposes on the basis of a "percent capacity" curve. This was a static device, dependent upon assumptions of a steadily declining utilization of available land with increasing distance from the central business district of a city.

A failing of the Chicago model was that it was insensitive to changes in accessibility within an urban region. If, for example, a new expressway were built, or even a fabulous new rail system, it seemed most reasonable to assume that this would change the places where people would build their residences and work places, since with an equal travel time they could live at a greater distance from the center. The Chicago model could handle this only subjectively. A situation like Staten Island before and after the construction of the Verrazano Bridge was beyond its powers. Clearly, this weakness had to be eliminated in an improved land use allocation procedure.

In the Niagara Frontier Transportation Study in 1963–64, concentrated effort was given to the development of a new model which would allocate activities to vacant land in a manner sensitive to the varying levels of accessibility provided by the transportation network.

The model that was developed can most easily be described in terms of a search procedure being followed by a hypothetical person trying to find a site for a new house. Starting at the center of the city, which represents a location where the newcomer would have the highest level of accessibility to all the profitable opportunities of a city, the newcomer would search outward for a site on which to build.

Let it be assumed that he has a given probability "*l*" of settling on a site once it is found. This probability will be substantially less than unity, because not all sites will be suitable. Some would be in commercial areas, some in blighted areas, some at too high a price, some too small, and so on. Thus, he will pass over many available sites in his search outward. As he searches outward, he comes upon more and more vacant land. At some point, he will find a site available which matches his needs, and he will build. In general, however, the newcomer would prefer to locate as close to the center as is possible, other things being equal, because in this fashion his transportation costs are kept low.

The sum of thousands of such individual searches and decisions, according to this hypothesis, results in the settlement pattern of the city. The urban area is almost completely built up at the center, as we can observe. However, as distance from the center increases, the percentage of development becomes lower and lower. This results in the same over-all pattern that was observed in the Chicago "percent capacity" curves.

Mathematically, the model is expressed as follows:[7]

$$A_j = A(e^{-lO} - e^{-l(O+O_j)})$$

where $A_j =$ the amount of activity to be allocated to zone j;
$A =$ the aggregate amount of activity to be allocated;
$l =$ probability of a unit of activity being sited at a given opportunity;
$O =$ the opportunities for siting a unit of activity rank ordered by access value and preceding zone j;
$O_j =$ the opportunities in zone j.

The operation of this formula is such that the probability of

[7] George T. Lathrop and John R. Hamburg, "An Opportunity Accessibility Model for Allocating Regional Growth," *Journal of the American Institute of Planners* (May, 1965).

settling per unit of available land is greatest nearest the zone from which the outward search is being conducted. This expresses the idea of a natural economy of effort in reducing transportation costs, communication costs, and other costs of linking people together.

In former years the probability value in this formula would have been higher, reflecting, perhaps not higher real transportation costs, but certainly a lower ability to pay for such costs. Recently, the increase in productivity and wealth has been such that people can afford to travel farther, build longer water lines, and in general pay for the other costs of living farther apart. This implies a lower "*I*" value.

The preceding formula was employed in conjunction with the highway network description system described earlier in Chapter V and with an extremely efficient algorithm to be described in Chapter XI. This algorithm permitted a computer to seek out the best path from a single point on a network to all other parts of the network. By these devices, the relative positions of all parts of a metropolitan area, *as defined by the speeds of available or planned transportation systems*, could be determined. In this way, the land use allocation model was made sensitive to changes in accessibility produced by changes in the transportation network.

To illustrate the effects of different kinds of accessibility upon urban growth, a prototype computer program was developed which was able to "grow" hypothetical cities having different assumed transportation systems. The development patterns of three of these computer-grown "cities" are illustrated in Figure 40.

In the upper right-hand corner, a city has been "grown" assuming a single high-speed transportation system running north-south over a background of gridded, slower facilities. The single high-speed line might be an expressway with a background of arterials, or it might be a rapid transit line with a background of bus service.

In the upper left is a star-shaped pattern, very similar to the urban development pattern of Chicago. This pattern was produced by assuming five high-speed radial transportation facilities.

In the lower left is a "city" which has been "grown" using only a gridded transportation system. For comparison, in the lower right-hand corner is the pattern of development actually exhibited by the

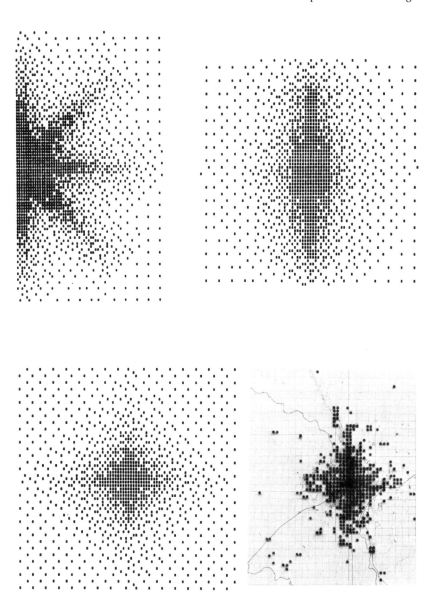

Figure 40.
Urban growth estimated by use of opportunity-accessibility model
as a function of alternative transportation systems.

Wichita, Kansas, urban area. There is a startling degree of resemblance between the computer-generated "city" and the reality of a plains city which grew up on a gridded street system.

The preceding graphics deserve a word of explanation. In the Detroit Metropolitan Area Traffic Study (1953–55) an ingenious method had been developed for using a tabulating machine's printer to print numerals directly on a map. In the Niagara Frontier study this idea was carried one step further, and a high-speed, computer-driven printer was physically adapted so that it would prepare dot maps such as have been shown in Figure 40.

The machine was altered by inserting a rectangular metal slug on the printing chain in place of one of the less-used typographical symbols. A computer program was written which used this slug to print rectangles in varying patterns of increasing intensity. The higher the intensity, the more rectangles were printed per square inch, until the paper was practically covered with ink.[8]

The time invested in the computer program, and in selecting combinations of dots which gave the impression of gradually increasing intensity (without obvious geometric patterns), paid off a hundredfold in the following years. The displays created by this device were used without further artwork for public meetings. They were reduced photographically for report illustrations. No clerical or drafting time was involved in transferring data to maps. All this meant a substantial increase in staff productivity.

Eventually, the Niagara Frontier model was programmed for a very large scientific computer capable of handling the 2,300-mile network of arterials and expressways and the 514 zones of the Niagara Frontier. Then, instead of using the model to forecast land uses which would then have to be converted to estimates of trips, the model was employed in estimating the future locations of trips directly. Since people and trips are so directly related to each other, such a use of the model was highly economic.

Two figures show the results obtained by the use of the opportunity-accessibility model. Figure 41 shows trips for 1970, and Figure 42 shows 1980 trips. In both cases the square mile is the

[8] Kendall H. Bishop and Steven C. Gibson, "Mapping by 1401 Computer Using Map01," New York State Department of Public Works, Albany, 1966.

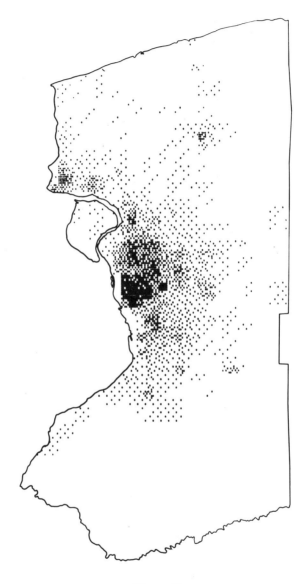

Figure 41.
Estimated locations of 1970 person trips in the Niagara Frontier.

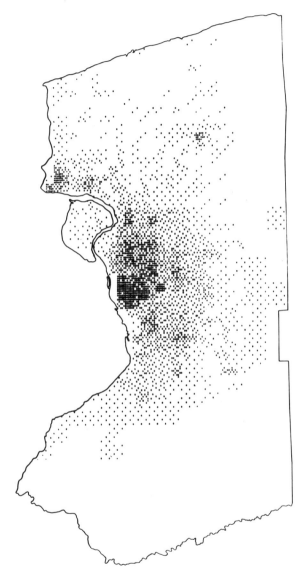

Figure 42.
Estimated locations of 1980 person trips in the Niagara Frontier.

smallest unit of area used for forecasting purposes; hence comparisons with the much finer grain (one-quarter square mile) displays of 1962 trips are unprofitable. Procedural problems account for the coarseness of the displays in the southern and northeastern parts of the study area.

What is clearly seen, however, is the rapid, sprawling growth of population estimated for the Niagara Frontier in 1980. The urbanized area has spread east, north, and south, with a near-merging of the three urban areas of Buffalo, Niagara Falls, and Lockport. Here is foreshadowed the growing together of three urban areas which were, in 1962, still largely separate. This is typical of the kinds of growing together which are producing megalopolitan complexes around the world. Anyone driving out from an urban area can observe this same kind of growth in action today, in almost any country.

The transportation system assumed to exist during the period of growth was Plan N-30, an extensive set of expressways serving the entire urbanized and urbanizing area. To see whether this made a substantial difference in the forecast or not, another forecast was run in which only those expressways were used which were already built or committed to be built—a total system of 120 miles as opposed to N-30's 246 miles. With the committed system, new growth tended to be slightly more compactly placed around the built-up area. The difference is just discernible when mapped. The lack of difference is explained by the fact that fairly good roads already exist everywhere in the rural parts of the two counties of the Niagara Frontier. Expressways speed up rural travel from forty or fifty miles per hour only to sixty-five[9] miles per hour. As a result, the effects of an extensive expressway system on urban growth were noticeable but not dramatic.

Evaluation

From the transportation planner's viewpoint, the main purpose of land use forecasting is to provide as good an estimate as possible

[9] This suggests, as will be shown later, that the greatest advantage from expressway construction comes in already built-up areas.

of future locations of people and their activities. The land use forecast must then be converted into an estimate of future trip ends, which in turn are used in the testing process that will be described in Chapter XI.

The quality of any such estimate is very difficult to appraise. The first criterion, from a pragmatic viewpoint, is that there must be an estimate—any estimate. Without an estimate of future activity distribution throughout the urban area, the long-range transportation planning process comes to a halt. Moving from just any estimate upward to a "good" estimate requires, basically, a better understanding of the forces which are at work in city building.

The difficulty here is that there are so many forces at work which shape cities. Transportation, communications, building materials, social pressures, educational practices, and community wealth, to name a few, all have a hand in affecting the way an urban area expands. Increasing the difficulty of making estimates is the fact that the estimates are made, not simply of numbers in time (as in population forecasting), but of numbers in time and across space. In effect, two dimensions are added to the problem. Geographic forecasting, furthermore, means forecasting by fairly small spatial units (one and four square miles in the high- and low-density areas of Chicago, for example) and this greatly increases the volume of calculations that have to be made. Under these circumstances, it is not surprising that land use forecasting procedures have taken years to develop.

The two models described in this chapter have been based on the assumption that the underlying force shaping cities is the desire for mutual proximity of people, but that this force is balanced by needs and desires of people for space. These needs and desires can be purchased in a wealthier society through more expensive and extensive transportation and communications systems.

All the evidence of the past three decades indicates a trend towards increasing real wealth in urban areas. With adequate purchasing power, people can purchase more space and at the same time can afford the extra travel costs which are needed to maintain mutual proximity. It would appear, then, that short of massive governmental intervention (of which there is no sign in the offing), cities will continue to spread out as they grow. This is what the forecasts of this chapter have shown.

Because forecasts of the locations and density of population settlement are important to the entire transportation planning process, a safety feature is needed. This is the continuing transportation planning process. By monitoring changes in land development and trip generation, technicians doing the continuing planning can observe whether actual development is in line with forecasts. If there are substantial changes, plans can be reviewed and revised if necessary to meet the new needs.

Conclusion

In a quiet way, the practice of forecasting future land use patterns for metropolitan areas, which was initiated by the Chicago study in 1957 and 1958, opened the door to a new way of thinking. The orderliness of urban growth patterns, which had been so surprising when data on land use were first displayed, surprised and shocked many others when it was employed in forecasting procedures. Intuitively, many people realized that where forecasting was appropriate, planning was not; that forecasting was proper in fields where controls could not be applied to alter events; and that planning was by this same token likely to be ineffective or unrealistic in such fields.

However, this new departure, instead of being destructive, actually contained ideas which will eventually lead (as we shall see later in this volume) to a far more effective and realistic means for dealing with urban problems. At a minimum, one of these means had to be the practice of dealing factually with land use and future land use requirements, with a tight accounting of numbers. Realism demands an accurate appraisal and measurement of fact; for too long planning had been dealing with inadequate fact, and this was now being remedied.

IX

GOALS

In previous chapters evidence has been presented which suggests that travel and the growth of cities are two phenomena which occur in very orderly patterns and that this order is the result of cumulative, intelligent appraisal by people of opportunities available to them in the short run. These patterns have something of the quality of the patterns of insect life; while the individual is conscious of what he does, he is not generally conscious of the larger order of which he is a part, and—most important—he is rarely conscious that this larger order, of which he is a part and which he is helping to create, may be destructive to him and his species.

This orderliness is useful in making projections, and it also has an immense fascination as a subject for impersonal, scientific investigation: the spatial organization and travel habits of an entire society, studied by a member of that society! However, the idea of the blind continuation of trends in a society of which we are merely antlike particles is very disturbing to most people. It seems dehumanizing. It offends us by seeming to remove two characteristics which we admire: our will power and our ability to see, well in advance, choices or alternative courses of action which we can select.

On reflection, of course, it will be seen that unless one is mesmerized by statistics, our will power is quite independent of these figures. And this will power is an extremely important element in planning. The skilled planner will not blink at statistics and wants all the scientific data he can get, projections included; but he must also have a very clear idea of the goals, values, objectives, and will power of his clients. These are the factors which, in combination with the largest possible stretch of foresight, produce the courage to make important adjustments, at very large scale, away from things-as-they-are-likely-to-be to the things-that-we-want.[1]

Therefore, it is important to take a close look at the goals which guide us in the choices we have to make. Unfortunately, as we approach this subject, we find that it is hazy and amorphous. The terms themselves—"goals," "values," and "objectives"—have multiple meanings. Anyone dealing with the subject soon finds that to bring them into the planning process he must set up some kind of system for dealing with goals. The following construct uses only the single term "goal."

Skirting the Quagmire

Let us start by defining a goal as a mental image which a person has of something which he would like to have, to do, or to be.[2] Let us assume further that this mental image is composed of some arrangement of molecules and electrical charges within a few cells in that person's brain—in other words, that it is something almost physical. Under this assumption the image or goal is as real as the object or state-of-being which it represents. It may, in fact, be more real, because the desired object may not exist at all.

Each person will have many of these goals or mental images. They may be temporary or they may be a lifetime commitment. They may be selfish or they may be unselfish. They will often conflict with one another. These goals will not be held equally strongly: some will be actively considered when a decision is to be made, and others will be set aside.

It is possible to persuade some people to delete or modify some of their goals or to add new goals to the set which they possess. But

---

[1] Of course, it could be argued that long-range planning, and actions made according to the recommendations of planners, are merely extensions of the kinds of actions which people make in reacting to events within a shorter time span. With this line of reasoning, long-range and comprehending intelligence is merely another extension of the same intelligence which the wasp uses in building the extra extension to his colony's nest at the nearest point to the center.

[2] For an excellent discussion of images and values, see Kenneth Boulding, *The Image* (University of Michigan Press, Ann Arbor, 1956).

for the most part, it is assumed that people's goals will remain constant.

It is important to remember that all goals have their sources with individual persons. Only people have these kinds of mental images. A goal or an objective is something which I, personally, want or which you, personally, want.

Some have suggested that we must consider the goals of future people, but under the foregoing construct, such goals do not exist. We may have goals for what we want our children and grandchildren to be, but these are our goals, not theirs. More pragmatically, the goals of future people cannot be counted in a ballot box, nor can they affect decisions that are made now. We must speak for ourselves; this is where the will power exists.

It cannot be overemphasized that a goal is of interest only at the point *where* and *when* a decision is to be made, that is, when a person is aware that a choice is in front of him. *Now* is the only time when decisions can be made.

In a democracy all individuals' goals count for something. The task at hand, then, is how to deal with the myriad goals which exist in the minds of an entire population, whether of a metropolitan area or a region. If these goals were objects outside people's brains, they could be sampled, classified, counted, and inventoried. However, they are not. Therefore, some mechanism has to be developed for seeing whether an accurate or reliable listing of goals can be obtained. This is a quagmire into which many sink who deal with this subject.

A variety of means have been proposed for trying to find out accurately what are the goals which people possess. Some have suggested taking polls, but this course is very difficult. People may not be able to frame their goals in words adequately, and their ideas of what they want to do when faced with an abstract problem may be quite different from their ideas of what they would do when faced with a concrete situation. Others have suggested that observations should be made of what people actually do and then deductions should be drawn concerning the goals which motivated them.

A simple and pragmatic solution to this problem is to have an individual or team propose a set of goals which are then subjected to debate and discussion. If the statement of goals survives the debate, it can be considered adequate; if it does not, it must be modified until it does survive. Provided that the debate is widely aired, this microcosm of the democratic process should produce a good representation of the common will.[3]

We have to realize, of course, that there can be no perfect expression of the common will because there is no set of images which is identical among all people. Any statement of goals has to be an approximation.

If the test of a good statement of goals is common acceptance, one wonders why more sets of goals are not approved officially by governments. There is, I think, a double answer to this. Most elected officials are extremely wary of committing themselves to specific statements which they realize they may not be able to live up to, or which may be used against them later ("See, your actions are inconsistent with Goal No. 4-b!"). On the other hand, the kinds of highly generalized goal statements which would be accepted by an elected representative of the people are not likely to be useful to the planner in helping him to make a decision. It may be, however, that with the spread of systems for evaluating governmental progress (like the planning-programming-budgeting system), goals of the kind described in the following section may become more widely understood, and people may require that they be adopted by governments.

The Requirements of Statements of Goals

Traditionally, goals have been written as statements of lofty ideals or conditions which people would like to see come about as the result of some planned construction program. A typical goal statement will be something like this: "We want the best possible transportation plan consistent with the ability of this region to pay

[3] One might speculate that the recent extensive concern with goals and values which dominates so many planning discussions is really a mechanism by which a professional fairly removed from the people satisfies his conscience that he is doing the popular will. If the public were directly involved in the decision-making, their goals would be expressed in their votes, and the whole subject of goals would collapse.

for it." Another might be "to provide a balanced transportation system which will encourage the development of our city as an outstanding environment in which people can live, work, and play."
   Nobody can disagree with these sentiments, but they miss the
real purpose for which goals are set. A goal is the thing which leads
a person to select a particular course of action when faced with a
choice of actions. Traditional statements of goals fail in this important assignment; they are so general that they fail to help anyone in
making a choice. The clue to their weakness lies in their use of un-
defined adjectives such as "best possible," "balanced," and "outstanding." What is a "best possible" system? Is it the best system
which is financially possible or the best system which is physically
possible? And best in what respect? And what is balanced? Seventy-
five percent auto and 25 percent transit, or the other way around?[4]
   So the author of a statement of goals has to search behind the
generalities for the basic things people want, which can then be used
in determining choices.
   Part of this searching is to reduce the goal statements to their
simplest, most basic components—components which cannot be reduced further. These might be called the "lowest common denomi-
nator" goals.
   It is essential that these single goals be those which people
want for themselves, and they ought to be stated as the wants of people. These are "first-generation" goals. Second- and third-generation
goals are the goals of institutions and programs, and while they may,
in fact, truly work for the good of the people, there is no guarantee
that this is always the case. For example, a goal of an agency like a
highway department may be to build Y miles of highway each year;
but the productivity of the last few miles built under such a program
may be very low and may not work efficiently to reduce the things
which affect people directly, such as reducing accidents or saving
time. So it is better to stick to the first-generation goals.
   Stated goals must be relevant to the problem, not only to a
broad problem area but to the particular level of dealing with that

[4] One metropolitan area considers a balanced system as one in which expressways are sufficiently congested that people will use transit; in other words,
congestion is the arbiter of balance.

problem. For example, the goal of beauty is relevant to transportation at the local scale but may be quite irrelevant in some cities when it comes to deciding upon a metropolitan system, since at the metropolitan scale beauty is very difficult to sense.[5] Where beauty does bear as a goal is in the selection of routes within a corridor, and even more in the design and placement of structures, landscaping, and "street furniture." A goal, if it is to be useful, must apply at the point where a decision is being made.

The criterion of relevancy, unfortunately, accents a dilemma of the transportation planner. How relevant does a goal have to be to be considered worthy of inclusion in a set of goals? Goals like safety and speed obviously affect transportation choices. But on the other hand there are many important goals such as better housing, better education, less crime, and lower disease rates whose relationship to transportation planning is unclear. The impact of these other goals on transportation decisions may be very slight in matters such as route location, or very strong when decisions are being made on the allocation of scarce governmental resources between transportation and, let us say, housing or education.

This dilemma is akin to the problem of whether it is possible to separate one aspect of an urban problem from all others in order to deal with it. Should not everything be dealt with simultaneously, since every part of an urban area affects every other part? The ideal of comprehensiveness is strong and has a logical appeal, but it is dangerous when it evokes the need for solving too many things at once.

It is constantly necessary to expand our ability to deal with more things, but there are limits to what can be done at any given time. In this book we are dealing with a very large subject, but one which must still be kept within reasonable bounds. It is for this reason—to allow advances to be made—that a list of goals is presented which does not contain reference to many goals which, although they are desirable and important, have less than immediate impact upon the transportation planning process.

---

[5] This is an assertion; others may hold contrary opinions. The reader interested in this subject should see Kevin Lynch's *The Image of the City* (M.I.T. Press, Cambridge, 1960).

The Goals of Transportation Planning

In the first chapter a list of problems was given which contains the things people dislike most about transportation. If these problems are turned around so that we see their obverse sides, they become goals. People dislike the danger of accident; the opposite of danger —safety—is a goal.

Thus, by taking the problems given in Chapter I and stating them in reverse, we have a preliminary set of goals. The following list contains goals which are related to the subject of transportation planning at the metropolitan scale.[6]

1. *Safety.* Trying to reduce the appalling toll of deaths and injuries which result from transportation accidents (mainly on the highways) is certainly one of the prime goals which should affect the planning and operation of transportation facilities.

2. *Saving time in travel.* History shows that whenever it has been made possible, people prefer to use, and will pay more for, faster means of transportation. This, for the most part, is not because they like the thrill of speed but because they would prefer to use their time in more productive or enjoyable ways.

3. *Reducing operating costs.* People prefer to spend less for an equal amount of transportation and resent any transportation expenditures they have to waste because of circumstances like stop-and-go driving.

4. *Increasing efficiency.* When people pay taxes or support bond issues for the construction of transportation facilities (distinguishing here between out-of-pocket spending for daily journeys and long-term investments in capital plant), they like to have it spent efficiently so that the greatest returns are obtained. Even when money has long since been spent (sunk capital), people want to obtain the greatest utilization from the past expenditure.

5. *Mobility.* Most people like to have the freedom of being able to get where they want to go, when they want to go. Mobility

[6] For a listing of the values of the scale of the community within an urban area, see the report "Transportation and Community Values," to be published by the Highway Research Board, Washington, D.C.

is an important goal connected with work, social life, cultural life, land development, and many other activities; it is a kind of freedom.

6. *Beauty.* People prefer to have attractive surroundings during their journeys; these surroundings include both transportation facilities and vehicles themselves and the rural or urban landscape beyond.

7. *Comfort and absence of strain, noise, or nuisance.* These values would be included on most persons' lists of things to be desired. The planning of transportation facilities has to take these values into account not only for those traveling but for those who live or work near a transport facility.

8. *Reducing air pollution.* This is a goal which, with a growing population, will become increasingly real and important to individuals.

9. *Minimizing disruption.* People want to minimize the disruptive effects of transportation facilities, particularly the forced dislocation of homes, businesses, and institutions arising from the construction of new transportation facilities, and particularly when it affects themselves or their friends and neighbors. Disruption of existing urban communities is felt very severely by poor people and minority groups, whose financial resources and ability to find replacement housing are most limited.

10. *Increasing productivity of the economy.* People would like to have transportation facilities built, located, and operated in such a fashion that the productivity of their region will rise, expecting thereby to get benefits for themselves.

11. *Ability to move about without an automobile.* At some time or other, most people find themselves without an automobile for varying lengths of time but still want to move about within an urban area. This goal is most acutely felt by the old, by those who cannot drive, and by those who are too poor to own a car.

It is often asked why goals like reliability and efficiency are not included in such a list. The answer is that these words contain compound ideas which can be expressed better in terms of several of the preceding eleven goals. Reliability, for example, is often stated to be a goal of transit service; actually it means (a) saving time—not having to wait for a late bus, for example, and (b) avoiding loss of comfort—not having to wait out of doors in inclement weather. Similarly, the goal of efficiency is a compound one, meaning greater output (of safety, for example) per unit of input (construction cost, for example).

Building the Bridge

One of the criticisms the staff of the Chicago study aimed at earlier transportation planning reports, and at many land use master plans, was that there was little or no connection between their goals and their plans. Reports would be issued containing fine statements of the objectives which were being sought, but when the plan was produced at the end of the report there was no accompanying proof —and in many cases no attempt to prove—that the recommended plan would help to achieve the goals previously stated.

So one of the tasks the staff set for itself was to build a formal bridge between goals and plan. We wanted to be able to prove that the plan we recommended for the Chicago area would be the best. If the Policy Committee to whom we reported approved our statements of goals and objectives, and our reasoning processes were correct, then they would almost automatically approve the plan, because the one had to follow from the other. The ultimate extension of this idea, of course, would be one in which a computer would be given a statement of goals for a given metropolitan area, together with the facts describing that metropolitan area, and then it would be pro-grammed to produce the best plan for the area automatically. We later achieved this, although only at a very small scale, in the opti-mum spacing formula, which will be described in Chapter X.

It was important to us that the quality of the workmanship of this bridge be very high. We knew, even at that time, that the plan we would recommend would propose capital improvements running into the billions of dollars. Further, as Burnham would have pointed out, a strong plan has a life of its own extending well beyond the presence of its authors. What we left behind in Chicago could be an influential factor for two or three decades, if it were well done.

The standards for connecting goals to plan should by right be much higher for transportation planning than for most of the other design-profession operations. The painter or the sculptor, using materials worth only a few dollars, can afford to judge his product emotionally. The architect similarly does what he wants, but unless he has a string of clients who agree with his taste, he does not get the commissions where that taste is an acceptable criterion. But the transportation planner can never—or should never be able to—persuade people that his judgment and taste indicate that a road or transit line should go in such and such a place. There are too many clients, the subject is too complicated, and the stakes are too high to indulge in this kind of imperial gesturing. The transportation planner must persuade people by the logic of his figures. He will never, of course, be able to persuade everybody because there are those who do not want to be convinced of anything and because there will not be universal agreement on goals. Nevertheless, the foregoing is the planner's professional responsibility.

It is instructive to see how the earlier transportation studies handled this problem. These studies listed goals such as accident reduction, time saving, and reduction of operating costs. The standard solution was then to compare the travel costs of the anticipated users of a new facility with the costs of that group of users if they were forced back onto the old network. The difference in costs was called a benefit. These benefits were then capitalized over the expected life of the facility and compared with the capital costs of building the facility. The result was a benefit-cost ratio.

The benefit-cost ratio suffered from two serious deficiencies. First, it did not measure the true costs of driving on the older street system; these costs varied as a function of the volumes using these streets, both for the driver who might use a new facility and for those who remained. For example, if a number of drivers used an expressway, all those remaining on the arterial would receive a real benefit in faster driving. Second, it was not applied to more than one facility at a time.

However, the benefit-cost ratio implied one significant idea: that the attainment of goals was a relative and not an absolute matter. Goals are things which people want to move *toward*, but perfect safety, infinite travel speed, and zero costs are unrealistic and cannot be attained. Any small degree of improvement toward these goals is desired, and the more improvement the better.

Progress toward some goals can be measured in quantitative terms. Accidents can be counted. The amount of time spent in travel can be measured or estimated quite reliably. The costs of building new transportation facilities can be estimated by engineers. The costs of driving automobiles and trucks or of operating mass transportation facilities are well known. Thus, if some technique could be developed which would calculate the performance of a plan with respect to each goal, the bridge between goal and plan would be built—for that individual goal, at least.

However, for other goals, this is not so easy to do, even conceptually. Beauty, comfort, the reduction of strain and discomfort, and increases in the productivity of the economy are very difficult, if not impossible, to measure as affected by different regional transportation plans. Furthermore, goals like beauty are visual images which vary markedly between people, and hence it is often difficult to obtain a consensus. Perhaps the only way to obtain an indication of how well a plan performs in respect to these goals is by the committee approach.

In the Chicago study this tangle was cut through pragmatically and quickly. Only those goals would be used (a) where the performance of a metropolitan plan could be measured in terms of that goal, and (b) which would be significant factors in determining the size and configuration of the transportation plan *at the metropolitan scale.*

Those goals which did not meet these criteria were set aside. This does not mean that they were unimportant or that we were trying to downgrade them in any way. It was simply that they could not be employed, given the technical skills which we had at that time.

Based on these criteria, four goals were proposed:

1. To increase safety.
2. To reduce time spent in travel.
3. To reduce operating costs (of drivers and transit users).
4. To reduce the capital costs of new transportation facilities.

The list of other goals which were proposed but not included as the basis for judging the performance of alternative plans (except intuitively) was as follows:

5. Minimizing disruption.[7]
6. Promoting better land development.
7. Making the city more productive.
8. Improving the appearance of the future city.

These correspond to the list defined earlier in this chapter, except for three goals:

9. Reducing air pollution.
10. Providing transportation for those without cars.
11. Increasing comfort and reducing strain, noise, and nuisance.

Air pollution at that time seemed to be only the property of Los Angeles. Chicago had a very extensive transit system in being in 1956 which was strongest in areas of low car ownership, so that there did not seem to be much point in setting up a separate goal for that. The comfort–lack of nuisance group of goals had to be set aside, because of inability to measure what it meant or how seriously people reacted to it.

These goals were discussed extensively with the study's Design Subcommittee, representing the State of Illinois, Cook County, the City of Chicago, and the Bureau of Public Roads. The members of this committee, and later the Policy Committee itself, approved of the list. Similar review processes have been followed in other transportation studies since that time.

Agreement was thus reached on four basic objectives—reducing time, reducing accidents, saving operating costs, and reducing capital costs. The performance of any plan could be measured in terms of these goals. The remaining objectives, rightly or wrongly, were set aside but not without regret. At that time (and the situation has not changed much since then) there was either no way reliably to measure plan performance in their terms, or these objectives were ones which could only be employed, after the metropolitan plan had

[7] Disruption of persons is measured to a large extent in the value of property acquired for right-of-way and thus is measured by goal 4 preceding.

been approved, by other teams of professionals working to locate the exact center lines of new facilities or designing them preparatory to construction.

The Problem of Conflicting Objectives

Simply having an agreed set of goals and objectives was not enough to build an adequate bridge between goals and plans. This was because the goals we had selected were not mutually compatible. The plan which cost the least to build would be one in which no new construction at all was proposed. And the plan which was fastest would certainly be very expensive and might conceivably not be very safe—especially if construction standards were lowered.

Here was a real difficulty, one which any person making decisions faces. Which goal is paramount? How will conflicts between goals be reconciled?

This problem could not be evaded. We had to have a single plan—the best one we could devise. To have a *best* plan meant absolutely that there could be only *one* objective or goal for judging which plan was best. In logic this cannot be disputed, although the idea is an uncomfortable one. As will be shown later in this chapter the notion of "bestness" is a limited concept and one which may not be useful at all in larger contexts, such as in regional planning.

What was this single objective to be? There was no single decisive moment when the answer to this question came to the Chicago study staff; it seemed to grow slowly, until suddenly it was there. We may describe the answer more easily in terms of product than in terms of the time sequence of its development.

Each of the four objectives was stated as a cost. Thus, hours of travel time were translated into time costs and numbers of accidents were translated into accident costs. Vehicle operating costs and construction costs were, of course, stated in dollar terms from the outset.

The value of time was obtained through synthesizing all the evidence which was available up to that time. Studies by G. P. St. Clair and Nathan Liederer, and Paul J. Claffey, had established

values of time for persons driving in automobiles.[8] These studies obtained their figures from a comparison of the choices auto drivers
made between free roads and toll roads. The value of truck drivers'
time was estimated on the basis of then current labor contracts. It
was concluded, based upon the known mixture of trucks and automobiles within the vehicle stream, that the value of time for an
average vehicle in Chicago in 1956 was $1.66 per vehicle hour.[9]
This number was consistent with all the evidence and with the prevailing value of time used by highway engineers in other states.

The cost of accidents was established by an extensive study.[10]
The costs of property damage, hospitalization, funeral expenses, and
court judgments were taken into account along with the losses of pay
of injured persons. Accident costs turned out to be substantial, averaging about 1.3 cents per mile of vehicle travel.

Operating costs were based on estimates of fuel, oil, and tire
costs which had been obtained from studies made by specialists in
this field.[11] The costs of depreciation of vehicles was not included because these costs were bound to be constant, as far as anyone could
possibly measure, between any of the plans to be tested and evaluated.

Construction costs of each plan were estimated on the basis of
the costs of similar jobs which had been completed in the Chicago
area in the preceding decade. These construction costs included right-
of-way costs.

It was then assumed that all these dollar costs were just that:
dollar costs. As such, they were all equal. A dollar's cost of accidents
could be treated like a dollar's cost of construction or a dollar's cost
of speed. A saving or reduction in any of these costs was equally as
good as a reduction in any other cost. This seemed to be heartless in

[8] G. P. St. Clair and Nathan Liederer, "Evaluation of Unit Cost of Time and
Strain-and-Discomfort Cost of Non-Uniform Driving," Highway Research Board
Special Report 56, Washington, D.C., 1960. Paul J. Claffey, "Characteristics of
Passenger Car Travel on Toll Roads and Comparable Free Roads for Highway
User Benefit Studies," Highway Research Board, Washington, D.C., January, 1961.
     [9] Chicago Area Transportation Study, *Final Report,* III (1962), 10.
     [10] Dayton P. Jorgensen, "Accident Costs and Rates on Chicago Area Streets
and Highways," *CATS Research News* 4, no. 4.
     [11] Various sources are cited in Hyman Joseph, "Automobile Operating Costs,"
CATS Research News, 3, no. 4.

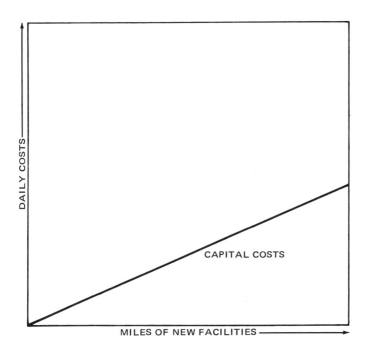

the case of accidents, and yet this represented realism, because the costs of accidents which were measured included all those judgments and awards which courts and juries were giving to the claimants in accident cases.

The single goal then seemed to leap out: *it was to develop that transportation plan which had the lowest total transportation costs.* All of the four basic objectives previously recognized were comprehended by this single goal. It was a compelling solution to the problem of reconciling conflicting objectives.

How this goal was used to select a best plan can be illustrated in the following manner. Suppose that a metropolitan community considers investing in ten different transportation plans, each larger and more costly than the one preceding. The capital costs of building each successive plan will rise, for all practical purposes, as a function of the number of miles of new facilities to be built. This is shown in the diagram above.

As the community invests more and more, it will change the

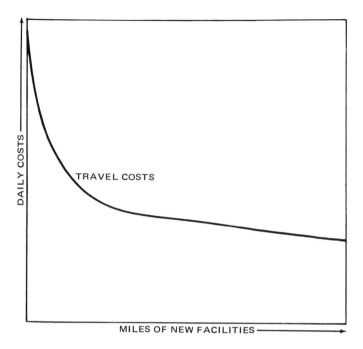

costs of travel within its region. Accident costs, vehicle operating costs, and time costs will be reduced. These costs will go down rapidly as the first improvements go in but less rapidly as more are put in. Eventually, further investment will produce very little reduction in the cost of travel. This is diagrammed above, in which travel costs of each plan are compared.

The sum of travel costs and capital costs is defined as the total transportation costs of the region. These are the sums paid out by individuals and corporations for their time, their accidents (mainly in the form of insurance), their vehicle operating costs, and their transit fares, together with governmental expenditures for right-of-way and construction.

At some level of investment, these total transportation costs will reach a minimum. That plan, then, which produces the lowest total transportation costs is the best plan for the region.[12]

_____

[12] To take care of any lack of precision in our measurements, and to make

If we look at this conclusion carefully, we shall see that it is indeed a very sensible criterion by which to evaluate a regional transportation plan. Providing that one can measure these costs, one would hardly recommend a plan which calls for the investment of money beyond the point at which that money will provide a return to the public in terms of reducing their accidents, time in travel, or operating costs. At the same time, one would not be likely to tolerate a

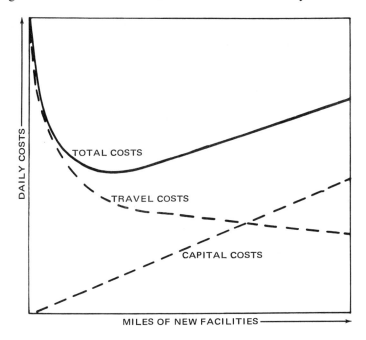

governmental policy which failed to spend money when that money could reduce accidents and travel time. Thus, the minimum total transportation cost expresses the optimum point between an inadequate and an over-extended public investment policy.

certain that all funds invested in transportation would produce an adequate return in competition with other possible investments in either the public or private sector of the economy, Carroll insisted that we use a 10 percent rate of return on any capital investment in transportation. This meant, in effect, that the last dollar invested by the best plan would return 10 percent interest. The first dollar would generally return much more and the *average rate of return* produced by most of the transportation plans we prepared was something in excess of 20 percent.

Summary and Evaluation

The task of planning transportation facilities at the metropolitan scale is one of making recommendations which will persuade people, both administrators and the public at large, to take actions and to make adjustments which are different from the normal drift of events. Planning for such changes, if it is done well, is a tremendous stretching of man's foresight in the dimensions of time and space and in his attempts to comprehend very complex phenomena of which he is only a small part.

But people will not support proposed changes unless these changes will produce things they want. So, inevitably, the goals of the people must be included in the planning process.

The difficulty with goals, however, is that they are so amorphous. Anyone dealing with this subject soon finds that to bring them into the planning process, he must invent a system, a set of rules by which to handle goals and to relate them to the choices which have to be made. A number of such systems have been developed which vary in their rigor and as a function of the kind of planning problem being faced.

The system developed by the Chicago study was tailored to the needs of planning transportation systems at the metropolitan scale. Basically, it consisted of four steps.

First, a fairly large number of goals was listed. These were debated and discussed with representatives of local governments. In this process they were refined to their essentials.

Second, the goals were screened. The most important screening was relevance: would different plans tangibly improve performance as defined by a particular goal? Different plans, for example, can produce measurably different safety records, and hence safety is a relevant goal. Put in other words, safety has an impact upon planning which makes it relevant. It was also felt to be extremely desirable that the performance of a plan be quantifiable in terms of whatever goals were selected, since measurement was better than opinion in making and justifying decisions.

Third, the goals selected were related to each other, so that gains in the direction of one goal could be compared to the losses in another. This was done by measuring plan performance in relationship to each goal in common units; the common unit happened to be dollar costs.

Fourth, these goals were then restated in terms of a new goal, which comprehended its component goals. The new goal was to minimize the sum of all transportation costs.

It is possible, in retrospect, to evaluate this manner of dealing with goals and relating them to alternative plans with some objectivity.

Within its limits the Chicago system was a satisfactory resolution of a very difficult problem. Four major goals were reconciled within a single overriding goal. These four goals took into account all of the costs which users of transportation facilities and the corporate public (i.e., government) paid directly for transportation.[13] The goal system was thus complete, within its limits.

In some respects we were very fortunate in being able to have a system which could incorporate four goals and still come up with an optimum plan. It happened that three of the goals (to reduce accident costs, time costs, and vehicle operating costs) all behaved in much the same way as a function of average speed of travel; they all were higher at low speeds and fell off as average speeds increased. If they had behaved substantially differently with respect to speed, a single "best" solution might not have been possible. Also, we were fortunate in that capital construction costs had a strong effect in reducing the three user costs. If they had not, then the clarity of having a good, sharp, minimum cost point would have been lost, and it would have been much harder to persuade people that a single plan was in fact the best.

The major difficulty with the Chicago system was the limited number of goals included in the effective goal set. We would have liked, then and in subsequent studies, to have included more goals di-

---

[13] It may be argued correctly that time is not a cost which is paid out in dollars; nevertheless, as an index of actions for which people are consistently willing to vote funds over many years, it is a valid goal.

rectly within the system. Goals such as improved land development, increased mobility of the population, and reduced air pollution are admittedly desirable candidates for inclusion.

Unfortunately, the inclusion of additional goals may become progressively more difficult, for three reasons. First, the measurement of what is good or better in many of these goals is extremely difficult. What precisely, for example, is "improved land development"? How can one weigh a metropolitan finger plan against a metropolitan satellite plan and declare which is better? Second, the effectiveness of different transportation plans in improving performance toward some of these goals is extremely small. Third, the inclusion of additional goals may eliminate the possibility of finding a best plan, almost by definition. The concept of "better" or "best" is in itself quite limiting. It is only possible to be best in terms of a single criterion. As one increases the number of goals, one also increases the difficulty of combining all goals into a single criterion. Thus, the multiplicity of goals or criteria defeats the purpose of trying to attain a clear-cut decision.[14]

One is therefore faced with the dilemma of being able to determine a best plan with a limited goal set, but not when more goals are added. This should not, however, be disheartening. The idea of finding the "best of all possible worlds" has long been held up as fatuous, and complete comprehensiveness may be an equal mirage. Nevertheless, the difficult problem of having some key goals not included in the system remains. This became very real when in the Niagara Frontier study we wrestled with how to incorporate mass transportation as an integral part of the decision-making process. How that can be handled will be reserved for a later chapter.

---

[14] Some people may be troubled by the emphasis here on "clear-cut decisions," especially as these are based on economic criteria which include a dollar value placed on time. The alternative, I would submit, is nonplanning. If we are to extend vision and conceive of superior systems of transportation, there must be a system created by which a social judgment can be employed to allocate resources consistently. Such a system we have devised. The social value of improved transportation, and especially faster transportation, is hard to deny when a long-term or world-wide view is taken.

X

EXPRESSWAY PLANNING: PART I

THE transportation planning process described in Chapter VI requires that a number of trial expressway plans be tested by using a computer to simulate future traffic flows over them. The trial plans will include a range of plans deliberately selected to examine substantially different policies on quantity, general location, and configuration of networks. The tests are long and expensive. It would be wasteful to submit poorly conceived schemes to the computer. Therefore, it is necessary to prepare trial transportation plans in a methodical fashion, and by intelligent preparation to limit the number of plans that needs to be tested.

There is a large body of data and ideas which must be assembled when a trial expressway plan is being prepared. Facts must be obtained which describe an urban area as it is, in its principal transportation and land use aspects. External factors such as the locations of nearby cities, of regional transportation facilities, and of major topographic features have to be mapped. The future density and placement of urban development has to be estimated. The pattern and spacing of expressways has to be approximated in an optimum fashion. And, finally, certain principles of joint planning of land uses and transportation facilities have to be applied.

All of these facts and considerations then have to be brought together. This is a process which cannot be organized neatly into a fixed sequence of steps because of the large number of interrelationships and feedbacks between the components. It is possible, however, to block out the major groupings of data and ideas and to suggest a rough ordering of operations.

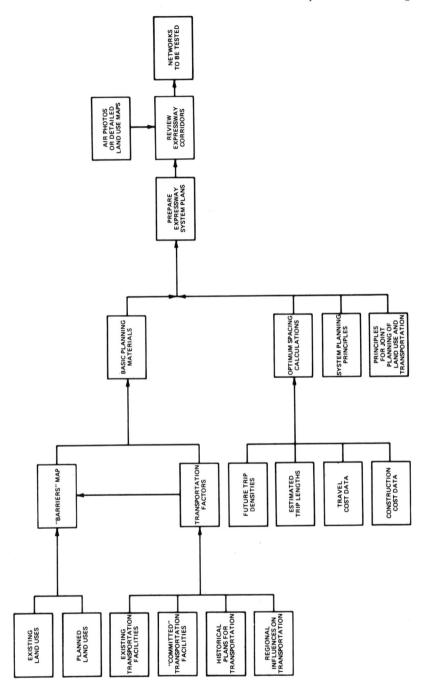

The process of preparing trial plans, as it evolved through the Chicago, Niagara Frontier, and Rochester studies, is illustrated in Figure 43. For convenience of verbal description, the steps in that figure may be grouped into five basic operations. These are: the assembly of basic planning materials, the calculation of optimum spacing, the application of system planning principles, the application of principles for the joint planning of land, use and transportation, and, finally, the preparation and review of trial plans and their component expressway corridors.

The first of these five operations, the assembly of basic planning materials, provides the planner with precise information describing the existing city with which he is working, together with certain "final" estimates as to its future density and geographic extent.

The second operation is the calculation of optimum spacing. This provides a preliminary indication of about how far apart expressways should be spaced. How this formula was invented is described later in this chapter.

System planning principles are then brought forward; these are the basic rules of thumb which indicate how segments should be linked up to form a network. System planning principles and optimum spacing are the two theoretical constraints which the planner must attempt to balance against the realities of the site in which he is working.

In addition, principles for the joint planning of land use and transportation facilities have to be brought into play. These principles deal with the spaces enclosed by transportation facilities and with lineal relationships between transportation facilities and land uses.

The trial plans themselves are then prepared. This may be done either as an assembly of completely independent plans (that is, Plan A is drawn up and then set aside while Plan B is drawn) or as a compilation of individual links forming a composite network (see Chapter XI) very rich in possible expressway corridors, from which all the plans which are ever going to be tested will be derived. In either case, the corridors proposed are subjected to detailed and exhaustive review on large-scale maps by planners and engineers representing the local governments of the area. At the conclusion of this step, various expressway networks can be readied for testing.

Transit and arterial street plans may be prepared at the same time as expressway plans or this work may be done later. Much depends upon the size of the urban area and the probable scope of the future transit system. In the largest cities transit planning should, if possible, proceed in parallel with expressway planning. In small cities, with fewer expressways likely, plans for arterials assume greater importance and should be prepared and tested along with expressway plans.

In the following pages these basic operations are described in greater detail.

Assembling Materials for Planning

As the transportation planner gets ready for the preparation and testing of plans, the kinds of materials which he needs begin to change, even though he is still working at the scale of metropolitan systems. Data collected by the major inventories of a transportation study and processed by machine to yield the regular relationships needed for research and forecasting are only partially useful when it comes to searching for good locations for expressway corridors. For such work, mapped data are required showing the exact physical boundaries of certain major cultural and physical features. These materials describe the realities of the urban area being planned, and they obviously influence the locations of new facilities. If they are well and thoroughly prepared, they will save countless hours because the system designers can work with correct facts at their fingertips instead of having to rummage around for data, or worse, to guess.

A very brief description of key materials is given below.

1. *"Barriers" map.* This is a map of an urban area showing the precise boundaries of certain land uses which are recognized barriers to the construction of new transportation facilities. Among these land uses are cemeteries, railroad lines and yards, public and private institutions, bodies of water and wetlands, airports, parks, forest preserves, and scenic and soil conservation areas.

2. *Planned land uses map.* This is a map showing plans for

future land uses, including residential neighborhoods, redevelopment areas, school "enrollment areas," and plans for institutional expansions.

3. *Regional transportation influences map.* This is a small-scale map showing the region extending out about 100 miles in all directions from the urban area being planned and showing major transportation routes, cities according to their sizes, and regional recreation areas.

4. *Urban transportation facilities.* This is a map showing expressways, arterial streets, rail transit lines, railroad lines, airports, and port facilities—in short, all physical transportation facilities except local streets.

5. *Detailed maps and/or air photos.* Detailed maps of land use, or air photos, at a scale of 1 inch = 400 feet or larger, are needed for evaluation of the practicality of corridor locations.

6. *Future land uses and population densities.* Sound twenty-year forecasts of future land use and population location are needed. Especially important are firm plans for extensions of land uses found in the barriers map.

7. *Future trip-making.* Twenty-year estimates of vehicle and person trip-making, the latter by mode of travel, are needed to define the quantity of roads and expressways which are needed.

8. *Previous plans.* A map compiling previous plans for transportation facilities, whether built or not, is a useful adjunct for planning.

9. *"Committed" plans.* In any given urban area, there will generally be a number of expressways or arterials which are, to a greater or lesser degree, committed to be built. The depth of the commitment will vary substantially, ranging from public statements of officials or the expenditure of funds for engineering design to the purchase of right-of-way. It is important to know about these "committed" facilities, although it seems most sensible never to accept any proposed facility as committed unless right-of-way has been purchased.

Except for item 5 preceding, all of these materials need to be assembled before planning can start. Item 7 preceding must be obtained before optimum spacings can be calculated.

Optimum Spacing

The main theme of the preceding chapter was the development of methods for connecting goals with plans in some rigorous fashion. This same idea, in microcosm, was the driving force behind the development of a better method for producing trial expressway systems for testing. To draw plans intelligently, that is, with cold reason and not intuitively, there must be an understanding of how the plan will work to achieve the goals which dominate the problem. There has to be reasoning behind the placement of each link, as much as there is in measuring the performance of an entire plan.

In reasoning toward an expressway plan, there are two critical questions that have to be answered. First, what kind of pattern should expressways form—grid, ring-and-radial, or some other regular or irregular pattern? Second, how many expressways should there be? This latter question is really a question of finding the correct spacing between expressways, since quantity (that is, length) is a direct function of spacing. More specifically, average spacing is defined by the formula

$$z = \frac{2A}{l},$$

where z is average spacing, A is the land area in question, and l is the length of expressways in that area.

In this section, attention is concentrated upon the study of spacing, leaving the discussion of patterns to a later part of this chapter. However, in order to study spacing, a particular pattern has to be assumed. The easiest pattern to work with is the grid. Fortunately, as will be shown, the grid and its relative, the warped grid, are from many points of view good patterns to adopt for major roadway systems. As a result, the conclusions drawn from theoretical studies of spacing have good transference to the real world.

The question of finding the best quantity, or spacing, of arterials and expressways was first formally raised in the Chicago study. As usual, the abstract question had a very specific origin. Two north-

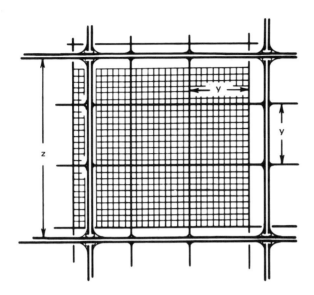

Figure 44.
Hypothetical gridded network showing arterial (y)
and expressway (z) spacing.

south expressways in the Chicago area seemed to be fixed at a distance of ten miles apart. One of these was the Dan Ryan Expressway. The other would be a new facility, running north and south along the line of the Des Plaines River, which had been proposed as an expressway as far back as 1946. Given these two facilities, it was logical to ask whether there should be zero, one, two, or three paralleling expressways between them. On what basis should a decision be made?

This question could then be generalized. Suppose, for example, that a city existed in which there were only local residential streets in existence, spaced grid fashion one-tenth mile apart on the average. A planner is given the assignment of superimposing a network of arterials and another network of expressways upon the grid of local streets. He is constrained to plan these major networks in a grid, as illustrated in Figure 44.

There are certain things which can realistically be assumed about these networks and the trips that use them. For example, the relative travel speeds attainable on each network can be estimated or measured. Speeds of fifteen, twenty-five, and sixty miles per hour may be found respectively on local, arterial, and expressway types.

The costs of building each of the types of roads can be estimated, based upon experience with building such roads. Local streets, for example, might cost $100,000 per mile to build while arterials and expressways might cost $500,000 and $5,000,000 per mile respectively.

The part of the urban area being studied produces trips at a known number of trip destinations per mile. Alternatively, future trip generation can be estimated. An area with a population of 5,000 persons per gross square mile may produce 10,000 to 12,000 person trip or 7,000 to 8,000 vehicle trip destinations per day.

These trips will, however, not all be of the same length. Some will be so short that they cannot use expressways unless they are spaced extremely close together. A typical trip length frequency distribution will be as follows:

Trip Length	Percentage of All Trips
< 2 miles	45%
2–4	22
4–6	12
6–8	8
8–10	6
10–12	3
12–14	2
14–16	1
> 16	1

All these trips take time and time has a value which can be assumed to be constant for all trips, regardless of their lengths. Each traveler, however, seeks to minimize the time of his own journey, and if he can, he will use a higher-speed facility in order to save time. We can include, within the single measure of time, other costs such as accident costs and vehicle operating costs.

Clearly, if it is desired to minimize the costs of all the travelers using the three networks, expressways would be built at impossibly close spacings (e.g., one-tenth mile apart) because on such roads travelers can drive most quickly and safely. On the other hand, if it is desired to minimize construction costs, no arterials or expressways would be built at all, since the least expensive streets are local ones.

The appropriate goal, therefore, seemed to be to minimize the sum of travel and construction costs since these represent the total transportation cost borne by the community, paid both through taxes and individually.

Accordingly, the total transportation costs for the part of the urban area under consideration were stated mathematically. The minimum cost spacing could then be found by differentiation, and the following formula gives the minimum cost, or optimum, spacing of expressways.[1]

$$z = 2.24 \sqrt{\frac{C_z}{KDV_{yz}P_s}},$$

where z = optimum expressway spacing in miles;
C_z = construction and right-of-way cost of expressways in dollars per mile;
K = a constant capitalizing the value of time;
D = number of trip destinations per square mile;
V_{yz} = $(1/V_y - 1/V_z)$ where V_y and V_z are respective speeds on arterials and expressways in miles per hour;
P_s = $\Sigma^{\infty}_{i(\beta)} F_i$, or that proportion of trips whose length is greater than β, which is the length where trips start to use expressways for some portion of their journeys.

When the optimum spacing formula was applied to different parts of the Chicago area, results were obtained which are shown in Table 19. These results were based on estimated 1980 vehicle trip

---

[1] Roger L. Creighton *et al.*, "Estimating Efficient Spacing for Arterials and Expressways," Highway Research Board Bulletin 253, Washington, D.C., 1960. For a later and more polished version of the derivation of the optimum spacing formula, see Chicago Area Transportation Study, *Final Report,* III (1962). 121–123. The mathematical solution to the optimum spacing problem should be credited to Morton Schneider.

densities because the formula was being used to calculate spacing estimates for the long-range plan for the Chicago area. The minimum cost spacings vary between 2.7 and 7.0 miles, as a function of the densities, speeds, and costs given in the table.

It is possible to give these numbers more meaning in everyday terms. Ring 3 in the Chicago area is an area with a population density of approximately forty families per net residential acre, which is dense apartment-style living. In such an area, expressways at 1956

Table 19. *Minimum Cost Spacing Determinants and Results, Chicago Area, 1*

Ring	Mean Distance From Loop (miles)	Vehicle Trip Destinations per Square Mile (thousands)	Expressway Speed (miles per hour)	Arterial Speed (miles per hour)	Expressway Cost per Mile (millions)	Minimu Cost Spacings Express (miles
2	3.5	28.7	45	15	$11	2.7
3	5.5	25.3	45	15	10	2.8
4	8.5	19.6	50	15	8	2.9
5	11.5	13.4	50	20	6	4.0
6	16.0	9.0	50	25	5	6.3
7	24.0	6.2	50	25	4	7.0

Source: Highway Research Board Bulletin 253.

costs and values of time should be spaced about three miles apart. In ring 6, population density is about six families per acre, which averages out to single-family development on 7,000–square foot lots. In such a region expressways should be spaced about six miles apart.

By examining the formula carefully, it is possible to develop some generalizations about spacing.

1. If the construction cost per mile of expressways rises, expressways should be spaced farther apart.

2. If the cost of travel increases (for example, if people's time becomes worth more), then it is better to build expressways closer together.

3. Where the densities of vehicular trip-making are high, expressways should be spaced closer together.

4. If trips become longer on the average, expressways should be built closer together.

5. If the speed of travel on arterial streets is increased (for example, through superior traffic management), then expressways should be built farther apart.

An Alternative Method. An alternative means of solving the optimum spacing problem was developed as a check. A simple graphical approach was used which, by arraying costs at various expressway spacings, permitted the observer to determine the least-cost solution by inspection.

The method graphed expressway construction costs per square mile and travel costs per square mile. Construction costs per square mile could be obtained by the formula

$$C_z = \frac{2A \text{ (cost per mile)}}{\text{spacing in miles}},$$

and travel costs per square mile could be obtained by the formula

$$T = DK(t_z + t_o),$$

where T = travel costs per square mile;

D = number of trip destinations per square mile;

K = value of time, capitalized for anticipated life of expressways;

t_z = travel time on expressways (mean expressway trip length divided by expressway speed);

t_o = travel time on other roads (mean trip length off expressways divided by nonexpressway driving speeds).

The sum of travel costs and construction costs was total transportation cost for a region, and this is what we wanted to minimize.

The key to determining these costs lay in finding out what proportion of each trip would use expressways. The proportionate use of expressways was obviously going to be affected by expressway spacing. How could we determine the use which trips of different lengths would make of local streets, arterials, and expressways at different spacings of these roads? Analytically, this is a very difficult problem which has not yet been solved satisfactorily for gridded expressway systems.[2]

We could approximate the distance traveled on local streets by computing the average distance each trip would have to travel on a gridded local street system in order to get to the nearest arterial street. This was a laborious process, involving counting little segments of local streets and computing the averages of distances which would have to be traveled, for we could assume an even distribution of trip ends and we could assume that all trips were long enough to reach an arterial street. This method unfortunately broke down when dealing with an expressway system. Many trips were so short that they could not use an expressway. Others were long enough, but the locations of their origins or destinations clearly influenced their choice, and these locations were random and trip directions were scattered. So our analytical attempts failed.

Another approach had some appeal. This was a process which copied the idea of the mathematician who determined the value of π by dropping needles on a floor ruled with many parallel lines spaced one needle's length apart. By counting the times when the needle touched one of the parallel lines, he was able to calculate the value of π since π enters into the equation which describes the angle at which the needle falls with respect to the parallel lines.

To conduct our experiment, we ruled off a large sheet of paper into a series of grids, one grid representing the local street system, another the arterial system, and a third an expressway system. Then, by taking sticks of different lengths, cut to represent air-line trips of two, four, six, eight, and ten miles, we made a large number of drops of these different sticks upon the surface of the paper. This was done at random. For each such drop, the distance was measured which the trip would make over each of three different street systems in order to reach its destination in the shortest possible time.

By this device, we prepared a graph (see Figure 45) which

[2] For a solution to parallel expressway systems, see W. Stearns Caswell, "A Theoretical Model for Determination of Expressway Usage in a Uniform System," Highway Research Board Record 238, Washington, D.C., 1968.

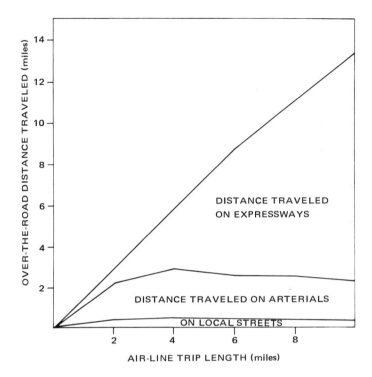

Figure 45.
Use of local streets, arterials, and expressways by trips of
different air-line lengths.

showed the proportions of trips of different air-line lengths on local
streets, arterials, and expressways. As can be seen, the results show
a reasonable pattern. Trips of all lengths pass a short distance on
local streets and a longer distance on arterials. As trips become
longer, however, all of their extra travel is placed on the expressway
system.

Two examples of the graphical method of determining minimum cost spacing are shown in Figures 46 and 47. The first example
(Figure 46) is for an area with 20,000 vehicle trip destinations per
square mile, expressways costing $8,000,000 per mile, and express-
way and arterial speeds of fifty and twelve miles per hour respective-

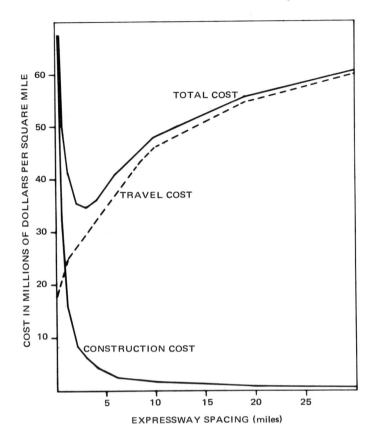

Figure 46.
Minimum cost spacing in a high-density region.

ly. This corresponds approximately with the data for ring 4 in Chicago. In the second example (Figure 47) there are 6,200 vehicle trip destinations per square mile, expressways cost $4,000,000 per mile, and expressway and arterial speeds are fifty and twenty miles per hour respectively. This corresponds approximately to ring 7 in Chicago. As can be seen from the graphs, the lowest cost points compare very closely with the results obtained using the optimum spacing formula.

For the nonmathematician, these graphs tell the story of optimum spacing very well. Close to the left-hand side of the graph, where expressways are spaced very closely together, total costs are extremely high because so much money is needed for construction. At the right-hand side of the graph, travel costs are very high because most travel must be driven on arterials and local streets when expressways are ten or more miles apart. In between, there is a point where the sum of travel and construction costs is least. This is the optimum spacing for expressways.

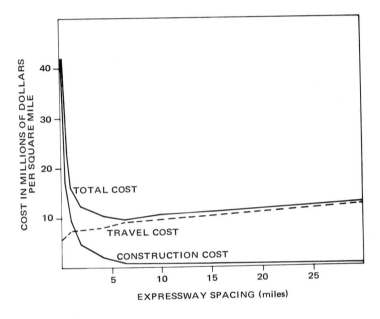

Figure 47.
Minimum cost spacing in a low-density region.

This minimum cost point is very sharply defined in high-density areas. In contrast, at suburban densities the minimum cost point is not so sharply defined. This suggests that it is relatively much more important to stick close to the optimum in high-density areas; at suburban densities it is possible to have a little more latitude in spacing, and considerations other than transportation economics may bear more weight.

Optimum Spacing: Conclusion. Optimum spacing is important to transportation planning for two reasons. First, it gives the planner a tool for making preliminary estimates of the optimum size of a transportation plan, through the successive application of the formula to parts of an urban area having different densities. Second, and more important, it shows that a rigorous connection can be made between a physical plan and the goal of minimizing total transportation costs. The optimum spacing device actually was developed before the linkage of goals with plans described in the preceding chapter, and played its part in creating that linkage.

These were significant gains, but the use of the formula itself must not be overplayed. The formula is an approximative device for use in preliminary planning, most applicable in metropolitan areas estimating a twenty-year population over a million. In an isolated city of less than 250,000, the formula is not very useful. For other cautionary statements, the reader is referred to the original documents.

Principles of Network Planning

Given a set of approximations of the best spacings between expressways, the next task in preparing trial plans is to link segments of expressways together to form either alternative networks or a composite network—both for testing purposes. (The definition of a composite network will be given in Chapter XI.) To combine expressway segments meaningfully, one must be aware not only of the best spacing but also of the principles of network design.

Large-scale network design was something few people had thought about at the time of the Chicago study. Very few people had devoted any time to this subject or had seen the need for good patterns of linking together the individual segments of roads which engineers were building with such care and skill. Most people were not even aware of the existence of networks as networks, let alone the idea of designing them in some superior fashion. We sat down, therefore, and began to develop a set of principles for the planning of expressway networks.[3] This work went forward in the Niagara Frontier[4] and other reports on this subject have since been issued.[5] The danger of this discussion comes from the realization that some readers may interpret these principles as unbreakable rules. A principle, in the sense of being "a settled course of action" (Webster) or a settled manner of design, is derived from a chain or process of reasoning, of which the principle is merely the short-hand statement of conclusion. Quite obviously, principles are untrustworthy guides for action to the person who does not know the background reasoning. In the real world the factors are more complex than in that limited, abstract world in which the principle is developed. Two-dimensional reasoning, thrust into an n-dimensional world, must often be upset.

Nevertheless, having statements of principles is necessary for the quick conveyance of certain ideas about design, so that these ideas can be used as rules of thumb against which to measure a portion of a trial plan as good or bad. In an area where there is so little knowledge, these ideas cry out to be articulated, even though imperfectly.

Principles of Expressway Planning. The first principle of expressway design is continuity. Transportation systems are lines for movement, and continuous, direct movement is made most easily over facilities which do not jog, but rather sweep or flow through an urban area. Stops, enforced changes in direction, or adverse travel are things which are undesirable *from the transportation viewpoint.* Other forces may require this principle to be compromised, but compromise here all too frequently results in problems which have to be

[3] Chicago Area Transportation Study, *Final Report,* III (Transportation Plan), 36–38.

[4] George T. Lathrop, "Principles for Urban Transportation Network Planning," Upstate New York Transportation Studies, Albany, November, 1962.

[5] "System Considerations for Urban Freeways," Institute of Traffic Engineers, Washington, D.C., October, 1967. See also Herbert S. Levinson and Kenneth R. Roberts, "System Configurations in Urban Transportation Planning," paper presented at the Forty-third Annual Meeting of the Highway Research Board, Washington, D.C., January 14, 1964.

alleviated later at substantial cost. Thus, the first principle looks like this:

As single expressways are put together to form systems, certain principles must be followed which limit the ways in which they can intersect with one another.

One general rule is that the design of an intersection should allow a driver to go in any direction he wishes. There is nothing so frustrating to the motorist as to find, when he gets to a major interchange, that there is some place he cannot go. Whenever this rule is violated, some conditions will change which will make the original designer wish he had been more generous.

Another rule of expressway interchange design concerns "lane balance." The number of lanes of expressways entering an interchange should be the same as those leaving it.

Because of the design requirements of interchanges (grades, minimum curves, sight distances, and weaving and merging distances), it is possible to design three-legged and four-legged interchanges.

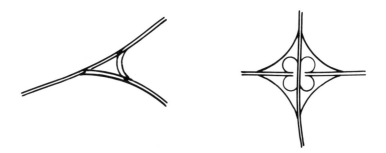

Five- or six-legged expressway-to-expressway interchanges, however, should be avoided. They are almost impossible to design without creating very confusing situations to the motorist and dangerously short and congestion-producing weaving distances.

These restrictions on the number of legs emanating on expressway-to-expressway interchange are very important because they limit systems so severely.

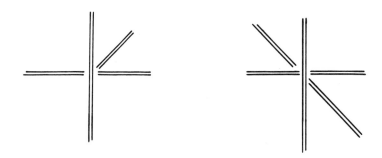

In addition to continuity and interchange principles, there is the principle of even distribution of investment. This is implicit in optimum spacing but needs to be restated because this principle is so often violated. Expressways are built to serve people—to serve people where they are living and working, but with a fair share all round. Thus it is unwise to have expressways crowded together in some places and spaced too far apart in other areas, as shown below.

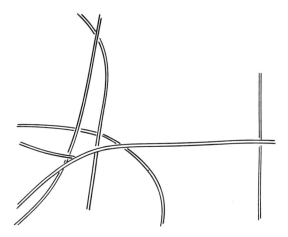

It is much better to have a fairly even distribution of service, as shown below.

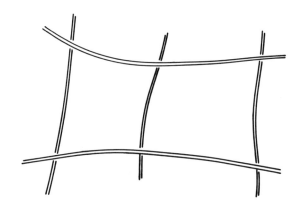

If a city or region were developed at one single density, the foregoing principles, in combination, indicate that a grid system of expressways would be the best.

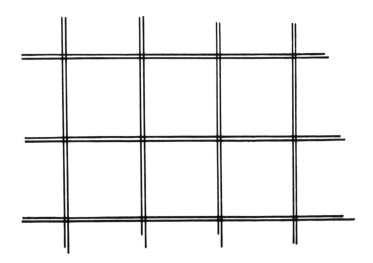

The grid is that system which provides continuity and even service to land area for the least length. No other regular, geometric form exists which competes with the grid. Triangular figures are plagued with six-legged interchanges; hexagonal figures lack travel continuity, although they are, in length-to-area ratio, more efficient.

However, urban areas are not built at uniform densities and so departures from the grid are necessary, since in those parts of the urban area where trip-end densities are higher, expressways must be built closer together. (In the very densest parts of large cities, additional systems such as mass transportation systems may need to be added in order to carry the very highest peaks of travel.) The regular system which satisfies these needs for urban areas whose densities peak at the center is the ring-and-radial system.

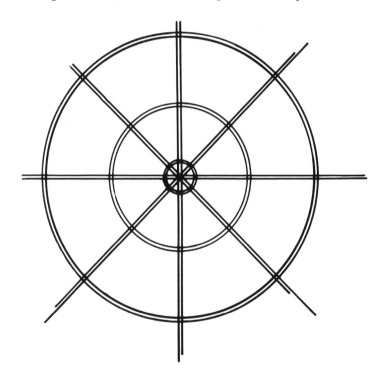

The difficulty with the ring-and-radial system is that it tends to concentrate traffic at the core of the city. Concentration of vehicular traffic on segments of road systems is to be avoided; dispersion is much the better principle. Obviously, any ring-and-radial which had all radials intersecting at the very core would be an impossible situation, but the often proposed radial terminating in a "ring road" around the city's core is not much better, because the ring road tends to become overcrowded both by those who want to go to the center and those who wish to cross to the other side of the city.

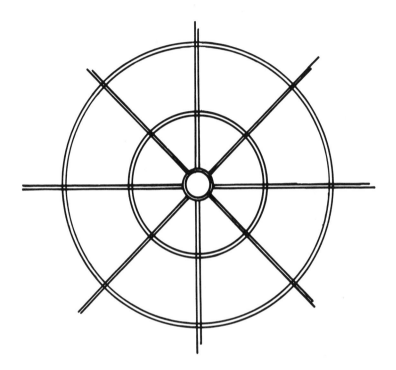

The best solution to this dilemma, from a systems viewpoint, is the warped grid. The warped grid is not a rigid geometric figure, but one which is adapted to each local situation.

The idea of the warped grid is that in regions of higher density the links in a grid are pulled in more closely to the center, at reduced spacing. This preserves continuity, maintains four-legged interchanges, and allows for optimum spacing according to the density in each part of the region. Warping the grid calls for great skill in design, so that an ideal can be fitted ingeniously to the city, within available rights-of-way, and can incorporate the inevitable pre-existing radial from a distant city or some other perturbation caused by previous lack of planning.

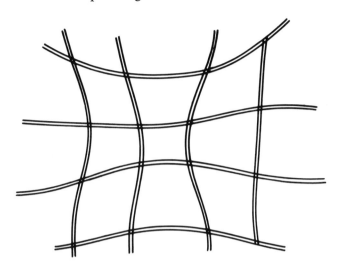

In fitting a network to an urban area, some specific rules of thumb are worth noting.

1. It is preferable not to have Y intersections of expressways in which the bottom of the Y is pointed toward the central business district of the city or toward an area of markedly higher density. This tends to overcrowd that part of the network, since two facilities are pouring their traffic into one. It is much better to divide an expressway as it moves toward the core, so as to disperse traffic in areas where there are more trip ends per square mile.

2. In proposing T interchanges, it is preferable (although not always possible) not to point the top of the T toward a part of the

city having higher density, because this will usually create adverse travel or a heavy unloading onto arterials.

3. Jogged interchanges are to be avoided wherever possible; they represent adverse travel and excess investment where the two facilities have a common link.

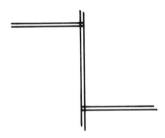

4. It is inadvisable to construct expressways with more than eight lanes. Investing too much money in one roadway is like having too many expressways cramped into one part of a city; it is better to provide an even distribution of service to all parts of an urban area. Expressways with more than eight lanes have the added disadvantage that vehicles have to be brought too far to fill it, and this means unnecessary travel which could be avoided if there were a better distribution of investment.

In addition to the foregoing rules, the network designer must be conscious of the interchanges each expressway link will have with other streets. The spacing of these interchanges is governed by very practical requirements of the flow of vehicles on expressways and the carrying abilities of the streets to which the expressways are connected. The following two rules are generally observed.

1. Interchanges between arterials and expressways in urban areas should not be less than one mile apart. However, at or near a

central business district, where the expressway is being used deliberately as a distributor facility with its high-speed, traffic-carrying function definitely submerged to the distribution function, on-and-off ramps may be located at closer intervals than one mile. The purpose of setting a lower limit to the frequency of interchanges is to reduce the turbulence to traffic flow caused by decelerating and accelerating movements.

As densities decline, interchanges should be spaced more widely, but not more than three miles apart within an urban area. The spacing should be determined by density, since it is desirable to keep the traffic volumes discharged onto arterial streets at a manageable level. Also, the objective of building expressways is to get an optimum amount of traffic (the optimum being determined by the least total transportation cost) onto the expressway, and this traffic cannot use expressways unless there are convenient interchange points.

2. The only streets which should be permitted to intersect with expressways are major streets (arterials). Traffic volumes would quickly submerge a collector or local street if that were used as the road interchanging with an expressway.

Principles of Arterial System Design. The long-range planning of arterial street systems is one of the weakest spots in the planning of American cities or transportation systems. A combination of forces has thrust them into the background. Already pointed out in Chapter VI was the lack of a consistent understanding of *systems* of transportation facilities. In addition to this difficulty, arterial streets in urban areas are divided between state, county, and local governments, none of which generally has responsibility for all major streets. Attention of state transportation agencies is naturally drawn to the largest facilities—the federally aided interstate and primary systems. The counties and cities, on the other hand, have had inadequate funds, nor has the need for long-range arterial system planning been adequately recognized.

Adequate studies should be made of arterial systems, especially in the growing parts of metropolitan areas where actions can be taken *in advance* to provide rights-of-way, to preserve set-backs, and to control development to the mutual advantage of the driver and the residential and nonresidential property owner. These studies are important because the arterial system, no matter how efficient the expressway network, will continue to carry 40–50 percent of the vehicle miles of travel in urban areas.

Such studies should normally be undertaken after a major transportation study has been completed which defines the expressway system for a metropolitan area. There are cases, as we found in Rochester, when it is necessary to test alternative arterial systems in certain critical parts of the city in order to find the best expressway system. But generally the largest system is planned first. Then attention can be given to the arterial system, and a declared public policy can be established on which streets will be arterials and where new rights-of-way will have to be dedicated. Once the future arterial system has been defined, actions can be taken to preserve its ability to move traffic and land uses can be adjusted to conform.

As in expressway planning, four principles should dominate the design of arterial street systems. These principles apply whether the system being planned is an existing system or a totally new one.

1. Arterial streets should have the quality of continuity.

2. The spacing of arterial streets should reflect the density of trip production, with tighter spacing in dense areas and looser

Table 20. *Approximate Volumes of Traffic on Arterials and Local Streets as Functions of Arterial Spacing and Density of Trip Destinations*

Daily Trip Destinations per Square Mile	½ mile Arterial Spacing		1 mile Arterial Spacing		1½ mile Arterial Spacing	
	Arterial Volumes	Local Street Volumes	Arterial Volumes	Local Street Volumes	Arterial Volumes	Local Street Volumes
10,000	7,000	230	13,000	430	18,000	600
15,000	10,500	345	19,500	645	27,000	900
20,000	14,000	460	26,000	860	36,000	1200
25,000	17,500	575	32,500	1075	45,000	1500

Note: These volumes are based on the assumption that 50 percent of the nonlocal vehicle miles of travel will be carried by expressways and that arterials will be able to carry the indicated load without becoming congested and forcing traffic back onto local streets.
Source: CATS, *Final Report,* vol. III (1962), Table 5.

spacing in low-density areas (see Table 20). Allowance must be made for the proportion of trips going by transit and the proportion of vehicle miles of travel expected to be driven on expressways.

3. Intersections of two arterials should be at right angles.

4. There should be no five- or six-way intersections.

These principles imply an arterial system in the form of a grid, although the grid need not be rigid. An arterial system should be warped to fit topography, changing densities of development, major land uses, historical areas, and the location of major generators of traffic. The basic system must allow easy movement in all directions for medium-length trips. Arterial streets should, of course, be the ones which connect with the ramps of expressways or parkways.

These principles of arterial system design are based on certain assumptions about the type of roadway being built. The arterial is conceived primarily as a four-lane roadway within a right-of-way adequate to permit the construction of left-turning lanes at arterial-to-arterial intersections. While the original roadway may only be two lanes wide throughout most of its length, its right-of-way, placement of driveways and sidewalks, and street tree planting should always be such as to permit easy reconstruction to four-lane width. The six-lane arterial almost always exists where there are not enough paralleling arterials or where there are discontinuities. The ideal should be to plan arterial systems so as to disperse traffic rather than to concentrate it in expensive, and hard-to-manage, superarterials.

Principles for Joint Planning of Land Use and Transportation

It is important in the course of expressway and arterial planning to think not only of systems considerations, but also of the relationships between the roadways which are being planned and the land uses which occupy the spaces between and adjacent to the roadways. Land uses are, after all, the activities which are being served by the roadways and it is important in serving them not to harm or destroy them. This is not to say that there can be no changes in land use, but rather that transportation planning should be sensitive to the requirements of people in their site-based activities.

In the following paragraphs it is possible to mention only a few general principles for the joint planning of land use and transportation. These principles deal basically with two types of questions: the viability of areas within the mesh of expressway and arterial systems, and the relationships of arterials to abutting properties. It is not possible to discuss here the design or aesthetic relationships between roadways and land uses—a field with a rapidly growing literature. Also, it is not possible to discuss the layout of local (as contrasted with arterial) road systems within the residential, commercial, or industrial districts which are bounded by arterials.

The Enclosed Spaces. An important principle of joint land use and transportation planning is that the spaces which exist within the mesh formed by major roadways should be areas which can readily contain efficient and pleasant groupings of activities or land uses.

This principle is not hard to attain within an expressway network; the spaces which are enclosed by expressways when they are at their optimum spacings are much larger than commonly thought. They can support almost any conceivable combination of uses. In the city of Chicago, for example, expressways spaced three miles apart (near-optimum spacing) will bound nine square miles of territory and a population of 150,000–200,000 persons. This is a small city in its own right. In suburban areas of metropolitan Chicago, expressways spaced five miles apart will normally bound 100,000 or more population. Parenthetically, in the former case the expressways will take up about 3 percent of the land area while in the latter case about 2 percent.

When it comes to the arterial network, more care has to be exercised, but arterials can usually be designed to bound viable groupings of land uses. Spacing and density are closely interrelated, so that there is a mutual influence between land use and network.

Most often people think in terms of the residential neighborhood as the basic land use building block. The residential neighborhood should be planned so that through traffic is discouraged from traversing the neighborhood. A population of 5,000 persons will usually have enough children to support an elementary school, which can be located at the neighborhood center so that small children do not have to cross any of the arterial streets which bound the neighborhood. At higher densities (20,000 persons or more per square mile) such a neighborhood can be planned within an arterial system spaced at half-mile intervals. At suburban densities a neighborhood can readily be accommodated within the space bounded by arterials spaced one mile apart.

For commercial and industrial districts a greater freedom is possible. Both types of land use require arterials to bring people and goods near their buildings. Hence, the arterials may need to penetrate the commercial or industrial area. However, in the case of shopping centers, governmental centers, institutional areas, and central business districts, there is a distinct trend toward creating traffic-free islands or even platforms which are separated from arterials to permit more pleasant and efficient carrying-on of the activities located thereon.

Fortunately, with a well-planned expressway system, the arterials which are spaced conveniently from the land use viewpoint are also spaced at intervals which give them traffic volumes that are not excessive. As shown in Table 20, traffic volumes vary as a function of spacing and of the number of trip origins (or destinations) generated per square mile.

One of the key principles of joint land use and arterial planning is that there must be enough miles of arterials (in other words, a fine enough spacing) so that traffic volumes do not overload arterials. If arterials do become overloaded, there is a strong possibility that traffic pressure will increase to the point where it "backs up" into neighborhood streets, with resulting increased danger to children and blighting effects upon property values. One of the benefits of a good expressway system is that it takes a heavy load off arterials—as much as 40 percent of all vehicle miles of travel, depending upon the part of the city being relieved.

Lineal Relationships with Land Uses. In addition to enclosing areas, arterials and expressways have an immediate relationship with adjoining land uses. This is a relationship which exists along the entire length of a roadway, and it consists of influences which the road and its traffic exert upon land uses and vice versa. Hence it may be called a lineal relationship.

In the case of expressways, the principal influence is from the expressway to adjoining land uses, because expressways are legally insulated by access-free ownership (and frequently by fencing) from interruptions to traffic flows. With careful design, landscaping, and adequate right-of-way harmful influences such as noise and air pollution can be held to acceptable levels. Increasing care is being applied to design of urban expressways and also to the coordination of building types and locations with the expressway design. Certainly joint design of land use and expressways is a desirable principle to follow.

Arterial streets have a more intimate relationship with land uses along their lengths and with the local streets and collectors which connect with them. This is because arterials have traditionally been dual-function roads, serving traffic and providing access to land uses. Consequently, arterials have to be planned not only as major traffic-carrying systems but also as integral elements of the urban community. Unfortunately, the incremental manner of urban growth is such that the design of arterials has been poor in its land use relationships as well as its relation to the system.

There are two obvious areas where improvements could be made in arterial–land use relationships. One is in limiting the number of local streets and collectors entering onto arterials, probably to not more than four per mile. From a traffic flow and safety viewpoint as well as from an aesthetic viewpoint, such an arrangement is likely to be superior to one in which residential streets debouch onto arterials at 300-foot intervals.

Second, land use planning should strive to minimize the number of activities which have direct access onto arterial roads. Commercial and industrial uses must, of course, be served by arterials. But any good planner can arrange a subdivision so that no residential units front on arterials; they should face onto interior roads. Where possible, extensive land uses such as golf courses, cemeteries, universities, and major industries should border arterials; these uses need only one or two driveways and the rest of the arterial frontage can be left friction-free for traffic.

Laying Out Trial Plans

When the necessary materials have been assembled and optimum spacings calculated, it is possible to proceed with the task of laying out plans to be tested by computer. This is a task of synthesis: combining the influences collectively imposed by optimum spacing, network and land use design principles, and the realities of land use and pre-existing expressway and transit lines.

The initial layouts should be made on small-scale maps, at the scale of 1 inch = 1 mile or smaller. This will often require weeks of work to produce an adequate range of plans for testing. Those who do this should not attempt to develop a best plan but should strive to define the realistic options and strategies which need to be tested by computer. In preparing initial layouts, all previous plans should be assembled and carefully considered. It is also important for those who do these metropolitan designs to have a thorough understanding of the area, such as can only be obtained by many hours of driving through the area.

Once the initial layouts have been made on maps at the metropolitan scale, they should be transferred to large-scale maps or aerial photographs (1 inch = 400 feet or larger). Each link must then be examined on these maps to determine the impact of the new highways and to estimate problems of land takings, relocation, connections with the arterial system, and costs. These detailed studies should be done in close cooperation with local and state officials, whose programs may relate to or be affected by any of the new links to be tested. The object of this scrutiny is to uncover all the facts and issues, not to find trouble-free links, because there are none.

Each of the plans is then documented. Each route is described, with what factors suggest or dictate its location, how well it intersects with other streets and expressways, how it fits in with plans for the city, what it means to various neighborhoods, and how it relates to parks and playgrounds. This documentation should be printed in a staff report.

It is extremely important for there to be careful and thorough documentation of data and thinking as the process of preparing trial plans goes forward. Transportation plans do not come with the flash of genius or inspiration. The real "pro" at the business knows the fallibility of his memory and the possibility that he may not be around to complete the process; therefore he leaves a clear track for his followers. This is not to suggest that rules should be followed rigidly or that the ideas and practices presented here should be followed like a formula. But in planning large public works it is an insult to the public not to have in the files a full explanation of the reasoning behind a plan.

XI

THE TESTING MECHANISM

Given any trial expressway plan such as might be prepared by methods suggested in the preceding chapter, there remains the task of determining, as rigorously as possible, whether it will be able to carry the traffic of some future year, or whether parts of it will develop excessive traffic loads. Equally important, the plan has to be examined to see whether as a policy for public investment it is better than other plans.

If it were possible to time-machine oneself into the future, or better yet into a series of alternative futures, one could observe conditions resulting from the construction of different transportation systems. One could count accidents and measure time spent in travel, the costs of operating vehicles over a highway network, and the costs of building and maintaining a highway network. These results could then be used to evaluate alternative networks.

Time machines obviously do not exist; yet the need to test alternative plans remains. So the future has to be simulated and with a great deal of accuracy and care. Although this is a costly and difficult process, it is clearly less expensive than trial and error. From the simulations the same kinds of measurements of the costs of accidents, time, operating costs, and capital costs can be made as if one were evaluating the performance of today's transportation system.

Basically, the idea of testing was not new to transportation in 1957–58, nor was it a practice limited to the field of transportation. All kinds of planning operations and decision-making processes employ the concept of testing. For example, a businessman considering whether to borrow money will calculate his interest costs under alternative financing plans. An engineer will calculate how many hundredths of an inch key parts of a bridge will deflect or deform under expected loads. These might be called "if-then" calculations: "*If* I do something, *then* this will be the consequence." Testing is the calculated predetermination (not by trial and error) of expected future performance of any system or phenomenon. Implicit is the idea that after the consequences have been determined they will be evaluated against some given goal or set of goals.

In the Chicago study and later transportation studies, testing attained a formal status and importance in the planning process which set a whole new standard for transportation planning. And this new standard, in its turn, stands as a challenge to metropolitan and regional planning.

To appreciate the improved standards of testing, we have to look at the tests made by transportation studies prior to 1955. Typically, origin-destination data would be gathered and traffic counts would be made. Street capacities would be compared with traffic counts. From these data, indications of needs—present and future —would be obtained and plans would be prepared, but rarely more than two or three. Traffic flows on proposed expressways would be estimated, but not for other streets. Some adjustments would be made to the expressway layout on the basis of the traffic volume forecast, and the plan would then be frozen. Subsequently, benefit-cost ratios might be calculated, but these would be used mainly to establish priorities rather than for purposes of justifying the plan.

The failures of these early procedures were the following:

1. They did not demonstrate whether a greater or lesser amount of new construction would be better for an area.

2. So few plans had traffic assigned to them that no proof was presented that a better plan did not exist.

3. The methods of expressway traffic estimation did not take into account changes in origin-destination patterns likely to be caused by expressway-induced changes in accessibility.

4. The methods of expressway traffic estimation did not provide feedbacks which would simulate the effects of congestion upon drivers' choice of routes.

5. The testing mechanism did not relate plan performance to goals.

In sum, the testing procedures of those times determined only a very few consequences of proposed actions; these were mainly the traffic consequences, and these in turn were limited to the new roads being planned. This is not meant to disparage what was done in those years, but simply to point out that the testing of early plans was not conclusive. Again, this does not mean that the plans produced were bad, but simply that they were not proven to be the best.

The preceding failings were eliminated and positive results achieved in their place as a result of the work of the Chicago study. Instead of dealing only with a limited expressway network, *all* of the inventoried arterial street system was included in the traffic estimation procedure. The effects of traffic congestion were taken into account, both on expressways and arterials. The hypothesized existence of a planned route would alter origin-destination patterns, as might be expected. The testing mechanism was rapid enough—and gained in speed in later studies—so that many plans could be tested. And lastly, the performance of each plan could be read off in terms of the goal of minimizing the sum of all transportation costs and of its components of reducing accidents, reducing operating costs, saving time, and reducing capital expenditures.

Basic Logic

The basic logic of the testing mechanism is illustrated in Figure 48, and in the following paragraphs.

1. The process starts with files of data on magnetic tape which represent first, the network of streets and highways in an urban area and second, the numbers of vehicle trip origins and destinations in each zone in that urban area.

2. Next, a computer is programmed to determine, for each zone of origin, the paths through a street network which will be used by the vehicles starting from that zone and going to all other zones in the urban area.

3. The computer is then instructed to distribute vehicles out-

ward from each zone of origin to their destinations, over the paths previously selected. The computer stores in its memory the total number of vehicles that pass over each link of the network.

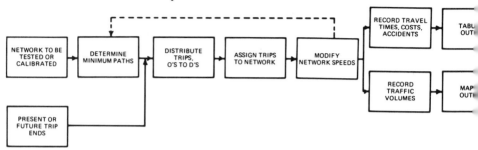

Figure 48.
Generalized travel simulation procedure.

4. Next, the computer modifies the speed of travel on each link as a function of the number of vehicles that have used the link. In the opportunity model, this modification is immediately fed back to that part of the operation which selects the paths from each zone to all destination zones.

5. At the conclusion of this process, the computer prepares magnetic tapes which contain the results of the simulation. These output tapes are then used to produce maps and tables which permit the plan to be evaluated.

In the following sections, the preceding listing of the major steps is amplified to give a more complete idea of the processes involved in simulation. The various steps are not, however, described in technical detail; for further information the reader is referred to the technical publications cited in the footnotes.

The Story of a Breakthrough: The Shortest Path through a Maze Algorithm

One of the crucial problems in simulation is to determine, in some reliable and very efficient manner, the way people move through a complex network from origin to destination. There are two reasons for needing to do this. First, the network of transportation facilities (whether a road or a transit network) is the only way by which people can move, and the paths which are chosen by people define the distances, times, and costs between different parts of a city and hence influence the destinations they are likely to select. Second, if a computer is to be instructed to assign vehicles or persons to a network, it must have rules which will enable it to select the right links for the vehicle or person to travel upon.

This is not a simple problem. Even in the smallest network the number of *possible* ways by which one can go even a few miles is astronomical. There are enormous numbers of combinations of paths, and a computer would have to grind for days if it tried to calculate them all. Man, being smarter, can zero in on a best path after a few days in a new city and even adjust to anticipated congestion at different hours of the day.

Prior to 1956-57 this problem had been handled only in the simplest of ways. Relationships between zones were calculated upon the basis of air-line distance—a fixed and unchanging quantity which could not be made sensitive to changes in speed or cost occasioned by the construction or improvement of transportation facilities. And, estimates of what paths drivers would take in going from origin to destination were made by hand, with the map as the principal tool. This was true even as late as the Detroit study. As a result, assignments of trips to networks had to be limited to relatively small systems, such as the expressway system, leaving out the much larger arterial network altogether.

In the Chicago study it was realized that these hand methods could not be tolerated any longer; a method was therefore sought for determining the paths people would choose which would include not only expressways (and rapid transit lines, in the transit world) but also *every major street* (and in the transit world, *every bus line*). This demand increased the size of the technical problem enormously. In the Chicago area with its 5,170,000 people in 1956 there were 2,800 miles of major streets, made up of at least 4,000 individual links. Some of these were two-way, some one-way. The number of possible ways in which a person could go from origin to destination was nearly infinite. What rules did people abide by in selecting their paths? How could this infinite number of possible paths be reduced to a very few paths or to a single path?

This became the subject of an intense effort. The study staff enlisted the aid of the Armour Research Foundation, and they produced, at first, two little gadgets. One of these was an electrical circuit made exactly like a small section of a street network, with a tiny neon bulb at each intersection. When two electrically charged probes were connected to the circuit—one at the origin of a trip and the other at the destination—the neon bulbs on the path of least resistance lit up. This was very effective as a demonstrator of the least-time or least-cost path, but it was too clumsy for large-scale use. Another device was a fishnet of string, made like a street network. Grasp two knots representing origin and destination and pull: the shortest path came taut and the rest of the network fell slack. This was not only cute, but accurate; but we could not pull $(500)^2/2$ knots and record the taut links.

Subsequently the people at Armour Research Foundation brought to our attention the existence of an algorithm (an algorithm is simply a method of notation or a procedure used to calculate a solution to a problem) capable of determining the shortest path through any maze or network. This algorithm had been invented by Moore shortly before.[1] They were given a contract to study this matter further, and in due course they reported back with a computer program which applied the minimum path algorithm to our problem of finding the shortest path between any origin and destination.

To illustrate how the minimum path algorithm works, consider the very small network shown in the following diagram. This network has only thirty-six links in it. (By contrast, the network of arterials in an urban area of a million population may have 2,500 links in it.) The time, in minutes, which it takes to traverse each link is printed beside the link.

What is the shortest path from A to B?

To find the shortest path from A to B, one starts out from A along each link emanating from A.

---

[1] Edward F. Moore, "The Shortest Path through a Maze," paper presented at the International Symposium on the Theory of Switching, Harvard University, 1957.

When reaching an intersection, one notes down at that intersection the time it took to traverse the link, plus an arrow pointing backwards along the path just used. Thus, at C, one would have an arrow pointing toward A, with time "2."

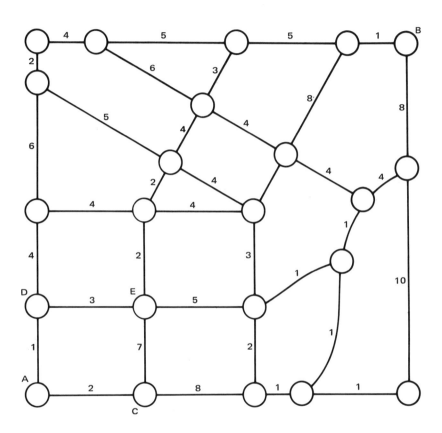

From each intersection which one has already reached, one starts out again, but this time, when reaching an intersection, one notes down the *cumulative* time it took to reach that intersection: thus, when going from C to E, one would draw an arrow at E pointing towards C, with the number "9," which is 2 plus 7.

However, when coming via D to E the cumulative time is 4, which is less than 9. Obviously, it is shorter to go from E to A via D than via C. So, one erases the arrow and the number at E, inserting the lower value of 4 and pointing the arrow towards D.

This same procedure is followed from intersection to intersection until B is finally reached. Then, starting from B, one simply follows the arrows back to A, the arrows pointing out the minimum path.

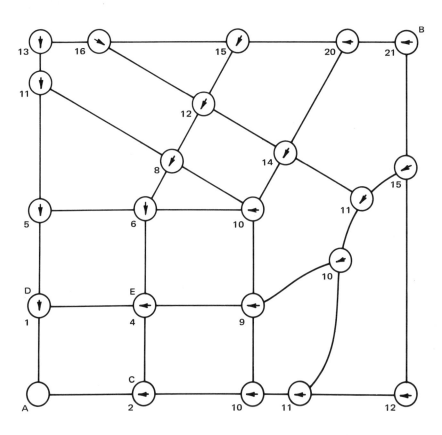

This method produces not only minimum paths from A to B, but from A to every intersection in the network, as shown in the following diagram. This is an example of a minimum path "tree." It has the property of relating all points in the network temporally (or by any other parameter used to measure the network) to the point of origin.

The use of the minimum path algorithm in transportation planning was based upon the assumption that drivers knew, and would employ, a minimum path in going from origin to destination. This assumption was sometimes challenged. People would insist, quite

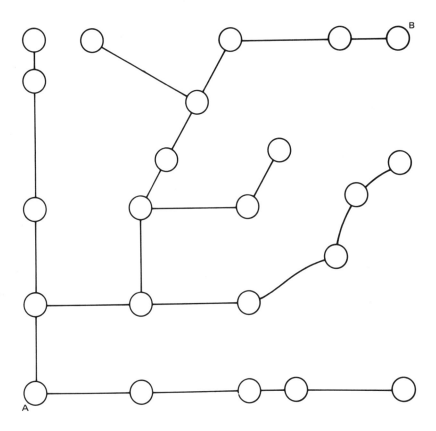

correctly, that some drivers would not use a minimum of any kind but would drive out of their way, if only to enjoy a more beautiful view. However, this argument ignored the fact that computer simulation was dealing with groups of drivers, not individuals (the average zonal interchange in the Chicago area, for example, was thirty-five vehicle trips). Assumption of a group's choice of the minimum seemed eminently reasonable.

The fact of the matter, however, was that the minimum path algorithm was such a cheap yet powerful tool that it had to be used. There was no alternative. Before this algorithm came along, there were only the crudest of hand methods for simulating traffic flows. With the minimum path algorithm, the vast mazes of transportation networks were pierced through and a way was found by which a digital computer could—almost—catch up with the man behind the wheel.

Distributing Trips between Zones

Given a means for rapidly calculating the shortest path through a network, the next step in the simulation process is to estimate the number of vehicle trips going from each origin zone in a metropolitan area to every possible destination zone in that metropolitan area. This step is frequently called the distribution process or trip distribution.

For convenience in analysis and forecasting, person trips and vehicle trips throughout the urban area are grouped within geographic units called zones. There were, for example, 582 zones in the Chicago study area. These varied in size from a quarter square mile in the Loop itself to one square mile in the city of Chicago and adjacent suburbs and to four square miles in the remainder of the study area. The zones were set at these sizes in order to keep the number of people and trips in each zone nearly of the same order of magnitude.

As described in Chapter V, these analysis and forecasting zones were tied numerically to the network. The numbering of the network's nodes actually incorporated the zone numbers. And in the approximate center of each zone was one node, called the "load node," from which all the vehicle trips coming from that zone emanated; it was at this point that they were placed upon the network.

The actual calculation of the number of trips which move between one zone and all other zones is done by computer, using, generally, either the gravity model or the opportunity model. In the gravity model, a formula of the form

$$T_{ij} = P_i \frac{\dfrac{A_j}{d_{ij}{}^b}}{\dfrac{A_1}{d_{i1}{}^b} + \dfrac{A_2}{d_{i2}{}^b} + \dots \dfrac{A_n}{d_{in}{}^b}},$$

is used to estimate the number of trips (T_{ij}) moving between zone i, which has P_i trips to export, and any other zone j, which has A_j potential trip destinations. The distance or travel time between the two zones is represented by d_{ij} raised to some power b, depending upon the type of trip interchange being simulated.[2] (In the gravity model, several classes of trips, such as work trips or shopping trips, are estimated separately.) The distance (or time or cost) between each pair of zones can be calculated using the minimum path algorithm.

In the opportunity model the trip distribution calculation is essentially done at the same time that the minimum paths are calculated. As described in Chapter III, the opportunity theory of trip distribution has travelers searching outward from a zone of origin and looking for a suitable destination. Each traveler (or group of travelers) has a defined probability of selecting a given destination, and this probability is modified so that it becomes lower and lower as more and more opportunities for successfully completing a journey are passed by in the outward search. This concept of travelers searching outward from a zone of origin corresponds perfectly with the mechanics of the minimum path algorithm. As described in the preceding section, that algorithm is also an outward-searching procedure. As in the case of the gravity model, several classes of trips are assigned, each of which has a different probability value.

What the computer does is to take one zone of origin at a time,

[2] *Calibrating and Testing a Gravity Model for Any Size Urban Area,* U.S. Department of Transportation, Federal Highway Administration, Bureau of Public Roads, Washington, D.C., 1966 (reprint).

determine the minimum path from that zone to all other zones, and then distribute trips outward over the minimum paths. As each possible zone of destination is reached, the number of trips destined to that zone is calculated by the probability formula

$$V_{ij} = V_i \, (e^{-lV} - e^{-l(V + V_j)}),$$

which was previously explained in Chapter III. The V values in the preceding equation are obtained by keeping track of the number of destination zones previously inspected as the computer sweeps out along the branches of the minimum path tree.

Assigning Trips to the Network

Prior to the advent of large-scale computers, each step in the estimation of future traffic volumes on expressways was done independently, and it was possible to talk about trip distribution and traffic assignment as separate operations. Records of trips were obtained from the travel surveys; these records were expanded to represent future zone-to-zone trips; and these trips were then "assigned," generally by hand and using maps, to the best route between origin and destination. The concept of assignment is one of adding up the numbers of vehicles that pass over each link in the network so that estimated future traffic volumes will be known.

In the various computer programs developed since 1955 which estimate the distribution of trips between zones, the recording of the number of trips using each link can be done integrally with the distribution process. The term "assignment," therefore, has become dated, although it is useful in explaining the fact that vehicle volumes using each link of the network are stored during the course of the computer operation.

Altering Travel Times

It was shown in Chapter V that speeds on expressways and arterials decline as traffic volumes build up on them. To be able to simulate congestion-induced delays seemed to be an essential part of any complete traffic simulation process. Without recognizing the fact of congestion, one would not be able to get an accurate idea of travel costs associated with any given plan, nor would all the points of traffic congestion show up.

Therefore, a refinement called the "capacity restraint" feature was developed in the Chicago study. This routine was designed to simulate the effect of congestion in slowing down travel speeds on crowded links. It operated by keeping track of the number of vehicles using each link. When the number of vehicles using each link reached a certain point, the speed of travel on that link was reduced.[3] As minimum path trees were built later in the course of a test, some links would be found to be so slow to traverse that different minimum paths would be selected than would have been the case if the capacity restraint feature had not been used.

The capacity restraint feature thereby approximated the condition in the real world where people will drive around areas known to be congested. It produced a more realistic simulation of driver behavior. Without capacity restraint it would be difficult to estimate travel costs reliably. Furthermore, capacity restraints are needed to improve the planner's ability to spot potential points of traffic congestion.[4]

The Outputs

The outputs from the computer simulation of traffic flow take two forms: tables and maps.

The tabular presentations are based upon the link summaries of

[3] Speeds were never reduced to zero because the traffic which was being simulated was 24-hour traffic; congestion is never so great that a link will be bottled up for that long a period of time.

[4] "Unrestrained" or "free" assignments have the advantage of indicating what links the drivers of automobiles and trucks would choose in going from origin to destination if there were no other vehicles on the network. Volumes greater than capacity on links in an unrestrained assignment indicate where some congestion would be, but not all points, since when drivers find a bottleneck they will spill over onto other streets and there may create new bottlenecks. A restrained assignment helps to identify these.

the numbers of vehicles using each link, and also of the accumulated time spent by all vehicles in traversing each link. Since the length of each link is known precisely from the inventory of transportation facilities, it is possible to calculate average speed. These data can then be converted to time costs, to vehicle operating costs, which are known to be functions of average speed,[5] and to accident costs as well, also a function of speed.[6]

```
BENEFIT COST SUMMARY FOR ASSIGNMENT NUMBER   76      LINK TYPE 3456      NETWORK N30

     TOTAL TRIPS                      10646832.

     TOTAL LINK MILEAGE                  437.0  MILES

     TOTAL LINK TIME                      10.47 HOURS

     VEHICLE MILES OF CAPACITY       17072100.

     VEHICLE MILES OF TRAVEL          8535600.

     VEHICLE HOURS OF TRAVEL          166685.1

     AVERAGE VEHICLE SPEED               41.8  MPH

     TOTAL OPERATING COST          $  266763.

     TOTAL ACCIDENT COST           $   26932.

     TOTAL TIME COST               $  226350.


     TOTAL ALL COST                $  522045.
```

ALL FIGURES ARE PRESENTED FOR AN AVERAGE TRAVEL DAY. COST ITEMS APPEAR IN DOLLARS.

Figure 49.
Economic evaluation of expressway portion of Plan N-30;
example of computer print-out.

The link data can then be summarized by analysis zone, and these summaries are then resummarized by districts, rings, and for the entire metropolitan area.

An example of a test summary is shown in Figure 49, which gives the results of a test of Plan N-30 for the Niagara Frontier. The

[5] George Haikalis and Hyman Joseph, "Economic Evaluation of Traffic Networks," paper presented at the Fortieth Annual Meeting of the Highway Research Board, Washington, D.C., January, 1961.
[6] Irving Hoch, "Accident Experience: Comparing Expressways and Arterials," Chicago Area Transportation Study, Chicago, 1959.

same kind of data were obtained for Chicago, but the output format for the New York studies is clearer for the nontechnical reader.

The second type of output of the computer traffic simulation program consists of maps of estimated traffic volumes on each arterial street and expressway in the entire metropolitan area. An example is Figure 50, which shows traffic volumes for a small part of

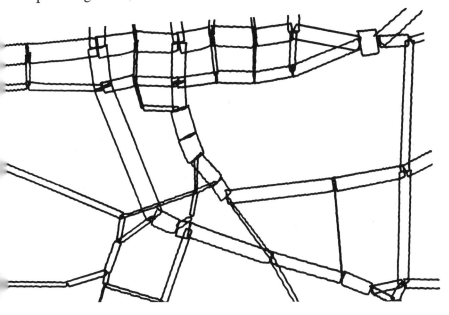

Figure 50.
Portion of computer-driven plot of traffic volumes on an
urban road network, at original scale.

the city of Buffalo, reproduced at the same scale at which it was drawn mechanically by a computer-driven plotter.

The story of these maps is an interesting sidelight. In the Chicago study, maps such as the foregoing were prepared by hand, and each map took weeks of effort by a crew of skilled and experienced clerks and draftsmen. When we moved to New York we realized that we would have to prepare dozens of such maps because we were preparing transportation plans for six upstate metropolitan areas—and, as it turned out, many minor cities.

So it was arranged to do this task by machine. A computer program was written which instructed the computer to calculate the geographic coordinates of a little box whose length was the length of a link of the road system and whose width was proportional to the volume of the road link in question. These data were placed on magnetic tape and were then fed through a small line-plotting machine, which mechanically drew the volume flow map shown in Figure 50.

A map covering an entire metropolitan area might take four or five hours for the plotting machine to draw. This was an enormous increase in speed over hand methods and permitted a large increase in the number of plans that could be tested. In addition to traffic volume maps, maps of street capacities could be drawn, or maps showing the differences between volume and capacity—in other words, traffic overloads.

For the planner and engineer, such volume flow maps were an obvious boon; they indicated where traffic volumes were heavy and where more or fewer lanes were needed. In short, they provided a great deal of the basic information needed in reviewing plans and proposals.

Calibration and Reliability

Before the traffic simulation program could be used in its intended role, that is, as a means for testing plans, it had to be tested for reliability itself. There were several tests which could be successively imposed on the computer model, the network, and the traffic estimates.

One of the first tests was to take the tables of origin-destination data (that is, the records of trips obtained by interviews) and assign these to the existing network of arterial streets and expressways. In such a test, the freedom given the computer was minimal; the destination of each trip origin was specified, and all the computer had to do was to thread the trip through the network on a minimum path. This kind of test served mainly to check the accuracy of the network coding. Any errors became apparent when the volume flow maps were prepared and compared with actual ground counts.

The next operation was both calibration and test. The known present-day numbers of trips were fed into the computer, but without specifying the known linkages between origin and destination. The computer then had to employ the probability formula to determine the destination of each zone's trips and had to assign them to the existing network. This process was done several times until the correct probability values of "*l*" were determined. Correctness was determined by comparing the known vehicle miles of travel with the simulated vehicle miles of travel in each ring. When these were brought into balance, the model was considered to be calibrated for the base year, which was the year in which data were collected.

Volume flow maps prepared from the calibrated simulations gave persuasive evidence of how well the computer program worked. Because mechanically prepared maps were readily available, Niagara Frontier evidence is presented here. Figure 51 shows actual 1962 traffic volumes in the central portion of Buffalo; Figure 52 shows simulated traffic flow volumes for the same area.

As can be seen, simulated and actual volumes are extremely close. Differences do exist which examination will disclose, but for the most part, the computer program is putting "correct" volumes on each street. It must be remembered that the so-called "actual" counts are themselves subject to error, and that even in as extensive a counting program as we conducted in the Niagara Frontier only a 20-percent sample of the links was actually counted, and most of these were short counts of two hours' duration.

When it came to the final phase of making estimates of future traffic, the "*l*" values had to be recalibrated. Once again, vehicle miles of travel was the control number to be met by the computer. Future vehicle miles of travel could be estimated quite readily, based upon the numbers of vehicles estimated to be in the study area as of the target year, as described in Chapter VIII.

With these kinds of tests and calibrations, the simulation program could be considered as a reliable means of testing future plans. It was by no means a perfect tool; no forecasting device ever is. But statistically and visually it held up. It reproduced current travel, and if it could do this, there seemed to be good reason for thinking that it could simulate future travel.

Figure 51.
Actual 1962 traffic volumes in central Buffalo.

But there was one more reason for being content with this simulation package. After all the work and care which went into its development, it was used in action not as an instrument for making *estimates* but as an instrument for making *comparisons*. As will be shown in the next chapter, one plan was to be compared to another, and all future plans were to be compared to a "null plan" which was for all practical purposes the present system. In using it as an instru-

Figure 52.
Simulated traffic volumes in central Buffalo.

ment of comparison, any failings in the model would be washed out, since the only variations between the different plans were the plans themselves.

The Composite Network

The main energies of the Chicago staff had gone, over a period of several years, into creating the improved testing mechanism which has been described in this chapter. As can be imagined, this was a hand-tailored process, and each plan which was tested was individually coded by hand and checked by machine. These operations sometimes consumed two or more weeks of time, but under the circumstances of having to prepare plans for only one metropolitan area this pace could be tolerated.

When the Upstate New York Transportation Studies were set up, we had a substantially different mandate. The task which we had in New York State was to develop plans for six metropolitan areas, and this had to be done by July of 1965, according to federal policy as expressed in the Highway Act of 1962. The outside pressures for speeding up testing were reinforced by our own desires to develop a more thorough testing program, and this could only be done by cutting down the time it took to test each plan.

The laborious parts of the Chicago testing procedures had been the coding and checking of the network prior to testing, and the posting of test results to maps after the computer runs. The computer runs themselves took only three or four hours. The output bottleneck was broken by the mechanical plotting of traffic volume maps, as described earlier in this chapter.

To eliminate the input bottleneck, a new technique was developed called the "composite network technique."[7] The essense of this technique was that instead of coding each expressway plan separately, all the links of all possible new expressways were assembled on a single map and then coded and checked only once. Then, whenever a plan was to be tested, those expressway links which were to be employed in that plan were identified, a small computer was instructed to create a complete network including those links, and this complete new network could then be tested by the giant computer.

The composite network was prepared by assembling all the plans for expressways which had ever been developed for a metropolitan area and superimposing them upon a single map. This was in itself a useful task, because it forced us to pay attention to the thinking of the many engineers and planners who had labored over plans in the preceding two or three decades. These plans contained some

[7] Kenneth W. Shiatte, "Composite Networks—A New Planning and Testing Tool," *Traffic Quarterly* (January, 1966).

insane ideas, but also some very carefully conceived ones. All the distinct expressway corridors (that is, generalized locations for expressways) were placed on the composite network map.

All of these corridors taken together constituted the composite network for expressways. An example of such a network is given in Figure 53. All of the corridors were then coded, but in a more simplified fashion then used for existing expressways while still accurately representing their lengths and speeds. Each link in the composite network bore (in addition to its regular network coding numbers) a three-digit number which identified it uniquely.

The intention and advantage of the composite network was to establish a large but fixed number of possible links, from which would be selected a few which would form the plan itself. Planning thereby became almost a search process rather than a process of synthesis or design. Practically this had great advantages: the composite network was coded only once and thereafter it was literally only a matter of an hour after a system had been selected for a tape to be ready to be threaded onto a giant computer for the test.

Conclusion

The testing mechanism described in this chapter was developed in response to urgent needs to be able to evaluate alternative transportation systems for entire metropolitan areas. Just as plans have to be prepared methodically and on the basis of reasoning which is connected to the goals which people are trying to achieve in transportation, so these same plans have to be tested carefully and in relationship to the goals of society.

It is very difficult to conceive, without actually experiencing it, the immense complexity of dealing with large networks serving cities having populations living at varying densities who generate trips of varying length and direction. To attempt to calculate mentally, or by hand, the volumes of trips which will use new networks in the face of these complexities is a kind of self-deception. Even formulas such as the optimum spacing formula are inadequate except under the

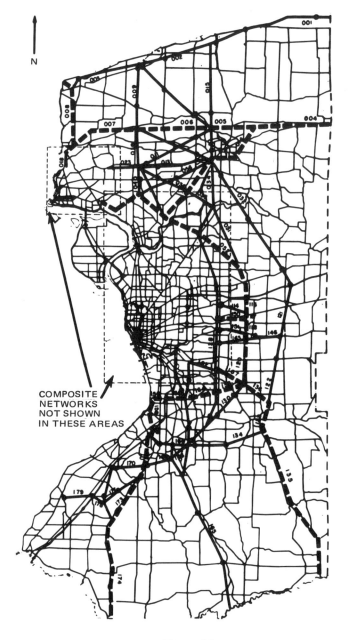

N

COMPOSITE
NETWORKS
NOT SHOWN
IN THESE AREAS

Figure 53.
Portion of composite network for Niagara Frontier showing links
(dashed lines) selected for testing.

most ideal conditions. For these reasons, some form of computer traffic simulation is needed to test plans.

The computer programs described in this chapter do reproduce present traffic remarkably well. There is every reason to believe that they can produce good estimates of future travel. Simulations of future travel can be checked against control estimates of vehicle miles of travel in the urban area being planned and in its parts; there are internal consistency checks available as well.

No forecasting method, of course, is perfect, and it is realized that there is judgment as well as science in making these forecasts of traffic spread across the transportation systems of an urban area. But the acid test of the testing mechanism is to ask whether one would be willing to certify a plan as being the best for a metropolitan area without having gone through the labor of testing it by computer traffic simulation. For those who have carried the responsibility, there is no substitute.

XII

EXPRESSWAY PLANNING: PART II

UP TO 1958–59 the mechanical problems of estimating traffic on hypothetical new road systems had been so severe that only a very few schemes—two or three at the most—could be tested for a metropolitan area. And these early tests did not provide estimates of the total costs of transportation; they dealt only with travel on the roads being planned and did not cover all major streets in the network. But from 1958–59 this was all changed. The ability to test an entire transportation network by simulating the flows of future traffic over that network and comparing results with the results obtained from tests of other plans opened up a whole new territory rich with opportunities for planning of transportation systems.

As a result, transportation planners in those cities where thorough transportation studies were conducted could begin to contemplate networks with detachment—not as designs in which they had personally invested so much time that they would fight to preserve each link, but as puzzles which could be twisted, turned, and manipulated in an impersonal search to find the best combination. Strategic questions could be asked. Should the expressway network really be this big—or this small? What *is* the best arrangement or configuration of components: a ring-and-radial scheme, or a grid, or some irregular shaping? Should more expressways be built in the growing parts of the city or in the older, denser parts? Is there a logical order of priority for building a plan once a plan is settled upon?

These were exciting questions, not so much because they were new but because the possibility existed that they could be answered with reason instead of supposition or assertion. There was a sense that the tests were valid, that the reasoning was sound and persuasive, that if the various authorities could get together (as they were being drawn together in policy and planning committees), there was no reason why a "best" transportation plan could not be built. And this was all the more dramatic when the sheer magnitude of the proposals was realized: massive channels for movement, embracing entire metropolitan regions and providing for the free, safe, and speedy travel of millions of people going about their daily affairs.

In this chapter, the final steps of planning and testing expressway systems for urban areas are illustrated by the use of two case studies. The first of these is that of the Chicago study, which was preparing and testing plans from 1958 onwards. The Chicago study was the first study to test plans in a conscious effort to find an optimum plan where optimality was defined by a single criterion, such as least total transportation cost. The second case study is that of the Niagara Frontier, where planning and testing took place in 1964–65.

Preparing and Testing the Chicago Expressway Plan

The strategy of planning and testing employed by the Chicago study was simple enough in its broad outlines. But this simplicity belied the immense amount of work which went into the preparation of each plan being tested, to say nothing of the weeks of time represented in coding each network, checking it for perfection, running the assignment tests, and then decoding and interpreting the results.

The main thrust of the Chicago tests was right down the center: the optimum spacing technique was employed to estimate the approximate order of magnitude of the new plan, and then a system was designed with expressways at this spacing. The barriers of cemeteries, railroad yards, water features, and public open spaces were considered; and, more positively, the various networks were designed to serve major generators of commercial and industrial land use and to provide access to major parks. System planning principles were used. Out of this emerged Plan K (see Figure 58) which

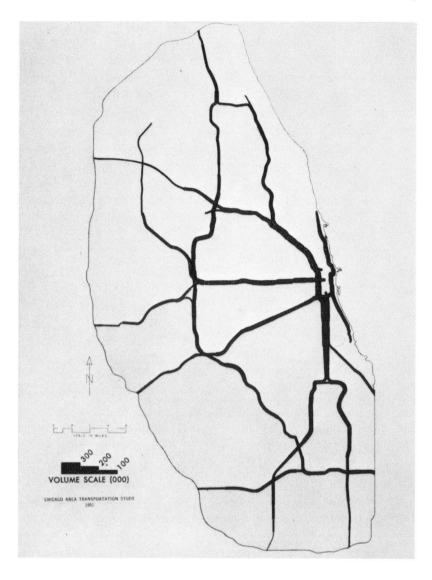

Figure 54.
Plan A.

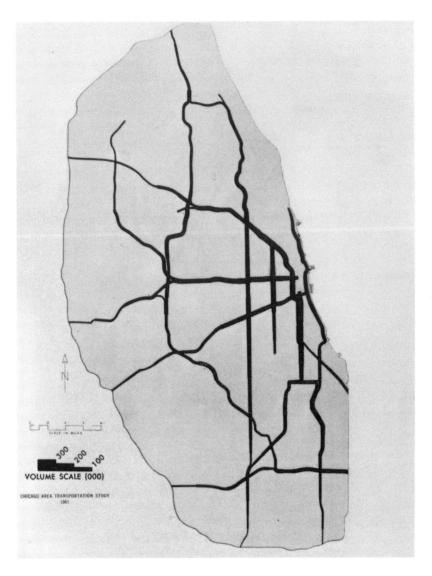

Figure 55.
Plan B.

proposed building 466 miles of expressways at a capital cost of $1,797,000,000.[1]

To check the scale of this plan, four other plans were tested having widely varying amounts of expressways. Two were at the lower end of the scale, and two had significantly more mileage than Plan K. The plan with the greatest mileage of expressways also employed a different type of facility in order to see whether a radically different system would pay off well. Once these tests had verified that Plan K was of the right order of magnitude, attention was directed again toward the middle-sized plan, and this was refined and tested to settle on minor improvements.

It is worth examining these plans in greater detail, both the extremes and the refinements, in order to convey better the interplay of ideas and procedures which helped to narrow the search toward a best plan.

The Low Investment Plans. Plans A and B (Figures 54 and 55) were drawn up and subjected to testing to determine whether it would be wise either to stop building expressways altogether or to build only a very limited number of additional facilities. Plan A was the more drastic of the two; only those facilities considered as being absolutely committed for construction were included. Plan B provided two north-south facilities which distributed traffic more evenly throughout the central part of the Chicago area and helped to reduce the overloads at the center caused by the radials composing Plan A. Plan A had 288 miles of expressways and Plan B had 327; thus they differed only by about 12 percent, and both represented a policy of extremely low future investment in high-speed roadways.

The consequences of pursuing such a policy would have been dramatic. The population of the Chicago area was expected to increase by 51 percent between 1956 and 1980, and per capita car ownership was expected to rise by 28 percent. The combination of these two growth rates (1.51 times 1.28) meant an increase in automobile registrations of 93 percent and a similar increase in the

---

[1] All data in this section are as reported in Chicago Area Transportation Study, *Final Report,* vol. III (1962).

vehicle miles of travel driven daily within the area.[2] This near doubling of travel would have been funnelled into a street system very nearly the same as that existing in the Chicago area in 1960. Even with the expected widenings of many arterial streets, the rise in congestion and loss of time can be imagined.

Since the number of accidents per million vehicle miles of travel was known by street type, the number of accidents in 1980 could be estimated, assuming Plan A to be the plan that was built. The estimates were formidable; in 1980, slightly over 500 accidents per day were predicted, as opposed to 330 per day at the time the plans were being tested. Fatalities per year from roadway accidents would have risen from 500 to 781.

Thus, although these two plans stood for a very conservative policy of government investment in new expressways, they turned out to be very expensive to the community as a whole because of their high travel costs. And these travel costs outweighed the savings in capital investment by far. Table 21 shows the costs of these plans in comparison with other plans.

Plan J—The Maximum Plan. A major interagency debate took place while these plans were being prepared. Representatives of the City of Chicago realized the severe problems of human dislocation created by construction of expressways within their city limits. The example of the Eisenhower Expressway was still fresh in their minds: the last links of that facility within the city of Chicago were only opened in 1960, more than ten years after it was started. More expressway construction in a politically sensitive city would mean greater problems, unless the expressways could use nearly vacant land, as was to be the case with the southwestern expressway.

Knowing these difficulties, and knowing also that traffic congestion was increasing on existing streets, the City's representatives searched with some diligence for a solution. One of their ideas was to develop a new, intermediate roadway—one designed to be superior to a conventional arterial but less expensive than a full-scale expressway.

[2] Since 1940 the number of miles driven in the average vehicle has remained relatively constant. See U.S. Statistical Abstract, 1967, Table 812.

Table 21. *Measured Performance of Alternative Trial Plans for the Chicago Area*

Characteristics	Plan					
	A	B	K	I	J	L-3
Miles of Proposed Expressways (including existing and committed expressways)	288	327	466	681	968[a]	520
Cost to Complete (after 1960, and including $350 million for arterial improvements) (millions)	$ 907	$1,274	$1,797	$2,457	$3,180	$2,007
Daily 1980 Costs (thousands)						
Interest and Principal (on construction costs)	294	413	583	797	1,032	651
Travel (accident, time, and operating costs)	6,177	5,837	5,490	5,259	5,292	5,377
Total	6,471	6,250	6,073	6,056	6,324	6,028
Estimated Annual Traffic Fatalities	781	698	638	606	638	626
Estimated Daily Traffic Accidents	504	450	378	346	416	359

[a] Includes "intermediate facilities" as well as full-scale expressways.
Source: CATS, *Final Report*, vol. III, Tables 11, 29.

Figure 56.
Plan J.

At the Chicago study, therefore, we undertook to test what the implications of this kind of road would be (see Figure 56). It was assumed that intermediate facilities within the city of Chicago and nearby suburbs would be built on existing major streets, which is to say that the existing major streets would be upgraded by widening pavements and by building a grade-separation at every major intersection, or nearly at one-mile intervals. In addition, many local streets entering the new intermediate facilities would be closed off. Raised medians and channelized intersections would be built. Where the major streets crossed under railroads or elevated lines (and this was quite frequently in Chicago), new structures would have to be built. All parking along these intermediate facilities would have to be eliminated.

It turned out that the cost of such a program of building intermediate facilities was extremely high—over three billion dollars. There were too many structures to be built. Railroad underpasses, medians, and street closings were expensive. The elimination of parking would have been extremely difficult. But in the long run, the most serious drawbacks to such a scheme would have been the continuation of very heavy traffic volumes on streets cutting the city at one- and two-mile intervals.

The computer test which was run on Plan J, which was the scheme using these junior expressways, showed that it had the highest cost of all the plans tested. This was made up of an extraordinarily high construction cost ($3.18 billion) and a travel cost which, while low, was not the lowest.

Plan I. While by no means as extensive as Plan J, Plan I was an extremely rich plan, with 681 miles of expressways proposed (see Figure 57). All of these expressways were conventional types. The main difference between Plan I and Plan K was that the former had a much more extensive system in the suburban parts of the study area. In the suburbs Plan I had expressways at four-mile spacings, and this was much tighter than the six-mile spacing indicated by the optimum spacing formula.

From the point of view of travel costs, Plan I was the best of all the trial plans tested. As shown in Table 21, the sum of daily

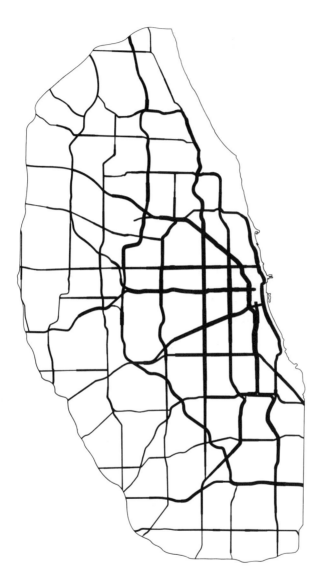

Figure 57.
Plan I.

accident, time, and operating costs for this plan was $5,259,000. The next best plan in this respect was Plan J. However, low travel costs would have had to be purchased by an investment of more than $2.4 billion, $660,000,000 more than Plan K. Hence this plan was quickly discarded.

Plans K and L through L-3. As previously noted, Plan K (see Figure 58) was prepared using optimum spacing, network planning principles, and data on existing land uses. Computer tests showed that from an investment standpoint it was superior to any of the other four plans tested. The search for a best plan could then correctly use K as a jumping-off point for further studies involving both small changes in investment and changes in configuration.

The configuration of Plan K, even though worked out on the basis of scores of trial drawings, was not of the best. The test results, when mapped, showed that some of the expressways carried very little traffic while some of the arterial streets carried too much. (Unfortunately, the scale of mapping which can be shown in this book is too coarse to display arterial volumes.) So the plan was adjusted to improve its performance and this resulted in the production of Plan L, which is shown in Figure 59.

Then, as noted in the Chicago study's final report (Volume III), and typical of the kind of detailed examination made of the plan,

> Three variations of Plan L were subjected to assignment tests. There was a question on alignment of Interstate 90 between its connection with Lake Street and North Avenue near Elmhurst and its junction with the Northwest Tollway. Two different alignments were tested, holding the remainder of the network exactly the same. The traffic assignment showed that one location was definitely superior. In one instance, impossible turning volumes at an interchange and overloading of a short section of the system were produced. These troublesome traffic problems were detected only after traffic loads were imposed on the network by traffic assignment.

The reader will be able to discern, by comparing Plans K, L, and L-3 (see Figure 60), the gradual refinement and smoothing out of the proposed expressway system. Where Plan K contained a T intersection with the top of the T facing toward the Loop (near

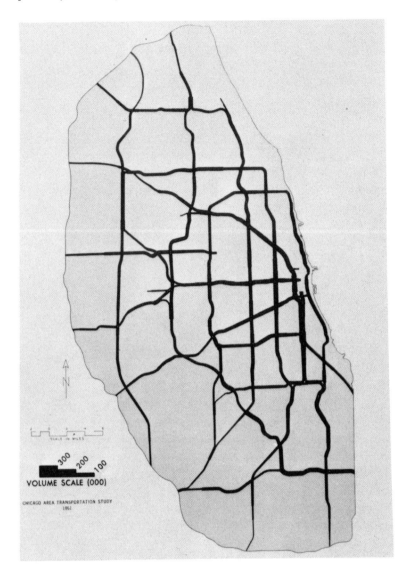

Figure 58.
Plan K.

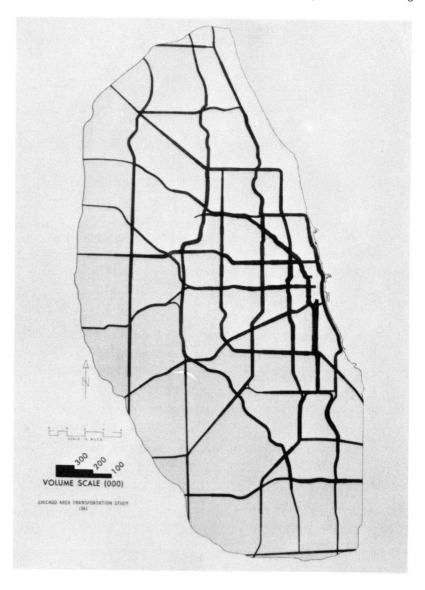

Figure 59.
Plan L.

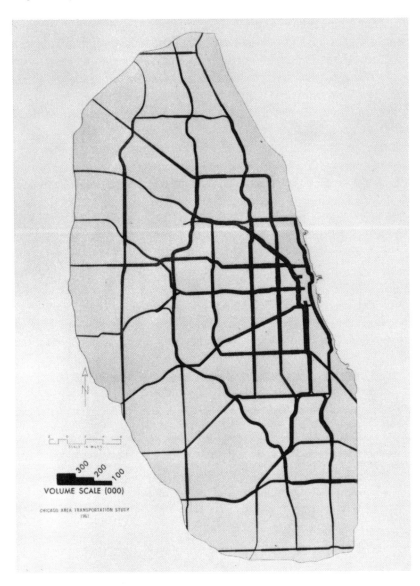

Figure 60.
Plan L-3.

center of map), Plans L and L-3 eliminated this. Plan K had some large areas in the south, southwest, and north unserviced by express facilities. Plans L and L-3 provided much more even service.

In the northwestern section of the study area a five-way interchange shown in Plan L has been eliminated in Plan L-3 while at the same time more even spacing has been achieved. In the south central part of the map a realignment of three roads has evened traffic volumes in Plan L-3.

Generally, Plan L-3 is a fine example of a warped grid which "flows through" a metropolitan area, subtly compressing its spacing as it enters regions of higher density. The expressways near the cordon line of the study area merge into the interstate and regional highways of Illinois and Indiana.

From an over-all economic point of view, Plan L-3 was the best, as can be seen in Table 21. However, the amount of improvement of L-3 over L, K, or even I was not very great—less than 2 percent. This seemed at first to be a fine margin for making a very large decision. Accordingly, marginal costs were analyzed—a form of analysis which exposed the differences in investment between the plans and thus expanded our ability to make a good judgment.

Table 22 compares the differences in construction costs and

Table 22. *Marginal Costs of Alternative Expressway Plans for the Chicago Area*

Plan	Marginal Investment over Preceding Plan (millions)	Annual Savings in Travel Costs over Preceding Plan (millions)	Marginal Rate of Return
A	—	—	—
B	$367	$115	29.3%
K	523	118	22.5
L-3	210	38	17.8
I	450	40	7.5
J	723	−11	(negative)

Source: CATS, *Final Report,* vol. III, Table 12.

reductions of annual travel costs of Plans A through J. Each plan is compared to the one which is next less expensive, and the rate of return on the additional investment is calculated. It had previously been determined that every new expressway proposed to be built would have to return a "profit," that is, a reduction of total transportation costs equal to or greater than 10 percent of the investment, if it were to be considered as a part of any plan. This rate of interest was established to reflect not only the going interest rate on any investment, but also a conservative desire not to overinvest in transportation at the expense of other public investments, such as in educational facilities, hospitals, or parks.

Plan L-3 was safely above the desired minimum rate of return, reducing time, accident, and vehicle operating costs by 17.8 percent, while the next larger plan (Plan I) returned only 7.5 percent. This provided another bit of corroboration that in L-3 we had that plan which was right for the Chicago area. The scale of L-3 was correct; the scale of the next larger plan was incorrect.[3]

Plan L-3 was re-examined for its service to land use and then taken to be the best of those tested.

Preparing and Testing Plans in the Niagara Frontier

Late in 1961 the New York State Department of Public Works began the program of urban transportation studies which was eventually to cover all the upstate metropolitan areas. The Niagara Frontier Transportation Study was the first in this series, but the task force responsible for survey work and the technical aspects of plan-

---

[3] It must be pointed out that this is an unusual form of marginal cost analysis. Normally, marginal cost analysis deals with the purchase or production of small identical additional units. Here we were dealing with entire networks, similar but not identical in their configuration and each filling the study area. Because of their similarity, it was reasonable to compare the Chicago networks' additional return to their relative additional cost; the comparison did expose the more profitable increments of investment. However, it turned out that this method could not be applied in the Niagara Frontier, where differences in the configuration and location of investment produced quite different returns even when investment was the same.

ning was soon given the name of the Upstate New York Transportation Studies (UNYTS).[4]

Our policy at UNYTS was to use the same basic planning procedures that were employed in the Chicago study, but to speed up the procedures centering around the computer traffic assignments so that more plans could be tested. There would have been very little profit in attempting to write a new computer traffic assignment program, but the work involved in mounting and dismounting each test could be substantially shortened. The techniques for speeding up these inputs and outputs have already been described in Chapter XI. They consisted of the composite network technique, which cut down the time needed to code and check planned networks from weeks to hours, and the use of an x-y plotter, which made similar reductions in the time required to plot out the results of the assignments. Turn-around time for an assignment became, in practice, a matter of about two days from the time a decision was made to test a group of plans to the time when the results were available for inspection.

With this kind of power, we could test many more plans than had ever been tested before for a given urban area. In the Niagara Frontier, more than twenty plans were tested; in Rochester, twenty-six plans were tested.[5]

As in Chicago, planning in the Niagara Frontier started with the assembly of basic materials—maps of "barriers," regional transportation influences, future land uses, and population densities. Then optimum spacings were calculated. These two sets of factors were then brought to bear upon the choice of expressway corridors, and a composite network was assembled.

Physically the Niagara Frontier area was a more complicated area to plan than Chicago. The two counties (Niagara and Erie) had three distinct but merging urban areas: Buffalo, Niagara Falls, and Lockport. The Niagara River made a deep identation in the main-

[4] This group is currently the Bureau of Planning in the New York State Department of Transportation.

[5] Rochester Metropolitan Transportation Study, "Basic Corridor Plan for Expressways," New York State Department of Public Works, Albany, 1967.

land area, and Grand Island was thereby physically separated from the rest of the area.

The various expressway systems which we selected out of the composite network for testing had to be woven across and around the physical features, and at the same time had to maintain spacings and stay within our principles of network planning. This was no small task. In involved fitting, testing, reviewing economic results, and checking traffic volumes on expressways and arterials.

There were two major problems which demanded especially careful attention in the Niagara Frontier. These were the problems of the proportional split between urban and rural expressway investment, and the problems of planning around existing expressways. These are taken up in turn.

Scale and the Urban-Rural Split. In contrast to the Chicago study area, which had an area of 1,236 square miles (46 percent in urban uses) and a 1956 population of 5,169,000, the Niagara Frontier had a larger study area—1,558 square miles—which contained a population of only 1,350,000. As a result, only 14 percent of the land area in the two counties was in urban use; the remainder was in agriculture or was vacant.

This high percentage of rural land in the Niagara Frontier brought to the forefront a question which had not really existed in Chicago: how extensive should the expressway system be in rural areas? Or, what should be the division of investment between rural and urban areas?

The temptation to plan large systems in rural areas was quite strong. Buffalo and Niagara Falls were focal points in a large region, and there was a natural tendency to extend radials out to nearby cities—to Rochester on the east and to the smaller cities of the Southern Tier counties on the south. Lake Ontario to the north was an attraction as well, not only for recreational trips but also as the site for a parkway paralleling the shoreline.

Two of our first computer tests, then, were for very large systems. Plans N-12 and N-14 (see Figures 61 and 62) had 395 and 363 miles of expressways respectively. But the capital costs of these

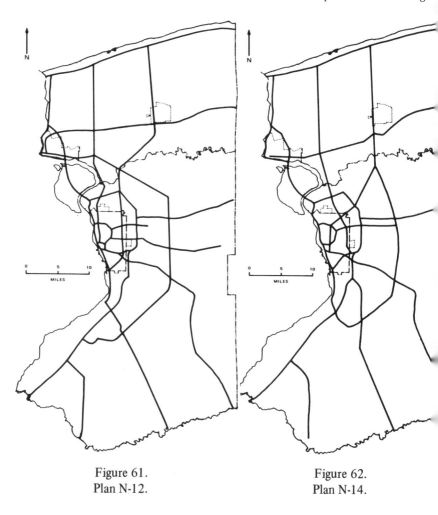

Figure 61.   Figure 62.
Plan N-12.   Plan N-14.

plans were very great—both over $500,000,000—and the reduc-
tions in travel costs produced by this investment did not offset the
greater capital costs when compared with other plans. And, more
tangibly, many of the expressways in rural areas were shown by the
traffic assignment tests to be carrying 1985 volumes of only 3,000–
5,000 vehicles per day. This was in contrast with the capability of
these same expressways to carry 50,000 vehicles per day without any
strain.

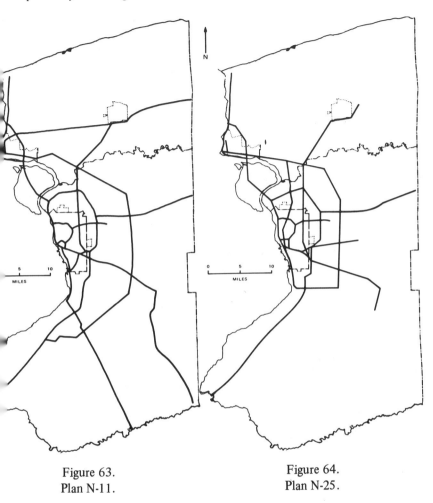

Figure 63.
Plan N-11.

Figure 64.
Plan N-25.

It became apparent that capital investment might be the same in two quite different plans, but that the geographic placement of the expressways might have startlingly different results on transportation costs. Plans N-11 and N-25 (see Figures 63 and 64) had construction costs which were, by coincidence, the same. As a preliminary report noted, "One contains a large amount of rural mileage; the other concentrates the investment in urban areas. Economic analysis of these two plans indicated that investment in urban areas, although it purchases fewer miles, yields far greater benefits than investment in extensive rural routes."[6]

We became curious about why this was so, because rural expressways were far less expensive to build than urban expressways, averaging in 1962 in the Buffalo area only $1,050,000 per mile in rural areas as against $9,620,000 per mile within two miles of the Buffalo central business district. And they attracted vehicles in about the same one-to-ten ratio. Where an expressway fifteen miles from downtown Buffalo might carry 5,000 to 8,000 vehicles per day, an expressway within three miles of downtown Buffalo would be carrying 50,000 to 80,000 vehicles per day. So the cost-to-volume ratio was nearly identical.

Our studies showed that the really significant difference in profitability lay in the *differences* between expressway and arterial travel costs in the city and in the country. In the city, expressways permit off-peak speeds of sixty miles per hour and average speeds, over a whole day, of forty miles per hour. Arterials, on the other hand, rarely average more than fifteen-twenty miles per hour over a 24-hour period and are at least twice as dangerous to drive on. The difference in travel costs in ring 2 in Buffalo we calculated at seventeen cents minus six cents or eleven cents per vehicle mile. In rural areas, however, ordinary highways classed as arterials provide fast service because they are so lightly loaded, and average speeds in excess of fifty miles per hour are not uncommon. Rural expressways at sixty-five miles per hour do not give the driver much of a cost advantage —perhaps 1¢ per mile over ordinary rural highways. This very simple explanation indicates why expressways within dense urban areas are so profitable: they provide travelers with more relief, and this relief extends to the people who don't use expressways as well as those who do.

Having established this principle of greater profitability of urban than rural expressways, we adjusted our planning accordingly, and

[6] Robert Breuer, H. Richard Etherington, and Henry L. Peyrebrune, "Planning Document Number 3—The Basic Corridor Plan," New York State Department of Public Works, Albany, 1965, p. 12. It should be noted that the last statement is based on the traditional urban economic analysis and does not take into account the as yet unmeasured effects of rural expressways on regional economic development.

most subsequent plans were of far smaller mileage with less of this mileage in rural areas. It was realized, of course, that this principle could not be extended too far. Some expressways had to reach out to connect the Niagara Frontier with adjacent cities and regions. We could not calculate the value of such roads on the basis of our user-benefit system, so we indicated these roads with a dotted "future" convention, leaving the decision on the timing of their construction to the statewide transportation planning process.

Adjusting to the Committed System. The second major planning problem in the Niagara Frontier was that of placing new expressways so that they would work in harmony with the existing expressways. This was by all odds the most difficult part of the entire planning task. Over 48 percent of the miles of expressways in what was to be our final, recommended plan (Plan N-30) were in 1962 either built or so far committed that their locations had to be accepted as fixed by the Planning Committee. The new links which we added had to work with the committed links, neither overloading them nor stripping them of traffic. This called for many careful adjustments.

Radial expressways constituted a particular problem. As they focused upon the central business district, they generally entered regions of higher trip density, and their traffic volumes increased. New expressways had to be located so as not to increase the radials' loads further, but instead to distribute the loads more evenly. This task was complicated by the presence of railroad lines, rivers, power lines, industrial districts, and residential neighborhoods.

Linking new routes sensibly with the existing and committed expressways was not made any easier, either in the Niagara Frontier or Chicago, by the presence of toll roads in those urban areas. In rural areas toll roads are wonderful devices in many ways. They provide high-speed service to those who want to use them and they do this well ahead of the time when state taxpayers can afford to provide them out of general funds. However, within cities they are nuisances. Most of them were designed just ahead of the time when transportation planning got its main start. The toll road planners selected their alignments with very little, if any, regard for the ultimate system of the urban area in which they were located. Because interchanges with toll barriers are costly to operate, they designed the urban sections with fewer interchanges than would be the case if they were free roads. This means that fewer drivers use them than would be the case if they were free roads, and more drivers must stay on slower and more dangerous arterial roads.

As expressway systems become more complete, new free expressways must intersect more and more often with the toll roads. In some cases, the location of the freeways is distorted so as not to disturb the locations of toll booths. Worse still, new free expressways are sometimes proposed which exactly parallel the toll roads, and at a few hundred yards away or less. This is the antithesis of good system planning. Prior to our network planning in Buffalo there was, for example, a serious proposal to parallel the east-west portion of the Niagara section of the Governor Thomas E. Dewey Thruway with a new expressway less than half a mile away. This was soon dropped.

As time goes on, the presence of both free and toll roads within an urban system is going to become more and more anomalous. One will be able to drive over most of an urban network without paying tolls, and yet a few sections will still be toll roads. As a result, fewer people will be served well than would be the case if they were free. Yet the extreme rigidity of toll road authorities as legal entities, separate from government and responsible primarily to bondholders, will doubtless prevent the changes from being made which would serve the public better. This is not just a problem in the two cities mentioned, but a severe problem wherever there are separate organizations building and operating parts of a total expressway system.

The Recommended Plan. The first series of plans tested contained six plans (the Base System, and Plans N-12, N-14, N-19, N-23, and N-25) which were used largely to determine the level of new investment in the Niagara Frontier which would minimize total transportation costs. The travel, construction, and total costs of these plans are plotted and shown connected by a solid line in Figure 65. It became apparent from these plans that the desired level of investment would be with a plan having about 250 miles of expressways. And the investigations into rural and urban investment had shown that it would be better if more of this investment were in urban areas and less in low-volume, rural expressways. Plan N-23 (see Figure 66) with 256 miles of expressways and an investment of $404,000,-000 seemed to be the proper point of departure for further study, both from the viewpoint of scale and of the urban-rural split.

The investigations and tests which went on after this point were extensive and detailed. The system had to be molded into shape, taking first one part of the area and then another, looking at estimated traffic volumes on the expressways and on adjacent arterials, and going over the results within the staff and with the Planning Committee at meetings in Albany and Buffalo.

One of these detailed investigations concerned the pattern of expressways in the southern part of the area. To determine the best solution in that portion of the study's area, five different plans were tested. In each case all the expressways north of a line which went east-west through the Buffalo central business district were held constant, so that the computer traffic assignment tests would reflect only the results of changes in the south. Plans N-25, N-26, N-27, N-28, and N-29 are shown in Figures 67 through 71. Economically, N-26 turned out to be the best, and its southern portion was used in the recommended plan.[7]

The plan which emerged from this work was Plan N-30, which is shown in Figure 72. This plan was slightly less costly than N-23 ($401 million as against $404), and its smoother and more efficient configuration gave it a daily travel cost of $1,818,000 as against $1,837,000. Some system planning principles had to be violated, notably in the southern part of the network. However, in general the plan stands out as a network flowing fairly smoothly through an urban area, connecting major population centers, serving industry, and providing access to recreational areas. The basic scheme is again

[7] This procedure of holding all parts constant while varying expressway configuration in one portion of an urban area was carried to its logical conclusion in the subsequent testing of expressway plans in Rochester. There the urban area could be divided conveniently into quarters by existing expressways in combination with geographic features. Various combinations of links were selected from the composite network in each quarter, and these combinations were then tested. Once an ideal pattern had been found in one quarter, the same procedure was repeated in another quarter, and so on. Some adjustments had to be made in fitting the quarters together, of course, but this procedure provided an excellent means for moving rigorously toward a best plan.

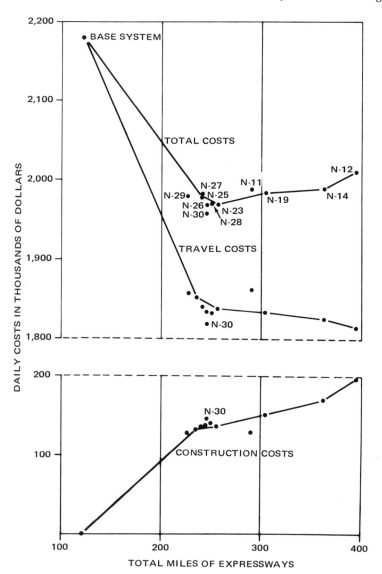

Figure 65.
Relationship of construction, travel, and total costs to
expressway length, Niagara Frontier.

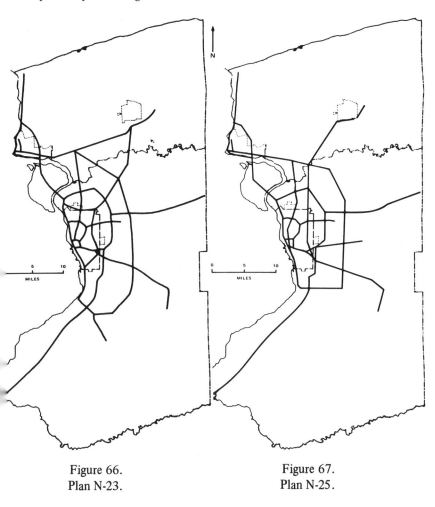

Figure 66.
Plan N-23.

Figure 67.
Plan N-25.

a warped grid whose spacing is compressed in areas of higher density but which maintains continuity of line and avoidance of abrupt transitions.

It must be noted here that while Plan N-30 was recommended as the best of those tested and was in fact published in 1965, two of its major links were defeated when the plan was being legislated. This is part of the game. The obligation of those working in planning is to put forward their best thinking. The plan and its components

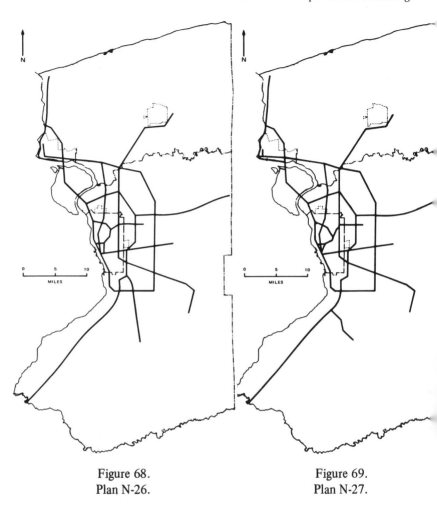

Figure 68.   Figure 69.
Plan N-26.   Plan N-27.

are always subject to review in the democratic process. In time, and with a continuing planning process, some resolution of differences will be achieved.

Conclusion

At the conclusion of the expressway planning process, we have to look backward once more to regain a sense of the reality which

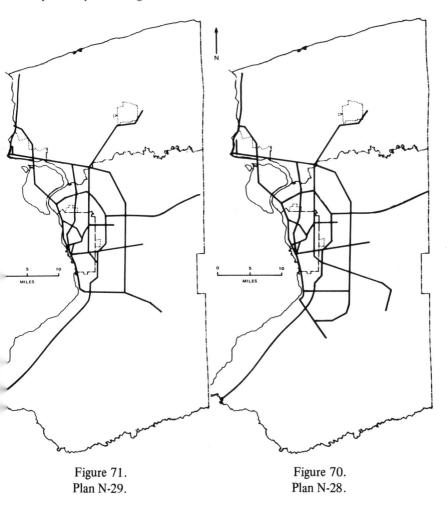

| Figure 71. | Figure 70. |
| Plan N-29. | Plan N-28. |

underlies the highly abstracted lines lying across these small-scale maps.

Large cities are continuing to grow, and their growth is not only in population but in wealth. People will inevitably spend all they can, and travel is one of the things they buy. The increases in travel are expected to be very large—between 80 and 100 percent within twenty years in large American cities. Most of this increase will be in

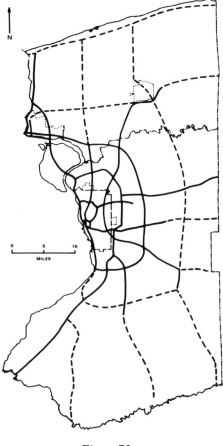

Figure 72.
Plan N-30.

automobile and truck travel, and very little in travel by mass transportation facilities.

Provision has to be made for increased vehicular travel. Vehicles could be left to use existing streets, but the service level of existing streets is limited by their too frequent intersection with other
streets and is worsened as traffic volumes rise. The most obvious alternative is to build new roadways, that is, to provide more space for
the vehicles. And of all types of new roadways, the expressway is the

most efficient type to invest in, when calculated in dollar costs per vehicle mile of capacity provided. It gains this efficiency because its design allows for continuous and uninterrupted vehicular movement.

Very simply, then, the strategic questions for transportation planning are how much investment should be made in these new expressways and where they should be built. In the major transportation studies a long and arduous process was developed which produced the kinds of plans shown in this chapter. New channels for vehicular movement were proposed to cut through existing developed areas, and ways were reserved for such channels in presently vacant land.

If expressways are built according to these plans, increasing proportions of daily travel will be driven upon them. In Chicago, 51 percent of the target year vehicle miles of travel would be driven on expressways while in the Niagara Frontier, the percentage would be approximately 40 percent—lower than Chicago's because of the greater proportion of the area remaining in rural use.

By attracting this proportion of travel away from existing arterial streets, a double advantage is gained. Those who use the expressways gain by traveling between two and three times as fast and as safely as they would on arterials. Those who remain on the arterials gain because traffic volumes are lower. The reductions in traffic volumes on arterials and the reality of increased off-expressway safety as a result of expressway construction have been carefully documented.[8]

The big picture is that the implementation of optimum expressway plans will provide space for travel, will save lives and reduce accidents and injuries, will save time, and will reduce operating costs. They will do this efficiently in terms of the dollars invested. More than this, the expressway networks will unify metropolitan areas, allowing people and businesses to specialize more and hence to become more productive.

If this planning were being done for a large assembly plant or for a new city on another planet, people would unhesitatingly declare that the whole procedure was laudable. But this planning is being

[8] Frederick F. Frye, "The Effect of an Expressway on the Distribution of Traffic and Accidents," Chicago Area Transportation Study, Chicago, 1962.

done for cities, and cities contain people who object to being moved or disturbed by expressway construction programs. The strength of the objections clouds the long-term, continuing gains which new expressways produce. As a result, construction of expressways in some cities has been delayed for years or blocked indefinitely.

One of the results of the opposition to expressways has been a search for alternative ways of transporting people, particularly by transit, and this subject is accordingly taken up in the next three chapters.

XIII

TRANSIT: DEVELOPING THE TESTING MECHANISM

FOR many persons who are concerned about the future of cities, transit is the area of greatest interest in the whole field of transportation planning. Expressways and arterials may be built in rural areas and suburbs—as many as are needed—and this will evoke only passing interest. Seemingly, nobody cares about these outer roads, although their influence pervades a region even to its core. But for these people the serious questions are about transit within the denser parts of the urban area, and particularly about transit as an alternative to expressway construction in the arterial city. What is the best policy on transit? What is a balanced system of transportation facilities? Will or will not the planning process produce recommendations for construction of new mass transportation facilities? What kind will they be? How many people will use them? Will they pay for themselves?

The transit questions are caught up with other, very difficult, urban problems. What will be the future of the central business district—can it be preserved without extensive rapid transit? Can the central city endure the impact of further expressway construction—and would not transit be an easier alternative? How can the poor and the ghetto residents move about without an improved, more extensive transit system? If transit is in difficulties, should not the city reshape itself with higher densities along transit lines so as to make transit viable?

Basically, these questions fall into two classes: those which focus on transit as a component of the total transportation system, and those which look at transit in relationship to other goals of the urban community such as supporting the central business district or aiding the ghetto resident. In this and the following chapter we deal with transit as a component of the total system of moving people within urban areas, leaving to Chapter XV the broader policy question of using transit as an instrument to attain various nontransportation goals of the urban community.

Having once established computer testing as the standard for examining alternative expressway plans, it is impossible ever to settle for a less exacting procedure for dealing with other forms of urban transportation. So the same general kind of planning must be used when dealing with transit as a component of the total transportation system. Data must be used to give scale to the problem. Data must also be employed to learn more about the choices which people make under given conditions. It is assumed that people make sensible choices in their own interests when faced with alternatives. Given several transit plans, the desired procedure is to estimate future usage and then evaluate whether it is worthwhile to make the indicated changes.

In the remainder of this chapter and in Chapter XIV, two examples are given to illustrate how transit systems can be tested. These examples are taken from the work of the Chicago Area Transportation Study, where the first computer assignments were made to a complete transit network, and from the work of the Niagara Frontier Transportation Study, where a greater variety of transit solutions was tested than for any other urban area. The Chicago technique was basically a pragmatic technique. The Niagara Frontier study estimated mode choice with a massive computer simulation model which was sensitive to changes in the level of transit and highway service, among other variables.

There are, of course, other transit planning and testing techniques.[1] The two testing techniques described here do, however, illustrate the important factors and problems encountered in transit planning and they show how important it is to simulate future usage,

---

[1] Martin J. Fertal *et al., Modal Split, Documentation of Nine Methods for Estimating Transit Usage* (U.S. Department of Commerce, Bureau of Public Roads, Washington, D.C., 1966).

taking into account the specifics of actual alignments and services in each city being studied.

The Chicago Transit Planning Story

During the time that new skills and techniques for highway planning were being developed in the Chicago study, work was also going forward in preparation for the planning of improvements to the mass transportation systems of the Chicago area. The Chicago study's transit planning was not an afterthought, although it came after and capitalized upon the big breakthroughs in techniques for highway planning. The minimum path algorithm, assignment of trips to a complete network, and the opportunity theory of trip distribution were all employed in the testing of transit proposals. Transit planning was a part of the original work assignment given to the Chicago study. This was the first time that a major transportation study had prepared and computer-tested plans for both transit and highways.

It is impossible to appraise the work of the Chicago study fairly without a basic understanding of the transit picture in Chicago, just as it is impossible to make accurate general statements about transit and cities without specifying the exact set of circumstances in each case.

The Chicago area had for many decades a very strong set of transit systems. In terms of route miles of bus lines and miles of subway-elevated lines and suburban railroads, Chicago's transit system is exceeded in the United States only by New York's.[2] The city's transportation had been until the 1930's almost completely dominated by the transit industry, and the starlike shape of metropolitan form even in 1956 attested to the strength of this influence. In 1956, despite the vast increase in automobile travel in the preceding thirty years, 24 percent of all trips were still made by transit, while 71 percent of the trips having destinations in the Loop on the average weekday were made by transit.

[2] "Urban Transit Development in Twenty Major Cities," Automotive Safety Foundation, Washington, D.C., 1968.

In terms of existing and potential rights-of-way for rapid transit service, Chicago was also very rich. Every major sector had at least one railroad line running outward from the Loop, and only one of these did not have an active suburban transit service already operating. (The remaining one was the line running out along the south branch of the Chicago River, through an area primarily industrial and with extensive sewage treatment areas, oil tank farms, and the like.)

Thus the transit planning problem in Chicago was not one of designing substantial new systems. The questions to be asked were these: should there be extensions to existing radial rail lines? Should suburban rail service be provided in the southwest corridor? Should cross-town or circumferential rapid transit lines be built? Were there any adjustments that could be made to the system to improve its performance and increase the number of its riders? These questions were not asked idly; everyone—highway engineer and transit specialist alike—was interested in and had a stake in trying to maintain and improve the performance of these transit systems, in order to wring the last bit of good out of the capital already sunk in transit rights-of-way.

Before any of the preceding questions of extension or placement of transit lines could be answered, it was necessary for the study to estimate the probable number of future transit trips likely to be made in each part of the Chicago area.

As we knew perfectly well at the time, estimating the number of transit trips without reference to the effect of planned improvements on choice of mode of travel was, to some degree, begging an important question. Improvements in transit service, reductions in fares, or the construction of new transit lines might substantially alter the number of transit riders. An improved transit system, by its sheer desirability, might be made self-fulfilling in terms of attracting greater usage. But whether improvements would in fact affect usage was not known.

There was at that time no feasible method for making such a determination. The large federal demonstration grant programs of the 1960's had not been started, and hence there was no experience on the effects of changes in the system. The very extensive computer programs developed subsequently in Washington and the Niagara Frontier were not available. Consequently, the effect of expanded or improved service had to be answered on a priori grounds and, although the reasoning was cogent and the conclusion basically correct, the answer was never considered satisfactory. Our logic went like this:

1. *Any* extension of mass transit service would, by its presence, attract some additional riders. There was no doubt about this; it was simply a matter of probability that, given a new facility, someone would find it convenient to use it. The question then became "how many will use it?"

2. It was assumed as a background fact that the metropolitan area was going to grow and extend outward at lower densities. It was assumed that no transit change would be significant enough to alter the nature or density of this growth pattern.[3]

3. Any extension of transit would therefore be into a less dense area of trip-making, or, if a circumferential line, would run in a direction serving a smaller number of trip desire lines than served by existing radial lines. In either case, the new transit facilities would be moving into less desirable trade areas.

4. The nature of transit, as a means of conveying groups of people, requires the assembly of these groups *before* transit can move them. This assembly must be not only at a place but at a point in time. Assembling people takes time and therefore imposes a delay. Once assembled, transit can move people efficiently.[4]

5. Because it must stop and start to pick up assembled groups of people, transit will inevitably be slower than any other form of transportation which offers a more continuous journey. The effective speed of transit in urban areas is predominantly a function of station spacing or the number of stops per mile.[5] Because of its slower

---

[3] It is quite a different thing for a transit system to alter the form of development of an urban area today when it is in competition with a majority form of transportation (the automobile) than when it was a monopolistic form of transportation as it was in the nineteenth century.

[4] Provided there are enough people. A train carrying ten passengers is not an efficient form of transportation.

[5] See Chapter V.

speeds, transit is not in a competitively strong position if it is extended.

6. It was assumed that the transit industry was and should be responsive to basic economics in considering extensions. In thinner trade territories, therefore, fewer transit vehicles would be scheduled and routes would be farther apart; the resulting poorer service would cause people to re-evaluate their choice of transit.

7. The fact that transit service had not been extended—had in many cases been contracted—was evidence that the economic limits of extending transit had already been reached.

To summarize these arguments, it was held that while new transit lines would attract some new users, the number of new users would be limited because the new trade territory was bound to be thinner and because transit, by its nature, was a slower form of transportation than the competing automobile. Under these circumstances it was very unlikely that extensions would have any substantial effect upon ridership. Therefore, it was concluded that ridership could be estimated independently and without reference to changes in the transit system.

In retrospect, one looks at these arguments with mixed emotions. By and large, the conclusion reached—that transit usage was not going to expand—was correct, and the data we have from the Chicago area since that time bears this out, even though some lines have achieved increases in patronage.[6] On the other hand, these a priori arguments made for an entire metropolitan area come across as too broad generalizations, without the kind of fine cutting edge which is desirable for planning purposes. But this was the fault of the times, and it was not for several more years that techniques were developed which could cut into this problem.

The purpose of describing the technique used in the Chicago study for estimating future transit usage is not to recite a history but

[6] The report, "1967 Cordon Count of the Chicago Central Business District," City of Chicago, Department of Streets and Sanitation, Bureau of Street Traffic, Chicago, 1967, shows a 1956 total of 533,000 transit and suburban railroad passengers entering and leaving the central business district of Chicago and a 1967 total of 504,500.

to illustrate certain basic concepts about transit which should be understood.

As we have seen, the first and most basic assumption was that choice of mode of travel could be estimated independently of the level of service provided by mass transportation facilities and, of course, independently of the level of service provided by the automobile. This was an undesirable assumption to make, although necessary at the time. However, it was mitigated by the fact that Chicago already had a very extensive rail transit system which extended out in all directions (except along the line of the Sanitary Canal) to the cordon line, while its main bus system was large and competently managed.

If choice of mode of travel were independent of service, then it had to be dependent upon circumstances at the origin and destination of each trip. The question was, which circumstances?

Looking at the origins and destinations of transit trips, the dominating fact in Chicago (as in most other cities) was that the central business district was the focal point of transit origins and destinations. More than 54 percent of all transit trips had their origins or destinations within the Loop and 81 percent had origins or destinations in the Central Area, which is that area within two and a half miles of the center of Chicago's Loop. The tremendous investment represented by buildings at the center mean that this was going to continue to be a magnet.

Based on this observation, the world of transit trips was divided in two portions: those trips having either an origin or destination in the Central Area, and all other transit trips.

Taking the Central Area–oriented trips first, their number was estimated on the basis of (a) the probable size or number of trips of all kinds expected to be in the Central Area in 1980 (the target year), and (b) the proportion of all those trips that was likely to be using transit.

The number of trips that were estimated to be destined to that Central Area in 1980 was based upon the plan for the Central Area prepared by the Chicago Plan Commission. This plan indicated a 5 percent increase in floor area by 1980. Total person trips to the

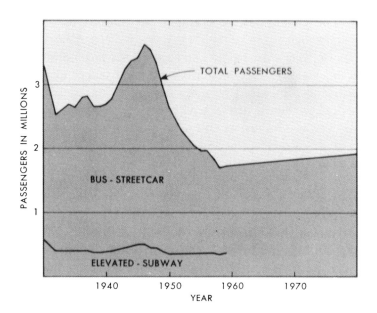

Figure 73.
Average weekday revenue passengers of the Chicago Transit
Authority, by mode, 1930-59 and estimated to 1980.

Central Area were therefore increased by 5 percent. It is interesting
that the actual number of person trips entering the Loop rose about
4 percent between 1956 and 1967.[7] The Loop attracts about 40
percent of the person trips destined to the larger Central Area.
Hence the closeness of the rise is only a general indication, but it
does suggest that the forecast was realistic in scale.

The proportion of trips expected to use transit was harder to
estimate. All the trend lines showed clear downward movements
(see Figure 73). A continued decline would have been the most
reasonable estimate. However, such an estimate would not have been
in keeping with the policies of the City of Chicago, which was working to try to increase transit usage to the central area. Assuming

[7] "1967 Cordon Count for the Chicago Central Business District."

that some of these actions would be successful, a slight increase in the proportion of transit users was forecast.[8]

Where would these transit riders come from? The specialized nature of the Loop, with its banking, shopping, personal services, educational, and business services activities, and all the specialized employment pertaining thereto, suggested that travelers to the Loop and the Central Area would come from all over the Chicago area, in direct proportion to the number of persons living in each part of that area. Data from the travel surveys showed that this was the fact in 1956, and it seemed reasonable to suppose that this situation would continue in the future. Hence, the origins of the Central Area trips were allocated across the Chicago area in proportion to the number of 1980 trips in each zone.

The obvious result of such a forecast was that new trips were estimated to be coming to the Central Area from farther out in the suburbs: logically, because the more distant suburbs contained most of the future growth. This meant that the suburban railroads could expect increases in travelers,[9] and that the average trip length would increase.

Turning to the other part of the forecast—the noncentral, or local, trips—studies showed that there was a relationship between transit trip-making and a variety of factors. These included automobile ownership, density, and distance to the central business district. Of these factors, automobile ownership was the most persuasive as an index of future change. With higher car ownership, the use of transit is eroded: first, the off-peak, recreational travel, where with multiple ridership the automobile is clearly less expensive per person; then, the shopping trip; last, the work trip.

The economic survey had estimated income, and the income estimates were used to estimate car ownership. Car ownership esti-

[8] In actuality, by 1967 a drop in total transit trips to the Loop had occurred, although subway and elevated trains carried larger loads.

[9] Unfortunately, no data on present trip length are available, but the records of the 1967 cordon count show that suburban railroads lost about 15 percent of their average number of passengers in the period 1956–67. Thus the forecast, which was always regarded as optimistic in favor of the transit system, was incorrect.

mates were checked against trend-line estimates of registrations. The car ownership forecasts were then employed to forecast the number of trips in each zone expected to make local (non–Central Area) transit trips. All told, it was estimated that local transit trips would rise from 1,417,000 to 1,446,000 daily trips, although the gains expected in the outer areas were offset by reductions in rings 2, 3, and 4, comprising the bulk of the C.T.A. trade territory.[10]

The forecast transit trips were then used to test out alternative transit plans. The trips destined to the Central Area could be assigned directly to the mass transportation network using the minimum path algorithm only, since both origins and destinations were known. "Local" transit trips were distributed to their destinations by use of the opportunity model and simultaneously assigned to their minimum paths, for the most part via bus routes.

The Niagara Frontier Testing Mechanism

Like the other major transportation studies, the goal of the Niagara Frontier study was to prepare a comprehensive plan for its area—a plan in which both highway and mass transportation systems would be included. However, despite the fact that the state had provided ample manpower authorizations and computer resources, it was impossible to prepare both transit and highway plans at the same time. More accurately, it was impossible to do these two tasks at the same time with the then current techniques *and* to produce a technical product which would be adequate in light of the transit situation in the Buffalo area.

Therefore we adopted a policy of preparing an expressway plan first and a transit plan second, promising to modify the expressway plan should the transit plan so require in the public interest. This procedure was supported by the fact that our organization was doing six transportation studies in rotation. The Highway Act of 1962

---

[10] These losses at least were correctly estimated. Annual reports of the Chicago Transit Authority show a decline in total transit usage from 621 to 511 million riders between 1956 and 1967, despite an upturn in usage since 1963.

required a transportation plan by July 1, 1965, for each metropolitan area. It seemed necessary for us to complete at least one expressway plan prior to that time as an evidence of progress, and to perfect our procedures.

By the summer of 1965, when the expressway plan for the Niagara Frontier had been published, it became abundantly clear that a heavy-weight effort in transit was necessary. The Planning Committee of the study, representing the technical leadership in planning and traffic engineering of the Niagara Frontier, was strongly in favor of a most careful examination of transit. Further, the Buffalo area, with a population of over a million, was the largest upstate metropolis; what happened in Buffalo would be indicative of what was likely to happen in other urban areas. So, methodologically and in regard to policy, the transit effort in Buffalo had to be excellent. Moreover, unlike Chicago, the Niagara Frontier area did not have a rail rapid transit system of any kind. Many options for transit were open, and so a fresh approach was necessary.

The clue to transit planning lay in being able to simulate future use of any transit facilities that might be proposed. This was simply an extension of the basic principle which had guided the development of expressway planning. In turn, the key to simulating future use of transit lay not only in assigning trips to the links of a transit or bus network, but also in estimating how many trips people would choose to make by transit instead of by automobile. The division of person trips between transit and automobile is called "modal split" in the jargon of the trade.

Modal split, as will be recalled, was estimated in Chicago on the basis of the characteristics of each trip's origin or destination. Transit trips to the Chicago Loop were estimated on the basis of a fixed proportion of all CBD trips; other transit trips were estimated on the basis of car ownership. This kind of estimating procedure may be called a static procedure or model because it is insensitive to changes in the network.

The Niagara Frontier staff wanted to develop a procedure that would be sensitive to changes in the network and to other factors as well, including parking costs. The procedure the staff developed is outlined in the following paragraphs and is worth careful reading because it illustrates not only a method but some of the evidence which helps one to judge the probabilities for transit use.

It was quite clear, to begin with, that choice of mode of travel is a very complicated matter. Each traveler living at a particular place within an urban area has a particular set of conditions to appraise. He has his own and his whole family's daily travel needs to consider. He has a purpose for making a trip, which may take him a few minutes or all day. He has a probability of going a certain distance. And finally, he is placed at just a certain distance from a bus or rail transit line or an arterial and expressway. From where he lives, these transportation facilities have a unique configuration which permit him to reach some parts of the community easily by transit and others only with great difficulty.

This simple description of what a single person must consider should shatter the confidence of those who make blithe generalizations about what any new transportation system "must" do.

The task facing the model builders was to break apart and categorize the variables influencing mode choice so that they could construct a model which would accurately simulate the choices people would make about the mode of their travel—for each trip they made, in fact.[11]

One of the dominating factors which had been known for some time to influence choice of mode of travel was auto availability. In the Pittsburgh Area Transportation Study it had been discovered that 85.3 percent of those using transit were "captives" in the sense that (a) they could not drive, (b) they owned no cars, or (c) someone else was using the family car or cars and therefore they had to use transit.[12] Almost 60 percent of those choosing to use transit who could drive, owned a car, and had it available but elected not to use it, turned out to be persons going to work in the Golden Triangle— Pittsburgh's central business district. For such persons other factors,

[11] For a description of the model, see John R. Hamburg and Charles R. Guinn, "A Modal-Choice Model—Description of Basic Concepts," New York State Department of Public Works, Albany, 1966.

[12] Louis E. Keefer, "Characteristics of Captive and Choice Transit Trips in the Pittsburgh Metropolitan Area," Highway Research Board Bulletin 347, Washington, D.C., 1962.

such as the longer journey and the higher cost of parking, evidently made the difference. Table 23 summarizes the Pittsburgh data. Using a different definition of automobile availability, the Niagara Frontier study found that nearly 71 percent of transit trips were "captives."

On the basis of such evidence, it was clear that an estimate of automobile availability was an important factor in estimating choice of mode. Automobile ownership in the Niagara Frontier was therefore estimated by family ownership category; families were broken

Table 23. *Captive and Choice Transit Trips in the Pittsburgh Metropolitan Area, 1958*

Type of Trip	Number of Trips	Percentage
Captive Transit Trips		
Trips from Noncar-owning Families	141,354	29.8
Trips by Nondrivers from Car-owning Households	142,132	30.0
Trips by Drivers from Car-owning Households with No Car Available	120,321	25.5
Total Captive Transit Trips	403,807	85.3
Choice Transit Trips	69,943	14.7
Total	473,750	100.0

Source: Keefer, "Characteristics of Captive and Choice Transit Trips in the Pittsburgh Metropolitan Area."

down into zero, one, and two or more car-owning families. Trips from families without cars were classified as "no auto available" and hence had the highest probability of using transit, although not 100 percent, because some of these people secure rides from friends. Trips made by families owning two or more cars were all classified as "auto available." Families with one car had their trips divided into "auto available" and "no auto available" in accordance with the proportions which the origin-destination survey showed to be existing in 1962.

A second factor affecting choice of mode is the purpose for

which the trip is made. Evidence indicated a substantial difference between work trips and all other trips. Work trips tend to use transit more. This is very reasonable: work trips are made generally in the peak hours when transit service is best, and choice of transit eliminates both a parking charge and tying up an automobile all day. Also, work trips tend to be more radially oriented, reflecting the historic (but diminishing) concentration of jobs toward the center of the city. Nonwork trips, in contrast, occur more frequently at off-peak times when transit service is poorer, tend to be short (which makes the transit trip with its fixed fare quite expensive), and are omni-directional, whereas transit is mainly radially oriented.

The two factors of auto availability and purpose were combined to make four categories of trips, as shown in Table 24. The percentages indicated show the proportions of all resident trips which use transit in each of these four categories.

Table 24. *Trips Made by Transit as a Function of Purpose and Automobile Availability, Niagara Frontier, 1962*

Trip Purpose	Transit Use as a Percentage of All Trips	
	No Auto Available	Auto Available
Work Trips	48.3	8.3
Nonwork Trips	9.4	1.6
All Purposes	12.8	3.9

Source: Hamburg and Guinn, "A Modal-Choice Model—Description of Basic Concepts."

A third and very important factor affecting choice of mode is the relative service offered by automobile and transit. It appeared certain that people would be influenced in their choices of mode of travel by the swiftness, pleasantness, and safety of the service provided. This had long been recognized, but the problem was how to quantify it.

The indicator selected to represent service level was travel time. This indicator was constructed so as to take into account, quite specifically, a number of variables which are recognized as affecting comparative service. These include, for transit, the time to walk to the bus or other rapid transit vehicle, waiting time, running time, transfer times (if any), and destination walking time. For automobile travelers these include time to walk to the vehicle, driving time, parking costs (expressed in time units), and destination walking time.

The use of time as an index of quality of service left out a number of recognized factors. One, for example, was the factor of comfort in buses *versus* comfort in cars. Another factor might have been convenience in carrying packages in alternate modes. A third factor might have been crowding. A fourth might have been comparative out-of-pocket costs. The difficulty with these factors was lack of evidence, especially when assessing their impact upon usage of a hypothetical system. There was, therefore, no real choice open to our research workers, and these factors were excluded.

In contrast, it was quite possible to get specific data on comparative journey times. The travel times between all zones could be measured by the minimum path algorithm in which the real network was accurately represented. The proportion using transit for each zone pair could then be learned from the origin-destination data. Where the Niagara Frontier data failed to provide information on fast transit service over longer distances (because there was no rail rapid transit in Buffalo), Chicago origin-destination records were imported to fill the gap.

A fourth and final factor was trip length. The data showed that for short trips of a mile in length or less, transit was used less frequently; for trips over five miles there was a very gradual decline in utilization. The very short trips are most frequently made by automobile, and for these trips distance may be a surrogate for cost, since with a fixed fare of, say, twenty-five cents, a one-mile journey is very expensive (twenty-five cents per mile). For longer trips, the slowness of transit begins to take an increasing toll; the absolute difference in travel time between automobile and transit may rise to fifteen minutes or more.

These four factors were then pulled together into a family of curves, which are shown in Figure 74. Here the different responses of a user are seen, and they are marked differences. If a user is going

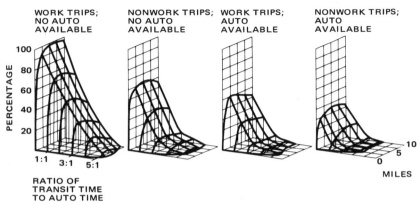

Figure 74.
Percentage of person trips estimated to use transit in the
Niagara Frontier as a function of purpose, auto availability,
trip length, and ratio of travel times, by mode.

to work, has no automobile available, is traveling five miles, and the speeds of transit and automobile are equal, he has a 70 percent probability of using transit. On the other hand, if he is going out to see a movie in the evening, has a car at hand, is going five miles, and the speeds of transit and automobile are equal, he has a 15 percent chance of using transit.

Given these four factors, a good estimate of modal split could be obtained which was responsive to the characteristics of the trip, the trip-maker, and the quality of service provided by competing modes. However, the staff wanted to go another step and to make the model responsive to the dynamic factor of accessibility—in other words, to make the model sensitive to changes caused by the construction of transit lines and expressways.

Accessibility and Mode Choice. If a series of zones are arrayed in space as shown in the diagram below, and then an expressway is built between two of the zones, as shown in the following diagram, the patterns of trip-making between the zones will change. Greater volumes of travel can be expected, for example, between zones A and B after the expressway is built than before. This phenomenon of increased traffic used to be called "generated" or "induced" traffic.

Such increases in volumes can readily be explained by either the gravity or opportunity theory of travel. These formulas showed that, if travel times or costs between certain parts of a city were reduced, the volumes of travel between those parts would be increased, at the expense of travel between other zones where travel times remained unchanged.

It seemed plausible to believe, then, that if a rapid transit line were built between A and C, as in the diagram below, that there

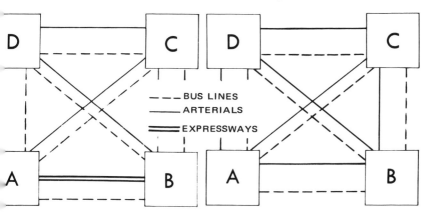

would not only be an increase in travel from A to C but also a shift toward an increased usage of transit at the expense of automobile travel. How much this shift would be, and whether it would even be significant, was not known.

It became clear, therefore, that changes in accessibility by transit had to be taken into account. These would affect not only the numbers of trips between pairs of zones but the mode of travel. A new transit line to a central business district would increase trips there and would tilt the balance in favor of transit. A new expressway would do the same, but would increase automobile travel.

The problem then became one of estimating how many transit and automobile trips would be made between each pair of zones, as affected by the different levels of accessibility provided by road and transit systems.

The modal split between each individual pair of zones could be estimated easily, given the four factors (auto availability, purpose, comparative quality of service, and distance) described in the previous section. But against what interchange volume would the percentage split be applied? The interchange volume calculated using the road network, or the interchange volume calculated using the transit network? These interchange volumes could be quite different. For example, in the previous diagram the interchange volume between A and C would be greater (relative to all other volumes) when calculated over the transit network, whereas the volume be-

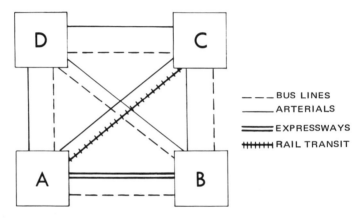

tween A and B would be greater (relative to all other volumes) when calculated over the road network.

The Niagara Frontier solution to this problem was as follows. Zonal interchanges were first estimated with *all* trips from every zone forced to go over transit, and then this process was repeated with *all* trips forced to go over the road network. The first interchange estimate would produce a pattern of travel in equilibrium with the accessibility created by the new transit system. The second would be adjusted to the road network.

Then the modal split proportion *for transit* (reflecting each zone's trip purposes, lengths, auto availability, and interzonal quality of service) would be applied against the transit interchange volumes. The *complementary proportion for automobile* would be applied against the automobile interchange volumes. Since the sum of all interchanges using this procedure did not necessarily add up to 100 percent of the number of trips exported from all zones, it was necessary after making the preceding calculations to normalize interchanges prior to making the final assignments to the two networks.

This compromise solution appeared reasonable. If, for example, a new transit line, as between A and C in the preceding diagram, boosted accessibility and hence volumes between two zones, then the transit proportion of the modal split was applied against that higher interchange volume estimated on the basis of the transit network. The same kind of situation obtained in the automobile world. Both taken together balanced the shifts in different parts of the urban area resulting from improvements in both the roadway and transit systems.

This completed the Niagara Frontier method for estimating transit utilization. Once the effect of new accessibility had been determined and the response of people to both accessibility and service levels had been estimated, it was merely a matter of employing the distribution and assignment procedure once more to place the trips upon the network and to record the travel costs associated with these patterns.

XIV

THE NIAGARA FRONTIER TRANSIT TESTS:
A CASE STUDY

THE "modal model" described in the preceding chapter was used in 1966 to test eleven different combinations of transit and highway systems for the Niagara Frontier. These tests were released to the public in December of that year but without recommendation by the staff or by the Planning Committee of the Niagara Frontier Transportation Study. It was recognized by these two groups that factors other than transportation economics would have a significant bearing on any decision reached by the Policy Committee or the community at large.[1]

In this chapter, the data and estimates produced as a result of these tests are used to illustrate the kind of work that has to be done as a first step if a sound strategy for mass transportation is to be developed in any urban area. Since these are first step tests, no attempt should be made, however, to draw conclusions from them or to extend these results to situations in other cities. The Niagara Frontier is a unique metropolitan area with its population of 1,350,000 occupying an unusual geographic site. The estimates obtained from these tests apply only in the Niagara Frontier. Still, much can be learned from observing the test results.

One of the things learned, for example, was the absolute necessity of laying out proposed systems on maps in order to deal with the

[1] Niagara Frontier Transportation Study, "An Evaluation of Alternate Public Transportation Facilities," New York State Department of Public Works, Albany, 1966.

realities of the site, of station locations and spacing, of probable speeds, and of the costs of equipment, rails, stations, and all the auxiliary facilities that need to be provided to make transit an operational reality. As an example, it seemed at first that all that would be required to establish a suburban rail service would be to buy engines and passenger cars, and to build a few stations along the numerous freight lines serving the Buffalo area. Investigation showed, however, that on several lines the condition of the trackage would not permit speeds of fifty or sixty miles per hour such as were desired for suburban service. Slower speeds were satisfactory for freight operations, but to develop passenger service, much of the trackage would have had to be relaid.

The Niagara Frontier was not an easy area for which to make transit proposals. There was no existing rail rapid transit service. The last commuter service in the area had been discontinued in 1961 when the New York Central Railroad eliminated its service from Niagara Falls to Buffalo because it was carrying only a few persons each day.

The shape of the urbanized and urbanizing area did not make things any easier. The city of Buffalo had expanded chiefly to the north and east of its business core which was located on the shores of Lake Erie, just north of the Buffalo River. The river, looping southeastward from the lake, created a broad band of marshy land which had later developed industrially. This band of river and industry continued to separate most of the city of Buffalo and the suburbs north and east from a much smaller urbanized area—the city of Lackawanna—which lay to the south along the lake shore.

North of Buffalo and the Tonawanda suburbs lay the city of North Tonawanda and twelve miles beyond that to the northeast was the city of Lockport. The city of Niagara Falls was separated from the main Buffalo settlement by the Niagara River and Grand Island. While transit lines might connect these communities, they would have to traverse circuitous routes or cover long distances which were sparsely settled.

A technique was developed which established in an objective manner those parts of the Niagara Frontier which would be most

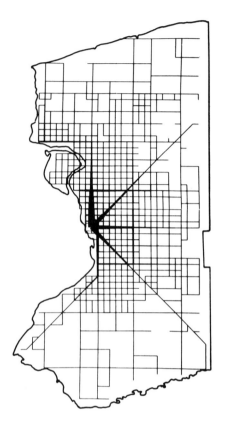

Figure 75.
High transit potential corridors.

likely to produce higher transit volumes.[2] An extensive network was generated, as shown in Figure 75. This network was fed into the computer as if it were a complete system of rail transit facilities with stops at one-mile intervals. The computer was instructed to assign

---

[2] Niagara Frontier Transportation Study, "An Evaluation of Alternate Public Transportation Facilities." Frederick F. Frye developed the technique for identifying high transit potential corridors. This technique was developed after some of the transit plans had already been tested, but its potential as a tool in initial planning suggests that it be described here in the text.

transit trips to this network. The results of this assignment have been plotted in Figure 75 with the width of lines representing the number of persons that would use each link of the "generated" network. Although the orientation of the network itself, and particularly its diagonals, had some influence on the results, Figure 75 shows quite clearly that the corridors of highest transit potential lay to the north and northeast of the Buffalo central business district. It was in these areas that the majority of new systems were proposed, although other proposed systems embraced the whole urbanized area.

The proposed systems were limited to those kinds of mass transportation facilities for which working prototypes existed. Thus, the types of systems proposed included suburban railroad trains (both diesel and electric), buses operating on expressways, conventional electrified transit trains such as are used in New York City, and the Westinghouse "transit expressway." Too little was known of the performance and costs of the more radical proposals to merit inclusion in a serious testing program.

Following agreement on each plan to be tested, the transit plans were coded, the highway network was modified (if modifications were being tested), and the resulting two networks were fed to the computer together with 1985 trip and 1985 automobile ownership rates estimated for each small part of the study area. After the split between transit and automobile had been made and these trips had been assigned to their respective networks, the results were printed out. Then the cost estimates for building the transit and highway networks and for providing transit equipment were prepared and the test was considered complete.

The Alternative Systems

In the following sections, six different kinds of transit systems are described. Some of these systems were tested in more than one configuration or with different assumptions about the expressway network serving the area, and thus eleven different computer tests were made. The order of presentation follows the order of increasing requirements for capital investment, starting with a "null" plan in which only surface buses operating on arterial streets would serve the area in 1980. In all cases, estimates of ridership are for the year 1980.

1. *No Transit Improvements.* The first test described in this series was made to establish a bench mark against which other transit proposals could be measured. This test assumed that no improvements would be made to the transit system of the Niagara Frontier between 1962 and 1985. This meant that the existing bus service provided by the Niagara Frontier Transit Authority and a number of smaller companies would remain exactly as it was in 1962. It was also assumed that the basic corridor plan for expressways, Plan N-30, would be completed and opened to the public.

With the expected higher automobile ownership rates of 1985 and with the more extensive expressway system, it was not surprising, therefore, that the computer estimated that daily use of buses would drop from 208,000 riders in 1962 to 189,000 riders in 1985. This drop seemed quite reasonable even though the population of the metropolitan area was expected to rise to nearly 2,000,000 persons by 1985. The figure of 189,000 riders was considered as the base against which ridership attained by other transit plans, with or without changes in the express system, could be measured.[3]

In this and the following tests, the estimates which are compared are restricted to the number of riders on the new transit facility itself, the number of riders on all transit facilities (the new transit facility plus the basic bus system), and the capital costs. The impact of proposed transit improvements on total transportation costs will be described at the end of this section.

2. *Express Bus Scheme.* From the point of view of capital investment, the scheme requiring the least additional capital investment was the express bus scheme. This scheme is shown on Figure 76. It consists of a radial system of buses focused on the Buffalo central business district and using expressways to provide service to Niagara Falls and Lockport in the north and to three suburban

[3] All estimates on transit usage are as given in "An Evaluation of Alternate Public Transportation Facilities."

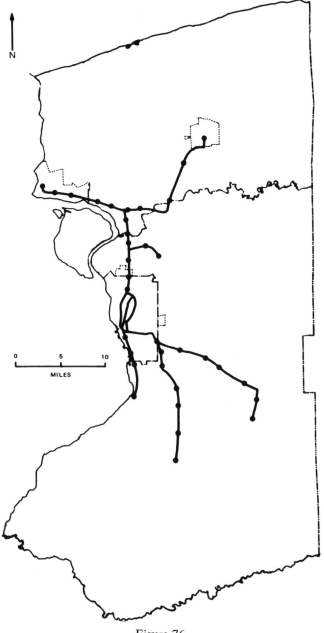

Figure 76.
Express bus plan.

areas to the south. According to this scheme, buses seating between forty and forty-five persons would use expressways of the basic corridor expressway plan with stops either at arterial crossings or at special stations built in the median strips of the newer expressways. Within five miles of the Buffalo central business district, exclusive bus lanes would be provided on all new expressways, at a capital cost of $15,000,000.[4] The staff estimated that 168 buses would be needed at $35,000 per bus and these would travel at three minute headways in the peak hour and at ten-minute headways in off-peak hours. The average system operating speed, including station stops, would be about thirty miles per hour. There would be 115 route miles of express bus service.

Actually, this was the second express bus system which was examined. The first provided a more specialized service in which buses, it was proposed, would circulate through a residential district in a loop pattern and then would run nonstop to the Buffalo central business district. It appeared, however, that this specialized service would attract too few riders and would not provide the total system accessibility of the plan that was tested by computer. The plan which was tested offered the feature of allowing local buses to connect at expressway interchanges with the high-speed service much as these local buses would feed any rail rapid transit line if such a facility were built.

On the basis of this extensive express bus system, the computer estimated that total transit ridership in 1985 would be 215,200 persons per day. Of these, 71,000 persons would be served by the express bus system, or about one-third of the total number of transit users. This was, in fact, the highest number of persons served by the high-speed portion of any transit plan tested.

With equipment costs estimated to be $5,880,000, and $15,000,000 set aside for the construction of special bus lanes near the Buffalo central business district, the express bus plan required a total capital outlay of $20,880,000. This was the lowest capital outlay required for any of the transit improvement schemes.

---

[4] This is for paving alone and does not include any share of right-of-way costs or structures.

3. *The "NYC" Rail Transit Line.* The study staff had been impressed during a visit to Cleveland by the possibility of using existing rail lines as the routes for new transit service. In Cleveland an existing rail line extending east and west from the Cleveland central business district had been refurbished and provided with modern self-propelled railroad passenger equipment. The provision of parking lots at stations had resulted in the creation of a new and apparently successful suburban service.

The best opportunity to do the same kind of thing in the Buffalo area appeared to be the tracks of the New York Central Railroad which ran for twelve miles north from the Buffalo central business district to the city of North Tonawanda, as shown in Figure 77. This route was fairly direct but unfortunately passed through a trade territory which tended to be more industrial than residential. Many prospective passengers would therefore have to come by buses to transfer at stations. There were eight of these stations between the terminals at North Tonawanda and the Buffalo central business district.

Because this was only a single line, it could not be expected to affect total transit utilization in the Niagara Frontier very much. Estimates of ridership on both buses and the new facility totaled only 198,700, of which 24,200 daily passengers used the "NYC" rail transit line. The capital cost for putting this line into operation was estimated to be $36,500,000.

4. *Suburban Rail System.* A much more ambitious trial plan was for a system of seventy-seven route miles (154 track miles) of rail routes using existing trackage to provide service to Niagara Falls and Lockport on the north and to a ring of suburban communities ten to fifteen miles east and south of the Buffalo central business district. The proposed system is seen on Figure 78. Stations were proposed to be spaced nearly three miles apart on the average in order to increase average speeds, and parking lots were proposed to be provided at all stations more than five miles from downtown Buffalo. Fifteen-minute headways were proposed for the peak travel periods and one-hour headways in off-peak times up to 1:00 A.M. in the morning.

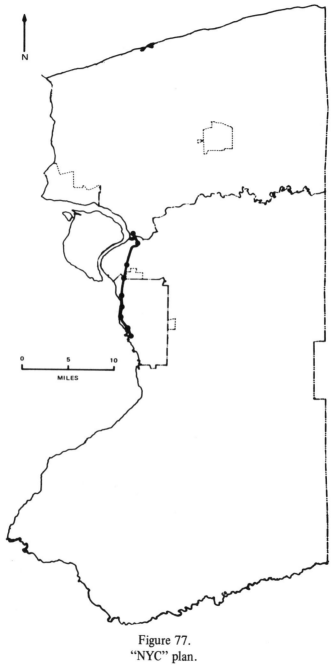

Figure 77.
"NYC" plan.

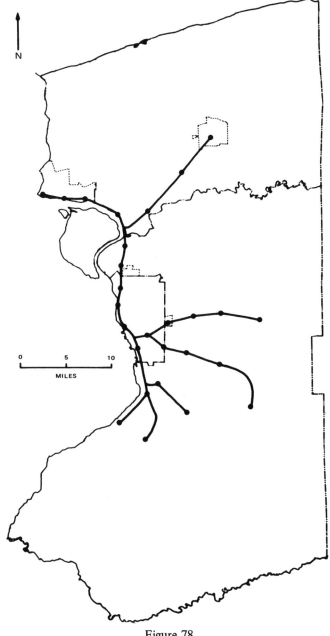

Figure 78.
Suburban rail plan.

With this extensive system, ridership on all mass transportation facilities in Niagara and Erie counties was estimated to be 210,000 passengers per day in 1985. Of this total, 50,000 passengers would use the rail system or about one-quarter of the total. This is fewer riders than would be found on the express bus system, an estimate which should not be surprising because of the smaller number of station stops, particularly in the more heavily built-up parts of the Buffalo urbanized area. Stations which are farther apart automatically freeze out the shorter trips. By providing higher speeds for the long-distance traveler, such a station configuration fails to serve the larger number of persons living in denser areas. This is a typical conflict facing the transit planner.

The costs of the suburban rail system as estimated by the study staff included $17,000,000 for new railroad equipment and $89,-000,000 for the upgrading of the railroad tracks. Many miles of tracks in the Buffalo area are adequate to serve freight operations but would be inadequate for the higher speed and smoother ride requirements of suburban rail service. Costs of building stations and parking lots were not, however, included in the total $106,000,000 capital cost of the rail system.

5. *The "Transit Expressway."* The areas north and northeast of the Buffalo central business district had the highest transit potential of any corridors in the Buffalo area. For these areas, two schemes were proposed which called for utilization of the so-called "transit expressway" or "sky bus." This transit expressway system had been developed by the Westinghouse Electric Corporation in collaboration with the Port Authority of Allegheny County, the U.S. Department of Housing and Urban Development, and others.[5] It was a system which employed a light-weight, electrically powered, rubber-tired, driverless vehicle operating on a separate right-of-way which could either be at grade or on a concrete or steel structure. Because each small vehicle is computer-controlled and labor costs are greatly reduced, headways of the vehicles can be kept very short. While speeds of these vehicles were assumed not to be quite as high as those

[5] "Condensation of the Report on Testing and Evaluation of the Transit Expressway," MPC Corporation, Pittsburgh, 1967.

of conventional rapid transit equipment, the low headway makes the average speed competitive with conventional subway or elevated transit equipment.

This kind of system was tested in two configurations as shown in Figure 79. The first configuration was the Kenmore alignment running north from the Buffalo central business district through the village of Kenmore to the city of North Tonawanda. The second configuration had an additional line which used the same trackage as the first line for about one-quarter of its length, and then proceeded independently northeastward to a terminus at the new Amherst campus of the State University of New York. Both of these lines would pass in places through areas with population densities exceeding 10,000 persons per gross square mile.

Ridership on the Kenmore line was estimated to be 40,000 persons per day and 63,000 persons per day on the Kenmore-university combination. Ridership on all transit vehicles in 1985 was estimated at 203,500 with the Kenmore transit expressway built and at 211,500 with both the Kenmore and the university lines completed.

The total amount of capital required to put these systems in operation was $60,500,000 for the Kenmore "transit expressway" and $102,800,000 for the combined system. Both these systems were assumed to be placed in operation along with all the expressways in the basic corridor plan for expressways.

6. *The Kenmore-University Rail Rapid Transit Scheme.* The final tests to be described in this series were of schemes which employed conventional rapid transit cars similar to those used in subway systems in Chicago, Toronto, and New York. These were proposed to run over two lines—the Kenmore line running between the Buffalo central business district and North Tonawanda, and the university line, which would share the Kenmore line for a distance of about three miles and then would run northeastward to the new campus of the State University of New York at Amherst. These lines were virtually the same as those of the transit expressway lines shown in Figure 79. Stations along these lines were proposed at about one-mile intervals, which meant that an average journey speed of about

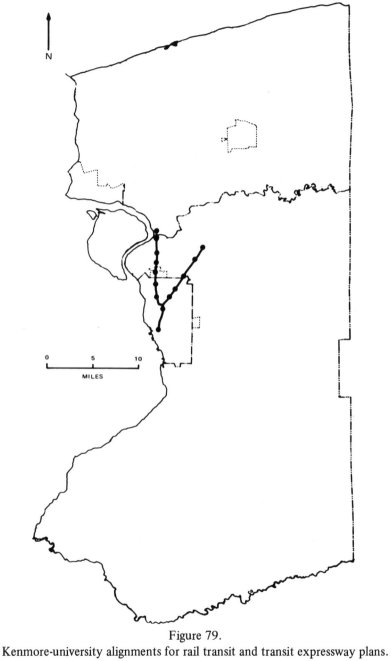

Figure 79.
Kenmore-university alignments for rail transit and transit expressway plans.

thirty-five miles per hour, including station stops, could be attained. Tests were made of the Kenmore and university lines separately and in combination.

Because the equipment on these lines was assumed to be slightly faster than that provided by the transit expressway (thirty-five miles per hour as against thirty miles per hour, including station stops), the usage of these lines was slightly heavier than in the case of the transit expressway. For example, the Kenmore line was estimated to obtain 42,000 daily riders, as against 40,000 for the transit expressway. But these 2,000 additional riders were gained as the result of equipment which cost $126,500,000, or about $66,-000,000 more in capital investment than the "transit expressway" system.

The costs of these rail transit systems, involving subway and open-cut construction and the purchase of fifty cars for a single line such as the Kenmore line and ninety cars for the Kenmore-university combination, at $130,000 apiece, would be very high. The estimated cost of the Kenmore-university rail transit line without the Kenmore expressway is $207,700,000 and the cost of the Kenmore rail transit line without the Kenmore expressway would be $126,500,000. Each of these costs would be reduced about $30,000,000 if the Kenmore expressway were built, since the expressway would be charged with the entire cost of right-of-way, utilities relocation, bridge construction, and similar expenses.

One of the subjects investigated in these tests was the question of whether a rail rapid transit line could eliminate the need for building a parallel express highway. The basic corridor plan for expressways had shown an expressway running in a corridor roughly north and south between the Buffalo central business district and the eastern part of the city of North Tonawanda. Passing through a built-up area, this corridor had evoked widespread opposition. Would the construction of a rapid transit line, partly in subway and partly in open cut, eliminate the need for such an expressway? This was a critical question which deserved a thorough examination.

The first tests were made of the single Kenmore rapid transit line, with and without a parallel expressway. When the expressway was assumed to have been built, the costs of the rapid transit line were reduced because it was assumed that this line would go down the median strip of the expressway. Without the expressway, the capital costs of the transit line would be higher because it would bear the full burden of acquiring right-of-way, relocating utilities, and building bridges.

The tests indicated that the use of the Kenmore rail rapid transit line would be almost insensitive to the presence or absence of an expressway. At first this seemed surprising, but on reflection, the computer's estimates seemed to be probably correct. The main reason for lack of change was the fact that the major determinant of transit usage was auto ownership. People without cars available to them (nearly 71 percent of all transit users) would use the rapid transit facility whether or not the expressway were there.

Much the same patterns of ridership were estimated when the Kenmore and the university lines were tested in combination. When these were tested with the assumption that an expressway would be built parallel to the Kenmore line, an estimated 68,000 passengers per day would use both facilities. Without the paralleling Kenmore expressway, 70,000 passengers would be served.

Reflections on the Tests

As in the case of expressway system tests in Chicago and the Niagara Frontier, the tests of transit helped those who observed them closely to learn more about the subject. In the world of simulation, as in the real world, events which are set in motion produce results which are sometimes surprising, sometimes expected, but always explicable *after the fact*. The advantage of simulation, of course, lies in the fact that the lessons are learned so inexpensively and quickly.

The results of the transit tests were on the whole negative from the point of view of transportation economics. Using the same procedure that had been used in evaluating expressway plans and evaluating both highway and transit together (including all capital costs and all travel costs), it was found that in no case did the construction and operation of a transit facility reduce the total transportation costs of the region. All the proposed transit systems resulted in slightly higher total transportation costs. This occurred even though the costs of transit improvements were estimated as carefully as possible, and whenever there was any doubt, the transit capital costs were understated.

The basic reason for this was that the transit schemes were for only a minority of the travelers of the region—for about 210,000 daily passengers (1962 level) in contrast with 2,669,000 automobile drivers and passengers. By investing sums up to $207,700,000 (about one-half of the cost of the proposed expressway plan), service to existing transit riders would be improved and a maximum of 23,000 automobile trips would be extracted from the road system. The improved transit service would, however, be insufficient to save people enough time and accidents or to reduce operating costs enough to offset increased capital costs, and total transportation costs would have risen slightly.

One phenomenon which was expected was the increase in transit ridership as a function of funds expended. In Figure 80 the various transit schemes are arranged in relationship to their capital costs and to the number of riders estimated to use each planned new high-speed facility. The "NYC" scheme, for example, has both low cost and a small number of daily passengers on it (24,200), while the rapid transit on the Kenmore-university line (without the Kenmore Expressway) has the highest cost and nearly the highest ridership on the improved facility itself. This result could be expected because investment produced increased average speed and made that speed available to more riders.

There was, however, a notable exception to this rule. The express bus plan is a maverick in this graph, having the highest ridership and the lowest cost. The reason for this, of course, is that the express bus system uses expressways as the specialized right-of-way by which it gains speed. But it only pays for paving extra lanes on a few miles of expressways close to the central business district where traffic might not move fast enough during the peak hour.

The same kind of reduction in cost with no loss of ridership occurs in the cases of the Kenmore and the Kenmore-university lines when these are built in conjunction with the Kenmore Expressway.

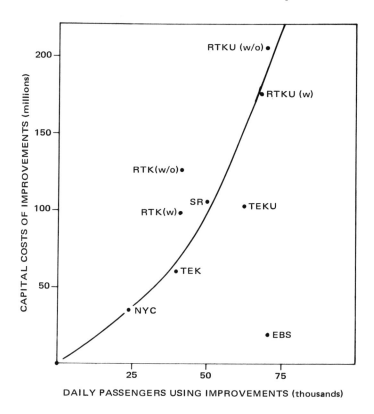

Figure 80.
Investment and estimated 1985 use of alternative rapid transit
improvements, Niagara Frontier.

By using the expressway's center mall as its right-of-way, the transit
line was able to reduce capital costs by approximately $30 million.
Thus, a second lesson which can be drawn from these tests is
that savings for transit can be effected by joint use of right-of-way.
This is a lesson which the transit industry knows very well: when the
transit companies were running street cars in the early days, they
paid for plowing snow and they even maintained their own strips
in the centers of streets—strips over which automobiles and trucks
could move. When they converted to buses, they eliminated most of

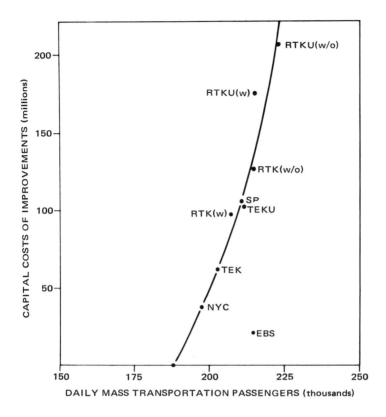

Figure 81.
Investment and estimated 1985 usage of all mass transportation
facilities, Niagara Frontier.

these costs, paying instead only the relatively small gasoline or diesel
fuel taxes.

Another lesson was that capital expenditures for transit tended
to increase total transit utilization, but only marginally. This is illustrated in Figure 81. The best that any of the tested plans could do
was to increase 1985 total transit usage by 18 percent or about
34,000 persons per day, which is the equivalent of taking 23,000
vehicle trips off the street each day. Some former bus riders are
given a faster and better ride and their ability to move about the

metropolitan area is improved to some degree, depending upon the configuration of the plan as well as the investment. But there is a serious question as to whether this kind of gain is worth the required investment.

If one steps back from the exact locations of the various transit systems and sees them distantly, some interesting comparisons can be made. Instead of eleven schemes, it can be seen that there were really only three types, with minor variations.

The first kind of transit scheme was simply the existing transit system which is, in the Niagara Frontier, a system of buses operating almost entirely over the major arterial street system. This is a service marked by frequent stops and close spacing, especially in the denser areas. It is not a high-speed system in any sense of the word, but one which covers the area, especially the denser area, with a fine-meshed service. However, the best service is toward the central business district.

The second kind of transit scheme is based on a policy of creating an *extensive system* in which service would be provided throughout all of the urbanized area of the Niagara Frontier. In one version, extensions and improvements of service would be made possible by the use of buses running over expressways. Low cost is attained because the transit system is not charged for any share of the cost of the expressways except where specific transit-oriented features are added.

Another version of extensive service is a CBD-oriented system using new suburban railroad cars running over existing rail lines. This system differs markedly from the express bus system in that stations are much more widely spaced and serve the dense areas near the core poorly; but having fewer stops in denser areas is the device whereby higher speeds are attained. Costs are high but are very much lower than they would have been had new rights-of-way been obtained and rails laid.

The third kind of system is an *intensive* system in which varying but substantial amounts of capital are invested to improve transit service significantly but in a fairly small part of the metropolitan area. Examples are the "NYC" scheme, the "transit expressway" scheme, and the conventional rapid transit schemes on the Kenmore and university alignments.

These three kinds of systems tap different market areas of transit users. The intensive plans provide substantial improvements in certain areas but do very little for the remainder of the metropolitan area. The suburban rail system is extensive, yet its primary focus is the central business district and it skips over the densely settled areas near the center. The express bus system has the quality of being least specialized, and yet this system is strongly radial, as are all the transit plans. None of the transit systems has the quality of universality which the road systems possess.

Reliability of the Transit Tests

It is proper to question whether transit was tested by reliable means. How good were these estimates? This is a matter which has to be approached within the context of the way in which the tests were used.

The technique of testing alternative transit systems, both separately and in combination with changes in proposed expressway systems, is, at its most basic level, a technique of comparison. Each system is compared with other systems, and all of these are compared with a "null plan," which for the Niagara Frontier study was simply the present system of bus service.

Because it is primarily a comparative technique, the first and most obvious way of obtaining reliability in transit testing is to use exactly the same kinds of computer procedures to test each scheme. In the Niagara Frontier eleven schemes were tested with identical procedures.

The second means of obtaining reliability is to assume the proper relative speeds, headways, and costs for each system being tested. This requires careful work and checking, because wrong speeds, for example, would give wrong relative results in the comparison of different plans. All of these basic assumptions were, however, readily visible and were subjected to verification by the study's

Planning Committee, which was composed of local engineering and planning officials.

The third feature by which reliability is judged is the ability of the computer model itself to simulate transit and automobile usage reasonably well. Even with identical procedures and very careful estimation of speeds and costs, the comparisons would be meaningless if the method of estimating transit and auto usage were substantially in error. But the Niagara Frontier estimates were good in the sense that they had simulated 1962 modal splits well. Moreover, every examination of the test results themselves showed that the model was behaving the way it ought to—predicting, for example, slightly more usage of a transit line when speeds were increased, or reducing automobile trips to the central business district when parking costs were raised.

Thus, for the purposes of comparison—which is, after all, one of the best ways of shopping for a best plan—the testing mechanism was extremely satisfactory. This is not to say that the estimated numbers of riders are within ± 2 percent of what would happen if the system were built and the city were to grow as predicted. There is no way of knowing how accurate any predictive device will be. Intuitively, one might suggest that the estimates would fall within ± 25 percent of "reality." This is accurate enough, since all comparisons are made by the same procedure and these errors of prediction are cancelled.

Conclusion

One should sense from these tests and observations the very particular nature of transit improvements. Transit is a thing, not a generalization. It is built or provided in very specific places, in given amounts. It is not cheap. It takes years to build and to bring into operation. And it operates within a particular area which has unique population characteristics and travel requirements.

With the help of a computer model which estimated volume usage on both road and transit systems, the Niagara Frontier study completed tests on a great variety of mass transportation plans. Every reasonable type of facility that might conceivably be built within the near future (i.e., that had a prototype in operation) and that was suitable for urban transportation was tested.

We have shown that when investments are made in new rapid transit lines, of whatever type, the usage of all transit increases as well. Whether the gains are worth the investment is a critical question. The tests in the Niagara Frontier suggest that the same kind of "profitability" which expressways attained could not be attained by transit.

However, these results did not permit a totally negative conclusion to be drawn. Other goals were involved. The City of Buffalo was hopeful of benefiting from the construction of some form of rapid transit—such as a subway—through the construction of more high-rise office buildings in the CBD and near the stations of a rapid transit line. The City's difficult financial position made this especially attractive. The study staff was concerned with the lot of the average bus rider who had, over more than a decade, obtained no improvements in speed of travel while automobile and truck drivers and passengers were receiving the benefits of an extensive expressway construction program. Relatively, the bus passenger was worse off than he had been.

It was beyond our ability to deal with such goals at that time, and so the results of the tests were released without recommendations. The great return from this work was the education which it provided. Much of what passed before had been just talk and loose speculation. The tests scaled the costs and estimated the ridership of the major kinds of systems that could be built in the Niagara Frontier. This provided a basis for more informed judgment, even though the results were not conclusive. The next question became one of how to achieve a strategy in the face of inconclusive economic results and of additional, noneconomic goals. This is taken up in the next chapter.

XV

TRANSIT: THE CONCLUSION

HAVING described methods of estimating future transit usage and having applied these methods to test a variety of transit systems, it remains to be seen whether these methods can in fact be used to develop a long-range policy for dealing with mass transportation in any given urban area.

Every community ought to have a strategic plan for mass transportation. A strategic plan may be defined as a broad direction for actions which can be followed for about twenty years and which will produce results which people want and which they are willing to pay for in view of the competing claims for investment or operating funds. The need for a long-range, committed public policy on mass transportation cannot be overemphasized. Any public actions which consist of making isolated transit improvements in piecemeal fashion would be as poor a policy as the piecemeal urban highway construction of the 1920's and 1930's.

No urban community should adopt a strategic plan for mass transportation—a twenty-year program—without a high degree of certainty that the actions which are proposed will be wise in the long run. This does not mean, of course, that a policy on mass transportation must be one which is finalized in all its detailed elements. The basic line of action should be defined and should either be profitable enough or desirable enough that it can be pursued, with the necessary adjustments, over the long term.

An example of a strategic policy plan is the system of interstate highways. This system was conceived in the 1940's, approved by Congress in 1956, and will be completed about two decades later.

This system is being built more or less as originally planned although shifts in the alignments of various routes have been made. Although a number of individual interstate projects have been criticized, there has been in general a continued acceptance of this system for the more than twelve years since it was approved by Congress.

Another example of a strategic plan is the basic corridor plan for expressways in any major metropolitan area. The corridors in such plans are not exact locations of expressways but indicate approximately where the expressway center line will be; the corridors may be a quarter mile wide in the built-up parts of the city and a mile wide in rural areas. The plan does indicate, however, the kind of facility, how many of them there will be, where they will be, and what the total cost will be.

There is an equal need to develop similar long-range plans and policies for the world of mass transportation. How much money should be spent? What kinds of transit facilities should be built or operated? Where should they be located? Clearly expressed policies on transit are rarities in American cities, unless one accepts the gradual abandonment of transit as a *de facto* policy. The private transit companies are quite clear about their goals: they want to survive and make money. But this certainty does not exist in the public sphere. This is the need which must be filled.

Developing a Policy: The First Steps

As we have seen in the preceding two chapters, developing plans for transit is a difficult technical task. The art of estimating future usage involves extensive research and computer assignments. These have to be done very carefully because transit has had a declining usage since 1945 and errors in judgment are not automatically swallowed up by expanding demands for travel.

Even when exhaustive tests have been completed, such as were illustrated in the preceding chapter, a ready solution does not stand out. There is no obvious best plan as was the case in expressway planning. There are extensive, costly plans, and more limited plans of lesser costs. How can a choice be made among these?

Part of the difficulty of reaching a decision lies in the poorly defined treatment of goals whose achievement might be aided by transit construction. This is compounded by an inability to measure progress toward some of these goals, or to know for certain whether the improvement of transit will secure progress toward these goals. Another difficulty lies in the presence of uncertainties which cannot be dissipated with present planning knowledge or simulation techniques.

Faced with these difficulties, the procedure illustrated in Figure 82 and described in the remainder of this chapter is suggested as a good way of developing a policy on mass transportation.

In the ordinary course of events, the first step in developing a transit policy is to reduce uncertainty to the minimum level. Naturally, all uncertainty cannot be eliminated, and in fact some very serious uncertainties will persist, as will be seen. Nevertheless, things which are often left as unknown can be measured, and the future condition of the city with respect to some very important goals can be established.

The best way to reduce uncertainty is through the use of a data-based transportation planning process, but such a process *must be comprehensive*, with tests made of the use of both roadway and mass transportation facilities. Preceding chapters have indicated how this can be done. It must be emphasized that this must be done thoroughly and well; quite often only lip service is given to this kind of planning, with a few tests of one or two plans of one mode.

To give an indication of what is meant by adequate testing, tests of at least five substantially different transit schemes and tests of five substantially different road systems should be made. One scheme in each set should be a plan testing what happens when future travel is forced to move over the present system.

By using the comprehensive transportation planning process, some of the major uncertainties can be eliminated. For example, the often asserted saying that streets and highways can "never do the job alone" can be checked out. Such a statement is now true for Manhattan, but in many medium-sized and even large metropolitan areas, highway capacity over the past ten years has increased faster than the increase in vehicle miles of travel.

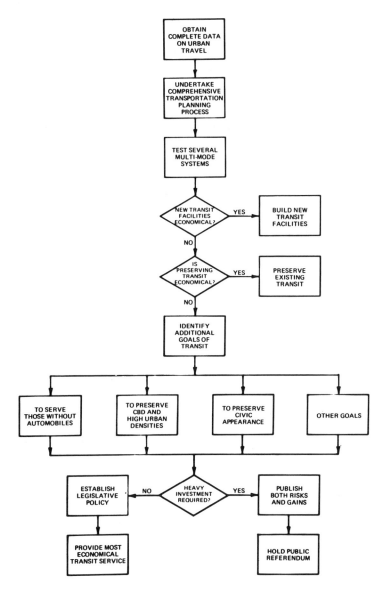

Figure 82.
Developing a strategy for transit.

For example, in the Niagara Frontier, the increase in vehicle miles of capacity, 1957 to 1967, was 3,030,000 while vehicle miles of travel increased by only 2,429,000. Equally important, by 1967 there were 5,510,000 vehicle miles of expressway capacity compared with a grand total of 9,959,000 VMT on all arterials and expressways. While the expressway capacity is not all in the right place, the massiveness of the capacity supplied, and its scale in relationship to total VMT, are facts which have to be noted. In the Chicago area in the nine-year period 1956–65, arterial and expressway capacity increased from 36,473,000 to 59,878,000 vehicle miles (or 64 percent), while travel increased from 33,161,000 to 46,282,000, or only 40 percent.[1] Three-quarters of the capacity increase was provided by expressways. If such trends continue, then the argument that highway congestion is continuously increasing is voided.

The use of the transportation planning process, especially as a result of the measurements obtained therein, will establish the proportions of the sizes of the different transportation problems. How many accidents are there? What is the parking situation? Where is mass transportation most used? What are the costs, both relative and absolute, of alternative system proposals? What will future usage be of different combinations of transit and highway systems? Getting things into proportion is a vital reduction of uncertainty.

Data obtained from the transportation planning process will establish the relative importance of the different modes of travel in carrying people in an urban area. Cities are strung along a continuum, with New York being the largest in the United States, Chicago second, Los Angeles third, and so on. Each metropolitan area has a different proportion of people carried by transit, ranging from 33 percent in New York area and 24 percent in Chicago to 7 percent in the Niagara Frontier. Each city has a different parking problem, different densities, different costs, and different financial resources. It is extremely important that generalizations true for Manhattan not be applied to Worcester, Massachusetts. The collection and full publication of data are important as the first order of business in developing a transit policy.

[1] Communication from John J. Howe, Chicago Area Transportation Study, 1969.

The next step in developing a transit policy is to apply economic criteria. The basic question which is asked is, "Will the construction and/or operation of mass transportation facilities result in the reduction of transportation costs in a given urban area?"

The economic question is the natural one to ask first. Making a profit on investment will naturally attract private capital, as it did in the early days of the transit industry. If private capital can be encouraged to move in, then a policy has been attained.

But things are not so easy now for any facilities involving the movement of people, and so social values like reduction of accidents and time saving have to be inserted as measures of profit. By observing how people behave, we can judge that they want these things and will vote to pay for them. Therefore, we can include them within our definition of profit. This implies government capital, as in the case of highways.

The same kinds of economic criteria that were used to justify the construction of new urban highway systems should also be used for judging transit systems. After all, both are parts of a total transportation system. If the construction or continuation in service of a transit line will produce reductions in operating costs, time costs, and accident costs, per unit of investment, equal to or greater than the reductions provided by highway improvements, then investment ought to be made.

It must be recognized, however, that there are two kinds of transit investment problems. One type has to do with the investment of funds in new rights-of-way, tracks, power lines, and rolling stock. The other type has to do with investment to preserve and operate a transit facility which is already in place. These two types call for different economic analyses. One type involves placing new funds into a fixed posture, in which case one must consider that the funds are being sought in competition with other kinds of public or private investments, and so one should obtain a high rate of return. In the other case, capital has already been sunk, and the wise policy generally is to obtain maximum use of the sunk investment.

Considering the possibility of new investment first, if reliable estimates, based upon a simulation of future travel over both mass transportation facilities and roadways, indicate that the construction and/or operation of new mass transportation facilities will reduce total transportation costs, then there is no question but that funds should be procured and the new system built and operated. Expenditures for mass transportation should be made up to the point where the return, in terms of reduction of social costs, on the last improvement proposed to be installed is equal to the amortization of the capital plus a suitable interest charge. There is no doubt that this is a wise policy, and such expenditures will be supported by the public over the long periods of time it takes to get most kinds of transportation improvements into operation. They will support these improvements because it is in their interest.

It is only fair to say, however, that this kind of justification for the improvement of mass transportation services will be fairly rare. Within the total transportation cost figure is the capital cost of improving mass transportation facilities. This is capital just as any other expenditure for housing or hospitals or parks is a capital expenditure. It should earn a high rate of return in reduction of time, accidents, and operating costs, just as other public expenditures should earn a high rate of return.

But earning a high rate of return in the world of transit is very difficult, even when time savings are included in the benefits as they are in highway planning. There are two main reasons for this. First, transit improvements—at least of the fixed rail type which are most often considered—are very expensive. Mile for mile their costs are of the same order of magnitude as expressways. The proposed Atlanta transit system was estimated to cost $11,000,000 per mile for the central 21-mile system and $6,500,000 per mile for the entire system of sixty-five miles.[2] The Bloor-Danforth Subway Line in Toronto cost $20,000,000 per mile.[3] Second, low unit costs per person mile of travel which are supposed to come from using transit lines are only obtained if large numbers of people do in fact use these lines. And large numbers will use these lines only if urban densities are high.

The preceding cost figures are given only to explain orders of magnitude. It is dangerous to generalize without specifics, so the only

[2] "Rapid Transit for Metropolitan Atlanta," Atlanta Region Metropolitan Planning Commission, Atlanta, 1967.
[3] "Transit in Toronto, 1849–1967," Toronto Transit Commission, 1967.

thing to do in any given urban area is to estimate the costs of the new facilities and to determine, through computer simulation, what the reduction in total transportation costs will be. Only then can a determination be made of the reduction or nonreduction in total transportation costs.

As part of these calculations, this question may be asked: "Will the construction and/or operation of new mass transportation facilities obviate the need for constructing additional expressways or widening arterial streets?" This question is answered by testing two identical transit plans, in one of which one or more expressways are included and in the other of which they are not.

If the results indicate that the elimination of one or more expressways through the construction of a transit line will reduce total transportation costs, then building a transit line is the proper course of action to take.

The second major type of transit investment problem occurs when an existing mass transportation facility is threatened with termination, as by bankruptcy. The preservation of an existing service may eliminate the need for construction of expressways. Since the facility is already in existence, capital needs are generally small. An example of such a case is the Long Island Railroad. This line, unable to be run profitably by private enterprise, was purchased by the Metropolitan Transportation Authority of New York for $65,000,000.[4] For the equivalent cost of building six miles of new transit line or six miles of expressway, an entire railroad of about 326 route miles was purchased. Here was a clear gain for the public.

Developing a Policy: The Final Option

If economic criteria fail to justify the construction and/or operation of new transit facilities, then both the planner and the community must realize that an entirely new situation exists. The rules of the game are changed; in fact, a new game has been entered. Let us see why this is so.

Economic criteria such as were used to develop expressway

[4] Metropolitan Transportation Authority, *Annual Report*, New York, 1967.

plans are proper justifications for transit improvements if applied to transit in identical fashion as to expressways, and if profits are shown. The results are determinative under that set of rules because the same kind of social gain is obtained through the means of transit. However, if these rules say that transit should not be built, then this decision must either be accepted or a new set of goals must be sought and a different game played.

It is perfectly legitimate and proper for people to decide that there are other reasons besides those of transportation economics for building mass transportation facilities. In fact, there are some very good reasons for so doing. Four goals stand out.

1. *There is a desire to provide transportation service to those without cars.* As noted earlier in this book, many people, including strangers in a city, do not have cars or cannot drive. Mass transportation offers these people a means of gaining access to the various opportunities of an urban area.

2. *There is a desire to have higher densities, particularly in the central business district.* There is a vocal group, including numbers of architects, urban planners, and writer-philosophers, who see the soul of the city in high-density living. These people note that throughout history it has been the city rather than the country which has given us our freedoms, our art, our literature, our commerce and trade, and most of our industrial productivity. They say that the central business district is the essence of urbanity, and for this reason the construction of rapid transit should be encouraged so that high densities and particularly the central business district will be favored.

3. *There is a desire to avoid demolition and to preserve civic beauty.* People want to preserve what is good in cities, especially the heritage of past centuries of fine buildings. And they want to avoid the trauma of carving wide swaths through built-up areas. Transit, especially subways, offers an attractive alternative to expressways.

4. *There is a desire for transit as a civic luxury.* People like a good, modern subway like Montreal's or Toronto's—not only for its smooth ride but for the appearance of its stations. Having a subway apparently puts a city into the big leagues and is a matter of civic pride.

When anyone appeals a negative, economics-based decision on

the basis of these goals, he is appealing his case (at least as of this moment in time) outside of the realm of the transportation planning process which has been so carefully erected. This is a frustration for the transportation planner, but it is a justifiable procedure.

However, having established a new goal or goals, it remains to be determined how much should be spent and what should be done to achieve them. The difficulty here is that goals such as those listed above are subjective. Luxury, beauty, service to those without automobiles, and the preservation of higher densities are things people want, but it is impossible to determine how much they are worth.

Under these circumstances, the only way in which a decision can be made is through recourse to the democratic process. If the people want to achieve certain goals of a subjective nature, then they can establish a public policy—an expression of the public will— either through their legislature or through a referendum.

The means by which the public will is established should depend upon the level of investment which is being proposed to achieve stated goals. If the investment is low-level—that is, if it does not require substantial capital to be placed in a fixed posture—then the decision can be made by a regularly elected legislature such as a city council or a state legislature.

However, if major public investments are required, as in the case of the construction of a rail transit line of almost any type, then the only way a decision can be made is through recourse to a public referendum. No planner, no professional engineer, and certainly no politician should move to spend hundreds of millions for transit unless a referendum has been taken. A favorable vote establishes a policy and indicates the course of action which can be taken over a long period. This is, in fact, the course that has been followed in San Francisco, Seattle, Atlanta, and elsewhere.

However, when votes are taken, it is presumed that all the facts will be laid upon the table, that a comprehensive planning process will have been completed as a first step, *and that the remaining uncertainties will have been plainly stated*. It is also assumed that certain sensible procedures will have been followed or at least considered, some of which are given below in relationship to three of the four preceding goals.

1. *The goal of providing transportation as a service.* It has been clearly established that the bulk of transit users are captives—people who do not own a car or cannot drive. There will always be a small proportion of the population that will be in this category. Giving these people mobility is something of importance for society, since otherwise they would not be able to play a full part: they would lead a more restricted life.

Providing public transportation for these people is a policy which should be expressed by a statement of legislative intent. Such a statement could be adopted by a city, county, or state legislature. The policy statement should define three things: the area that will be served by mass transportation facilities, the speeds to be attained, and the hours of service.

Having such a public policy should be advantageous from several viewpoints. Persons would know where public transportation facilities would be provided and where not. They could then adapt their building programs to suit. Governments would know where their obligations lie and would not have to face constant pressures for extension or contraction of service.

Once the level of service has been defined, the task of the transportation planner is to determine how it can be provided, that is, with what kind of system of transit and what kind of equipment.

Economically, the correct approach is to provide the required service at the lowest possible cost. In other words, the search for a solution will consider the cheapest possibility first and if that will not provide the required service, the next cheapest, and so on. In searching for such a solution, the transportation planner will naturally first investigate all possible solutions in which the right-of-way is free, is already developed, or can be shared with other users, since such a procedure will keep costs at the lowest level.

2. *The goal of reinforcing high densities.* This is a goal which is most frequently and directly stated with reference to the central business district. However, the implications are broader: transit needs high density at all stations and along its feeder lines because transit and high-density development are symbiotic. Some people may argue that high densities are undesirable, but for the sake of argument let it

be supposed that reinforcing high densities is something the people want and that high densities will be good for them.

Here is where the element of uncertainty enters. Very little is known about changes in central business districts as a result of changes in transit systems in recent decades. Historically, the development of towering central business districts is associated with transit. This happened in the era from 1880 to 1930 when transit was the dominant and almost monopolistic form of urban transportation. Whether transit can spur central business district growth today is an uncertain thing. This will be one of the areas in which research will doubtless make important advances in the next ten years. Those who vote for transit should know about this uncertainty.

3. *The goal of preserving beauty.* If one has a beautiful city, there is no question but that building a subway underneath it is going to preserve the appearance of that city where an expressway would clear a path 200 or 300 feet in width along its length. Subways are expensive facilities to build, but in many cases they are the only means of increasing capacity for moving people without substantially changing the face of the community.

In some cities the collective appearance of buildings is an almost priceless heritage, and in such cases their preservation is worth considerable extra expense. In the case of Washington, D.C., one of the strong arguments in favor of building subways is the preservation of the present appearance of our nation's capital. Of course, if one goes to the lengths of building subways for the purpose of preserving beauty, it is extremely important that auxiliary administrative means be employed to see that that same beauty is not eroded by having ugly buildings, billboards, or other claptrap enter the scene.

In many cities in Europe, Asia, Africa, and South America there exist large areas—sometimes the entire city itself—which retain the character of past centuries. Often the streets in these areas are completely inadequate as vehicular ways; they were designed for the pedestrian or for carts. They can be crushed by influxes of automobiles and trucks. These cities and their old quarters can rarely be replaced, although the fifteenth-century center of Warsaw, which was rebuilt completely following its destruction in World War II is an exception to the contrary. Under such circumstances, actions to improve transportation services by moving street cars and buses completely underground should be seriously considered.

Yet this is not an easy task. The populations living in these cities are bound to grow wealthier as the industrial and scientific revolutions reach more advanced stages in each country. The urge to spend increased wealth upon automobiles seems irresistible; the automobile is a vehicle of freedom. These vehicles must be garaged, fueled, and repaired. And they must be brought to work and parked. Under such circumstances, what happens to a truly medieval city? Slowly but steadily its compactness is eroded.

If a medieval city such as Krakow or Salzburg is to be preserved, it must in many cases change its functions. Perhaps the older quarters, which had mixtures of land uses, must become almost completely residential or educational, so that the pressures of the automobile will not be felt so acutely.

Through such examples can be seen the idea that transportation planning is not an independent kind of operation but must be related to the economic and land use factors of community growth and change.

Beyond Transit

The preceding sections of this chapter have outlined a procedure by which a long-range direction for mass transportation development can be established (see Figure 82): For most cities this is not the satisfyingly objective kind of procedure which was developed for the planning of road systems. Instead, if economic justifications fail, recourse must be had to the democratic process in order to establish the public's will for expenditures for things whose valuation is subjective or even uncertain.

Faced with this kind of decision-making process, one begins to see more clearly than ever before that transportation planning, whether for highways (whose need can be measured fairly readily) or for transit, is only a part of the story of planning.

The thing which brings this out so clearly is the peculiar dependence of mass transportation upon certain characteristics of the city. Mass transportation needs a high-density central business district as a focus and it needs high densities at its stations and generally along its routes. Without these things mass transportation cannot readily support its operations out of the fare box, let alone pay anything to amortize fixed capital improvements. Transit's great dependence upon density is reinforced by the increasing ability of people to pay more for their own individual means of transportation.

If transit is to work, then, it must have a good environment. But this kind of environment is not developing naturally these days, and it is unlikely to come about without controls or subsidies which will either directly or indirectly induce higher densities in certain parts of an urban area.

The proponents of transit suggest that new transit facilities will encourage higher densities along their lines through the improved accessibility which these lines provide. Up to this point, however, evidence upon this subject is clouded.

If the growth of the city has to be controlled in order to make a particular form of transportation work, then questions naturally arise. Should a whole city be altered in order to make one form of transportation work? Is the kind of city that would make mass transportation work one that people want? Overconcentration on transit can produce a kind of blindness to goals which are substantially more important. Increasing the productivity of the economy, providing better living conditions, giving people opportunities to develop more completely as persons—these are larger goals which should supervene. Transit or any other form of transportation is merely a means to an end—quite literally, only a way in which people can travel to their destinations. The destination is more important than the path, and this is why we must enlarge our vision and improve planning techniques in order to build better cities within better regions for the future.

XVI

CONCLUSION

WITH the preceding account of the testing of transit alternatives and the suggestion of a method for establishing a policy on mass transportation, this exposition of the transportation planning process is concluded.

This has been a special-purpose accounting: not a detailed exposition of either data or technique, but an attempt to describe key facts and planning methods that are inadequately understood. The underlying purpose has been to show that it is possible to deal rigorously with metropolitan networks of transportation facilities of several types, and to test which of several long-range plans or policies most nearly meets predefined goals.

Such a planning process gets its significance from the clamoring transportation problems which face cities in the United States—and, indeed, in all parts of the world. This is a grim business when the accident record is remembered. And congestion, air pollution, ugliness, high costs, and lack of mobility in some segments of the population are extremely serious problems as well.

Enormous resources of money, materials, and human energies are being allocated to the construction and operation of new and improved transportation facilities. These resources should reduce the problems of transportation markedly, but they have in the past been planned too frequently on a project-by-project basis. As a result, many investments earn poor rates of return; they reduce transportation problems but not as much as they should. Furthermore, individual projects do not always add up to an efficient total system and this further lessens their potential for reducing transportation problems.

Over many years, and particularly since 1955, techniques have been developed which permit transportation planners to prepare strategic plans for entire systems of metropolitan transportation facilities —both highway and transit systems. These techniques require careful measurement of cities. Extensive surveys have been made of daily trip-making, of transportation facilities, and of land use. These data show that urban areas are surprisingly orderly in their travel patterns and in their arrangements of land uses.

A series of important technical advances in the 1950's enabled transportation planners to create working representations of the city. This was made easier by the data showing orderliness of travel and land use. Theories of travel were coupled with operational descriptions of networks, and an extremely efficient search algorithm enabled minimum paths to be found through large networks. These advances made it possible to simulate travel for an entire metropolitan area, including choice of mode of travel. The growth of cities was also simulated.

To the extent that the future could thus be prelived, it could also be prejudged. But judging required some kinds of standards or criteria. Accordingly, statements of goals were prepared. These incorporated goals such as reducing accident, time, operating, and travel costs. A single goal was then specified: to reduce total transportation costs.

Trial plans were prepared. These were plans for both expressways and for rapid transit systems. They embraced entire metropolitan areas, and were designed following extensive and carefully organized preparations which included estimating correct spacing of major facilities and a study of the efficiences of alternative types of facilities.

The various trial plans were tested by computer simulation and their performance in relationship to the prespecified goals was ascertained. By comparing performances of different plans, a best plan for each metropolitan area was selected.

In the case of rapid transit systems, this procedure was also followed, but a conclusion could not be reached on the same grounds that justified highway investment. Therefore additional goals had to be given recognition. But it turned out that performance of transit plans in terms of these goals (mobility for those without automobiles, preservation of central business districts, and preservation of urban appearance) could not be measured. In the absence of demonstrated improvement toward the new goals, it was concluded that strategic public transit policies can only be determined by the electorate.

If one were to attempt to extract the essence of all this work, it would be this: the transportation planning process is an attempt to move the construction and operation of transportation facilities away from the short-range, incremental, and reactive kind of planning toward the development of strategic plans for metropolitan areas, using a methodical process featuring simulation to estimate the future behavior of certain phenomena, and evaluating performance of various plans in relationship to pre-established goals.

The Direction of Future Improvements

The preceding recapitulation has described the basic transportation planning process as it was developed during the decade 1955–65. This is a process which, like any planning process, has its limits. These include limits of the time period for which forecasts can reasonably be made, limits of the detail with which networks and travel can be simulated, limits on the number of goals that can readily be included within the evaluative mechanism, and limits on the ability of land use forecasting models to estimate such things as trip densities.

The fact that there are limits to the process should not suggest curtailment of this kind of work. The methods are there which can be used to evaluate alternative strategies for road and mass transportation systems. To abandon these would be like going back more than twenty years to the time when transportation systems were built piecemeal and when there were totally inadequate measures and understandings of urban travel. The appropriate question, instead, is in what direction future improvements should be made.

In this section, therefore, four areas are identfiied where the transportation planning process as it now stands may be improved.

1. *Adding More Goals.* A drawback of the metropolitan transportation planning process as it now stands is its limited set of goals. The effective goals are user goals (lowering time, accident, and operating costs) and the goal of reducing capital investments in new transportation facilities. It would be desirable to include a greater number of goals, representing other things that people want, when deciding upon a transportation plan for a metropolitan area. There are two ways in which this could be done, theoretically at least. First, certain goals might be stated as fixed, rather than variable, targets. For example, a minimum level of service and a minimum area of service might be prescribed for mass transportation. Then optimum transportation plans could be determined with and without the constraint. The difference in cost between the two optimum transportation plans could then be attributed to providing mass transportation service of the prescribed level. This cost could then be appraised by the executive and legislative bodies of the government or governments having jurisdiction over the area being planned, or the matter could be decided by referendum.

A second method would be to include the costs of making improvements toward one or more additional goals as part of the capital costs of building new transportation facilities; alternatively they might be related to the variable traffic loads moving over all transportation facilities. Noise and air pollution, for example, might be related to traffic volumes, and the costs of noise and of air pollution might be appraised as functions of the proximity of traffic volumes to populations in their vicinity. This is, of course, much more easily said than done; if it were only moderately difficult, it would have been done already. In more than a decade of metropolitan system planning, very little, if anything, has been done, in the way of successfully costing additional goals and incorporating them in the transportation planning process.

If it were possible to incorporate additional goals, it is possible that the results would be ambiguous. Investing funds to improve economic productivity, for example, might produce two different transportation plans with nearly equal minimum cost points—one where there is little investment for economic growth, and one where the investment for economic growth pays off in a new, low, total cost. It is ironic that the inclusion of more and more goals may well, as noted in Chapter IX, have the effect of making it more difficult to reach a clear-cut decision.

A more positive observation, however, is that the attempt to add goals to the transportation planning process should be accompanied by an expansion and improvement of other kinds of planning to make use of those kinds of actions which can deal directly and effectively with the problems which are the obverse of the goals under consideration. Thus, the goal of developing a better land use pattern can probably be attained more easily by planned actions in the land use field than indirectly by manipulating transportation facilities.

2. *Improving Arterial Planning*. Arterial system planning is one of the weak points in American city and transportation planning. At present, metropolitan transportation planning concentrates almost exclusively on the backbone network of expressways and rail rapid transit systems. This has been a conscious and, for the most part, a wise policy; the main networks have to be established before the lesser systems can be planned, and not the other way around. Nevertheless, the lack of arterial planning and to a lesser extent the lack of bus system planning has been a major omission which has and will continue to have the most serious consequences.

Although urban expressway systems are planned to carry between 35 and 50 percent of vehicle miles of travel in an urban area, the arterial system has to carry all except 10 percent of the remainder. (About 10 percent of vehicle miles of travel are on local streets leaving 40–55 percent of travel to be carried on the arterial system.) The arterial system is extensive, so that volumes on it may average only 3,900 vehicles per day, as in the Niagara Frontier in 1962 (or 9,400 as in the Chicago area in 1956), but these volumes vary upwards in many places to congest two-lane and in some cases four-lane roads in peak hours. In the Chicago area, 54 percent of all accidents were recorded as occurring on arterial streets.

Arterials have the further problem of being the natural and indeed almost the only appropriate sites for those land uses which generate large volumes of trips. Shopping centers and "ribbon commercial developments" have to locate on arterials. Industrial areas, although their trip generation rates per acre are of the same magnitude as residential areas, nevertheless have very high impacts on roads as work shifts change. The interactions between vehicles entering and leaving the traffic stream and the through vehicle call for additional street space and good geometric design of these roads.

Thus, the functions which arterials are called upon to perform require arterials to be well planned and built both as individual roads and systems—but historically this planning has not occurred. As cities grow, roads which were laid out to serve farming needs or to interconnect minor settlements are absorbed into the arterial system. Often these roads are discontinuous, spacing is poor and inadequate for urban needs, and pavement and right-of-way widths are inadequate. Because there is no planning and often very little in the way of land use controls, the new urban arterials are well encrusted with ribbon development even before the areas between them have been developed, so that widening is made difficult. Houses may occur every fifty feet. Subdivision streets may intersect with the arterial every 250 feet. There are unsafe intersections.

This lack of planning has occurred for a variety of reasons. One reason is that most of the miles of arterials brought into the urban system are the property of town and county governments. These governments have not had strong planning agencies. The state and metropolitan transportation agencies have been fully occupied with their major systems.

If this situation is to be remedied, substantial efforts will have to be made. The first step is to develop a system plan for arterials—a plan which will have sufficient capacity to meet travel demands when the area is fully developed and which will align the roads in a pattern that will meet the directional needs of travel. Then standards for arterial design and for land uses adjacent to arterials must be established and made into laws. These standards ought to limit access along arterials to those activities that need it: business and certain institutions. Residential buildings should face away from these heavily traveled streets, fronting instead upon interior residential or collector streets.

These are not basically new ideas, but they are ideas which need to be put into practice in widespread areas. If arterial streets could be as well planned as expressway systems are, urban areas would be much more desirable places in which to live. This is one of the great voids in American planning, and it is a void which needs to be filled as much from the local level of government as from above.

3. *Improving Simulation Models.* The processes of simulating urban growth, traffic flow, and choice of mode of travel—three key models on which present transportation planning is based—need refinement and improvement. Present models do creditable jobs and without them there would be very little certainty about systems planning. Yet there are several areas where gains can be made that will be of major benefit for planners.

First, there is a great need to develop a simulation model that will be useful in making plans for small areas. Current traffic assignment techniques are quite blunt tools; they are useful in estimating volumes on expressways and major arterials, but their abilities to estimate ramp volumes, turning movements at intersections, and volumes on lesser streets is restricted by a number of factors. Among these is the fact that, with current traffic assignment techniques, trips from zones are forced to enter and leave the network at only one point in each zone. In actuality, trips enter and leave the network at nearly every block face. Research is now underway which will at least start to remedy this failing.

A second area where simulation can be improved is in better estimation of future urban growth. The model described in this book improved urban growth simulation greatly, bringing changes in accessibility into the equations. But changes in density as a function of changed accessibility were not taken into account. Yet it is probable that the density of land development is affected by accessibility, among other things. And there should be some way of estimating the force of rising incomes upon densities. If people have money to spend, they will spend it, and space may be one of the commodities they want to buy.

A third area where improvements can be made is in the estimation of choice of mode. The present models used to estimate modal choice are brute-force programs requiring excessive amounts of computer time. Better theoretical statements are needed.

4. *Linking Systems Planning with Implementation.* More important than any of the internal improvements just described is the need for making transportation planning an integral part of the total job of building transportation systems. This need may seem remote to those who have not been close to problems of implementation of transportation system plans. After all, once a transportation plan is prepared, why should it not be scheduled and built, piece by piece? This seems very logical and simple, but it is too limited a view of reality.

The problem is that the construction of a transportation system involves a large number of organizations and skill groups working through an extensive series of progressively more detailed steps. There are federal, state, and local governments and a wide variety of private and quasi-public organizations operating at the community and neighborhood level. There are long-range transportation planners, the engineers, the traffic engineers, the city planners, the landscape architects, and other professionals who are concerned with urban renewal, housing, municipal government, and state finances. Finally, there are the residents of each area through which a new transportation facility must pass, who increasingly must be convinced of the value of the facility which may force them to move. Even after a transportation system plan has been adopted, it may take five years or more for a typical urban expressway or transit route to be completed.

Transportation system planning has to be followed by engineering, and engineering considerations have to be fed back into the system planning operations if there are any foundation, engineering design, or other problems which could not be anticipated at the system planning level. In turn, planning and engineering have to be brought together with governmental financing, so that long-range programs can be developed. The generalized locations of transportation routes shown in the system plans have to be studied further in route location studies (which tend to merge with preliminary engineering studies). At this point, coordination has to be attained with urban renewal, mass transportation, school planning, and the hundred other programs of local and state government which interact with a transportation facility. Coordination needs continue through all the succeeding stages of design, consultation with neighborhood groups, preparation for public hearings on the project, and even into construction itself.

To make a success of such a series of actions over so long a time span calls for administrative skills and communications of the highest order. It also calls for organizational unity and continuity, since so many people have to work together for so long a time.

Extension

It would not be right to conclude this work without considering the possibility of extending the methods which have been described in this book to the task of dealing with the much larger problems of metropolitan and regional settlement. There are a number of interesting parallels between transportation planning and the assignment of trying to deal better with changing regional settlement patterns. These suggest that regional studies could profitably be undertaken along fresh lines—coldly, inquisitively, and with measurements that seek to disclose the causal sequences of growth and change.

As in the case of transportation planning, it is possible to start with a list of problems which are commonly held to be serious in scale. The transportation problems of urban areas arose when urban population growth and changing technology imposed too many people and vehicles upon a fixed transportation system. Within the fixed system each person continues to make wise choices for himself, but the aggregate effect of these choices creates congestion, danger, air pollution, and high travel costs.

In the area of human settlements, actions taken by individuals within a limited geographic area create another set of problems. Cities and regions grow and change incrementally, as the result of individuals making locational decisions in their own best interests. In the past century most of the opportunities for individual advancement have lain in the cities because of the specialization of human activities made possible by mutual proximity of large numbers of people. The wealth that has been generated by cities has been great and fairly well spread, but along with the wealth came serious problems. These problems cannot be laid wholly at the door of urban size or at the door of the incremental manner of urban growth. Yet, both size (which is unplanned) and the blind manner of growth have contributed substantially to the magnitude and seriousness of these problems. For example:

1. *Pollution—air, water, and land.* People and their machines emit wastes which in small amounts are absorbed or eliminated by natural processes. As cities grow in size, the volume of polluting material is increased. Eventually, cities become so big that the former balance of man with nature is destroyed, and nature ceases to be able to recover locally from the pollutants that are injected into the air and water or are strewn on the land.

2. *Transportation problems—congestion, danger, and high costs.* The gradual growth of cities imposes successively larger burdens of traffic upon fixed street systems that were laid out in earlier times for smaller communities and different travel needs. The incremental processes of growth still cause arterial systems to develop inadequately.

3. *Loss of freedom; loss of individuality.* When urban areas become so large that a person cannot leave them except by monumental effort, then the city becomes a prison. And when man thus becomes constantly confronted by too many of his own kind, he becomes oppressed with a sense of loss of individuality and dignity. These sensations are more onerous for the poor than for the rich, because the poor have less means for escape and are more deeply buried, and at higher densities, in the urban mass.

4. *Class segregation.* There will always be a natural drawing together of people with similar backgrounds and tastes, but this phenomenon becomes distorted, acute, and increasingly unhealthy as urban areas grow in size. New housing built at the periphery attracts those who can afford it—the middle and upper income groups. (This is not a "flight to the suburbs"; it is simply the inevitable manner of incremental growth which existed long before there were suburbs to give it a name. The more well-to-do are the only ones who can

finance new urban growth.) The result of this process is that the poor are "selected out," in the sometimes expressive language of data processing, to remain at the core of the city.

In the larger cities these processes result in the existence of very large areas of segregated housing—segregated poor, segregated middle class, and segregated rich. But this segregation is most destructive to the poor and the minority groups who can become so isolated that they lose sight of both the requirements and the possibilities of self-improvement. As we all know, the situation can reach such a critical mass that destructive riots can ensue.

5. *Inability of the city to adjust to change.* The gradual enlargement of cities envelops older buildings closer to the core. Surrounded, and with a central geographic position that maintains and even increases land values, the older areas find it increasingly difficult and costly to adjust to changing conditions. And conditions have changed substantially. Automobiles are one example. And higher incomes have raised expectations while existing buildings deteriorate and become more obsolete with every passing year. Educational and other public service standards rise. And high densities make things more costly. Freedom to change ought to be planned into a city, but existing cities do not have this freedom and are thereby faced with terrible pressures.

6. *The ceiling on quality.* The incremental manner of urban growth imposes a severe limitation on the quality of urban development. Unified action and bold new schemes are impossible when building piece by piece. The urgency of individual actions and expectations clouds the community's vision of needs for parks, school sites, and other public places. Inadequate rural roads are encrusted with buildings and then are absorbed into the urban area as arterials. All this comes about gradually and subtly until suddenly a whole area is developed and has to wake up to repair things that never should have happened. In a word, incremental growth blocks planning—not necessarily, but almost inevitably.

All these problems are accentuated by a rising standard of national living. As productivity goes up, so do standards of what is expected or desired. Very rapid means of travel and communication break down the barriers behind which people were once isolated in a comfortable regional parochialism—content with a lower standard because that was all they knew.

To reduce these problems is one of the main objectives of government at all levels. And so, many programs are initiated—housing, education, health, pollution, urban renewal, and many others. All of these are vitally needed, direct responses to immediate and well-perceived problems.

However, it can be fairly stated that these programs do not have a base of strategy for dealing with the drift of urbanization. There is no strategic state or national policy about regional development. Where are our cities going, and our regions? Do their unhindered growth patterns accentuate the kinds of problems we have just listed? Are there other settlement patterns which would permit an equally productive economy with a lower total social cost? Are there other settlement patterns which would permit easier rebuilding of the cores of existing cities? What will the national human character be like in fifty years? Will our present regions grow to the point where all desirable options will have been foreclosed for our children?

If these questions are to be answered—if strategic plans for regional development are to be prepared—then certain conditions must be met. The three key conditions are the possession of adequate data, the ability to simulate important regional phenomena of growth and change, and the development of an agreed-upon list of regional goals. These conditions do not obtain adequately at the present time, and if they are to be met, an enormous effort will have to be made. It will be seen, of course, that these three conditions have a one-to-one correspondence with three of the five components of the process which is common to so many types of planning, including transportation planning. The remaining components, planning (or the suggestion of changes) and evaluation, can be undertaken whenever data, simulation capability, and goal statements are ready; prior to that time, however, planning and evaluation at the regional scale are weak.

We are not certain what data will be needed for studies of regional and metropolitan development, but experience from the transportation studies suggests a minimum list. This would include data on land use, land costs, density of development (measured, perhaps, by floor space), travel of people, travel of goods, population growth, and economic activity. Information on the migratory patterns of people within regions and metropolitan areas, and on rent-income and rent-dwelling condition relationships would be very useful. Except for the population data, most of these data do not exist for regions, and yet it is imperative that such data cover entire regions, just as travel data for metropolitan areas cover the entire area for which plans are being prepared.

The accent in this section is upon regions rather than metropolitan areas. This does not mean that data should be aggregated for metropolitan areas—quite the contrary. The emphasis on regions is purposeful because within regions containing many thousands of square miles and a number of cities as well as extensive rural areas, there exists the possibility for substantially different development strategies. This is not so clear a possibility in metropolitan areas, whose geographic areas are generally quite closely drawn in around the presently urbanized area.

Given present, limited knowledge of regions, a gigantic simulation model and computer program cannot be developed that would represent all the operations of a region, or even a metropolitan area. The task of simulating regional phenomena has to be broken down into a series of component models that will be able to reproduce the behavior of certain classes of happenings.

The first simulation models should simulate tangible human phenomena. The movements of vehicles, the birth of children, the construction and aging of housing, the migrations of population, and the production of goods and services are all tangible things. Data can be collected on these things and simulations can be checked. If practical results are to be achieved, a start must be made in this realm. Only after much progress has been made should intangibles like education and behavior be considered for inclusion within the regional planning process.

The following seven models might form the initial core of a regional planning process.

1. Population changes (births, deaths, aging).

2. Economic activities (production of goods and services, income, income distribution).

3. Travel (daily travel of people and movement of vehicles over the street system).

4. The construction and modification of the regional supply of housing and nonresidential buildings.

5. The migrations of people within the regional housing supply.

6. The movement of goods.

7. Water supply and sewage disposal.

Probably the two most important of these models are the models dealing with the construction and modification of the regional supply of buildings and with the movement of population within the regional housing supply. It is incredible, in many ways, that large-scale, data-based transportation planning covering entire metropolitan areas has been going on for more than a decade without comparable studies having been made in the field of housing. It is a matter of national policy that each urban area with a central city population of over 50,000 persons should engage in a transportation planning process that costs between one and two dollars per capita. But similar studies have not been made in the field of housing, where the total annual capital investment in private residential construction *alone* is three times the annual value of all highway construction.[1]

If these simulation models were developed and made operational, it would be possible in very large measure to describe the condition of a region at some future point in time. The impacts of governmental programs of various types could be ascertained. Simply describing the future region, however, would not be meaningful unless that region could be evaluated, and this requires that a list of goals be prepared. These goals would in turn have to meet certain conditions, the chief being that the condition of the region would have to be rateable in quantitative terms against the selected goals.

All the foregoing will require immense work and perseverance. But in the long term, it seems to be an essential kind of work if we are to maintain a pleasant and efficient tenancy upon this planet. It is not suggested, of course, that this is the only course of action that

[1] U.S. Statistical Abstract, 1967, p. 711.

should be taken. For example, a program of construction of experimental cities is greatly needed to develop new urban arrangements in a manner unfettered by our long habits of building cities incrementally. And there is continued need for applying better the conventional tools that are already at hand. Nevertheless, the work of regional studies needs reinforcement.

Conclusion

The work of the transportation planners which has been traced throughout this book began with the hope that through hard work and ingenuity methods could be developed which would assure that good plans would be developed for metropolitan transportation systems. In very large measure this hope was realized. Plans were developed which were demonstrated to be the best in terms of an agreed criterion.

As this work went forward, we gradually began to see that human settlements whose transportation systems we were planning had, within themselves, a high degree of order and some evidences of a natural economy of effort. The choices of individuals, made to secure their own advantage, had themselves to be economical of effort, or else the individual would not be maximizing his own benefits. The sum of all these individual economical efforts produced a regular order which could be perceived after certain surveys had been taken.

This orderliness was both comforting and disturbing. It was comforting in the sense that it indicated that people's actions are not, in fact, utterly chaotic and stupid.

But orderliness was also disturbing in that it showed that our largest aggregations of population were not being planned and could not be planned under prevailing conditions. Growth, especially within the framework of local government countenanced by the states, was beyond control. Sooner or later the forces of the economy, of population growth, of the opportunity represented by place near or within a city would result in changes being made—changes in the zoning laws, changes in transportation facilities, or other changes—whatever is needed to accommodate the thrust of expansion.

Here, then, lay a new challenge. Urban growth, being blind and mechanical, posed three problems. First, within that urban area growth would create pressures of an explosive nature. Second, growth would ultimately be so extensive as to impair permanently man's balance with nature and with himself. And third, the manner of growth, being incremental, results in a product whose quality is substantially below that which could be achieved by planning.

But perhaps the most troublesome aspect about this discovery is that we see ourselves as ants within a heap or as cells in a coral plant. If we cannot control our manner of growth, we cannot control our destiny. Failure in this regard sets a limit on our aspirations as individuals and as a people.

The challenge is to overcome these limits, both by study and by action and experiment at the largest scale. We want to extend our vision and understanding of the future, further than we now can see and know, in the comprehensive planning of regions.

In a sense, this planning is a bold dream: it is a further extension of man's instincts not to be dominated by events but to dominate them; to control rather than be controlled by animal instincts and reactions; to look forward and to combine the freedom and creativity of the individual with an order that will allow a continued and more graceful existence on this planet; and above all, to see things whole.

APPENDIX

The urban transportation planning process is a team operation. The following lists contain the names of the supervisory and principal supporting staff members of the Chicago and Niagara Frontier transportation studies, all of whom contributed to the work described in this book. It is unfortunately impossible to list the hundreds of others who also worked on these studies or who contributed in other ways.

CHICAGO AREA TRANSPORTATION STUDY
Supervisory and Supporting Staff
1955–61

R. W. Adams, *Operations*
Howard W. Bevis, *Economics Research*
A. P. Black, *Planning*
G. W. Blake, *Tabulating*
C. E. Browning, *Research*
E. Wilson Campbell, *Assistant Director*
J. Douglas Carroll, Jr., *Director*
R. E. Carter, *Planning*
Peter J. Caswell, *Assistant Director*
Roger L. Creighton, *Planning Consultant*
L. M. Doggett, *Publishing*
R. E. Eyestone, *Administration*
F. F. Frye, *Research*

E. L. Gardner, *Research*
S. M. Hadfield, *Land Use*
G. Haikalis, *Traffic*
John R. Hamburg, *Research and Forecast*
A. B. Hamilton, *Data Processing*
Thomas Heffernan, *Data Processing*
Irving Hoch, *Economics Analysis*
John J. Howe, *Data Processing*
Garred P. Jones, *Graphics and Publishing*
Dayton P. Jorgenson, *Field Services*
H. Joseph, *Economics*
L. E. Keefer, *Traffic Engineer*
C. Kramer, *Research*

E. Kramer, *Research*
G. A. Leeper, *Assistant Supervisor*
G. A. Letendre, *Systems Analysis*
S. McGee, *Administration*
R. J. McKinnon, *Research*
T. C. Muranyi, *Traffic*
A. Napravnik, *Administrative Secretary*
J. D. Orzeske, *Field Services*
A. S. Rathnau, *Cartography*

A. Reithofer, *Design*
W. Rifkind, *Office Manager*
Morton Schneider, *Systems Analysis*
R. H. Sharkey, *Land Use*
F. A. Smola, *Assistant Supervisor*
Robert E. Vanderford, *Data Processing*
N. Vivona, *Research*
B. F. Vrtis, *Cartographatron*
B. H. Wegener, *Cartographer*

K. Zerrien, *Assistant Supervisor*

NIAGARA FRONTIER TRANSPORTATION STUDY
Professional Staff
1962–64

Andrew V. Barothy-Langer, *Cartographic Supervisor*
Jeanne P. Bassett, *Senior Statistician*
Kendall H. Bishop, *Supervisor of Data Processing Section*
Mildred Black, *Senior Economic Research Editor*
Robert Breuer, *Associate Urban Planner*
Roger L. Creighton, *Director*
H. Richard Etherington, *Senior Urban Planner*
Jean M. Fatica, *Administrative Assistant*
Jere E. Fidler, *Senior Mathematician*
Donald R. Fisher, *Senior Computer Systems Analyst*
David I. Gooding, *Associate Economist*
Charles R. Guinn, *Senior Transportation Analyst*
John R. Hamburg, *Associate Director*

George C. Hemmens, *Associate Research Analyst (Transportation)*
George T. Lathrop, *Principal Urban Planner*
David B. Lemerise, *Transportation Studies Field Supervisor*
Ralph J. Marshall, *Associate Mathematician*
Frederick W. Memmott III, *Transportation Studies Survey Supervisor*
Henry L. Peyrebrune, *Senior Research Analyst (Transportation)*
Eliot M. Rowe, *Planning Delineator*
Kenneth W. Shiatte, *Associate Transportation Analyst*
Robert C. Stuart, *Associate Director*
Ronald W. Tweedie, *Transportation Studies Coding Supervisor*
G. Frederick Young, *Senior Urban Planner*

INDEX

Accidents: fatalities, xvi, 4, 6; costs of, 114, 206

Air pollution, 13

Arterial streets: defined, 94; principles of system design, 237–239; need for improved planning of, 358–360

Automobiles: car loading, 21; time use of, 28–29

Automobile trips: geographic distribution of, 37–40

Bus systems, 95

Bus trips: geographic distribution of, 43–44

Capacity: of streets, 102

Capacity restraint, 257

Cartographatron: described, 34–36; failure to record density, 39; used to study communities, 46–47

City: as a self-modifying system, xvii. *See also* Urbanization

Community: not identified by travel patterns, 44–47

Composite network, 263–265

Congestion, 8

Data: in the transportation planning process, xviii, 171; processing, 161–165

Data collection: in the transportation planning process, 137; evolution of, 149–150; geographic coding, 151; travel survey types, 152–153; home interview, 156–158; truck-taxi, 158–

159; roadside interview, 159; miscellaneous travel surveys, 160; processing of, 161–165; factoring, 163–165; vehicle miles of travel, 165–166; person miles of travel, 166–168; land use and floor area, 168–169; networks, 169–170

Desire line maps, 33

Evaluation, xix, 140

Expressway planning: basic sequence, 215; materials for, 216–217; optimum spacing, 218–223; principles of, 229–237; trial plan preparation, 243–244; testing, 247–248; composite network technique, 263–265; Chicago case study, 269–283; marginal cost analysis in, 282–283; Niagara Frontier case study, 283–294; urban-rural split, 285–289; and toll roads, 289–290; adjusting to committed system, 289–290

Expressways: antipathy toward, xxiii; defined, 94; vehicle miles driven on, 223–225; effect on traffic and accidents, 297

External trips, 41–43

Floor space: by type, 69–70; geographic distribution, 73–74; inventory, 168

Forecasts: in the transportation planning process, 138

Fratar method: use in travel forecasting, 52

A NOTE ON THE AUTHOR

Roger L. Creighton is president of Creighton, Hamburg, Inc., planning consultants, and adjunct professor in the Department of Civil Engineering at Rensselaer Polytechnic Institute. Born in Shanghai, China, in 1923, he received a B.A. degree, *magna cum laude,* in Engineering Sciences and Applied Physics from Harvard College, and a Master of City Planning degree from the Harvard Graduate School of Design. He served as planning director of the Portland (Maine) City Planning Board, 1951–55; as planning consultant for the Chicago Area Transportation Study, 1955–61; as director of the Upstate New York Transportation Studies, 1961–64; and as acting director of the Subdivision of Transportation Planning and Programming, New York State Department of Public Works, 1964–66. Mr. Creighton has published numerous articles and technical reports; *Urban Transportation Planning* is his first book.

UNIVERSITY OF ILLINOIS PRESS

———